44636 -2

GN
484.3   Brain, James Lewton
B7
        The last taboo

The Last Taboo

SEX AND THE FEAR OF DEATH

James Lewton Brain

ANCHOR PRESS/DOUBLEDAY
GARDEN CITY, NEW YORK
1979

Library of Congress Cataloging in Publication Data

Brain, James Lewton.
  The last taboo.

  Includes bibliographical references and index.
  1. Sex customs. 2. Sex (Psychology) 3. Death—
Psychology. 4. Taboo. I. Title.
GN484.3.B7   392'.6
ISBN: 0-385-14581-0
Library of Congress Catalog Card Number 78–20060

My sons, Charles and Peter

Contents

Acknowledgments

This book grew out of an article that was published in 1977. A number of friends who were not anthropologists read it and urged me to get some of the ideas to a wider public. It is not, therefore, an academic's book, though I hope anthropology and psychology will get some ideas from it. Originally I included many matters of debate for scholars in those disciplines, but have been persuaded to cut them out as being of little interest to the general public.

I must pay tribute to a number of people. First, to my wife, Mary Gordon, for her encouragement. Over the years a number of my students have come up with perceptions that have been important to me. Among them I am particularly grateful to Michelle Israel and Janice Holden of SUNY at New Paltz and Kerey Parnes of Vassar College. My editor, Elizabeth Frost Knappman, has been extremely patient and good humored in dealing with me. Finally, my great thanks to Maria Narvaez, who struggled successfully with my handwriting and typed the manuscript.

1

Reflections

I did not come to my profession in the ordinary way. I was a very bored and mediocre high school student. The kind of jobs that seemed to interest my fellows—medicine, law, engineering, banking, insurance—had no appeal for me. Instead, I elected to go to agricultural college, which offered the chance of outdoor work and possibly service abroad in what was then the British Empire. First, I had to spend a year working as a field hand. The year was 1939. I was just sixteen. By the end of my year all the colleges had closed, so I determined to go on working on farms until I was old enough to join the Army. It was a strange time, but for me a wonderful experience as I became aware of the marked differences in manners and mores between my own middle class and the rural working class. In 1942 I joined the Army, only to find another whole new world. At the end of World War II, I could not think of anything I wanted to do, and although I hated the stupidities of the Army, I thoroughly enjoyed the travel experience it made possible. So I stayed on until 1950 when I could bear no more. I had, however, been all over France, Belgium, Holland, and Germany, had six months in Egypt and six months in what was then Palestine, and a year in Hong Kong.

All this experience made postwar England seem unbearably dull and drab, and an advertisement for agricultural field officers

in Tanganyika (now Tanzania) sounded attractive. The job
proved to be wonderful, and I threw myself into learning Swahili
and trying to find out something about the people among whom I
was working. Finally, I met a number of anthropologists, and it
seemed to me that a combination of their theoretical knowledge
with my practical experience would make my work with people
more easy.

In 1959 London School of Economics accepted me as a (very
apprehensive) graduate student of anthropology. I did one term in
residence during a leave, went back to East Africa for three years,
collected material for a thesis in my spare time, and then returned
for a further two terms to complete my residency requirements.
There was no doubt that the training I had received made my
work better. Whereas before I was like someone finding his way
around in a room filled with furniture in the dark, now it was as
though someone had switched on the light.

In 1963 Syracuse University, in New York State, invited me to
come to the United States to help in the training of Peace Corps
volunteers. The Syracuse graduate school allowed me to register
for a Ph.D. program, and two years later I went back to Tanzania
for fifteen months to carry out field research. In 1968 I completed
everything and became that slightly odd creature—a Ph.D. with
no B.A. degree.

In one way, my study of anthropology had answered many
questions for me. Certain things, however, remained a puzzle. I
thought of various experiences over the years and tried to understand how they fitted together. I widened my reading to include
works on psychoanalysis and began to get more clues. Let me give
three examples of the kind of experiences that were puzzling me.

1942: Bovington Camp, Dorset, England. It was my first day in
the Army. A collection of unhappy-looking young men was trying
to make sense of the hundred and one items of equipment just issued at the quartermaster's office. Worst of all were the horrible,
hairy battle-dress uniforms, stiff with chloride of lime to protect
the wearer against mustard gas. They looked ugly and felt worse:
itchy, scratchy, smelling like a swimming pool. It was a warm
April, warmer than many English summers, but the only underwear permitted was that issued: heavy woolen undershirts and .

long johns. The shirts too were of heavy woolen flannel material. The combination of all these with intensive drill sessions on the barrack square over the next few weeks was to make the period one of such physical misery that today, more than thirty-five years later, it is still vivid in my mind.

While we were wrestling with our foul-smelling uniforms and wondering how on earth the old soldiers managed to look smart and well-tailored, an angry looking Irish corporal stamped into the barrack room.

"All right, then, you shower of shit! On your feet! Come on—move!"

We got up and stood awkwardly.

"Jesus, Mary, and Joseph! Look at youse! . . . Okay then, outside! Come on—at the double!"

Everything seemed to be shouted, nothing was muted or reasonable; nothing was explained. Under the prodding and pushing of our screaming corporal, we formed three ranks. Squads of soldiers passed us, their ironshod boot heels crashing to the ground, their heads high, their arms swinging absolutely straight and shoulder level, a hundred men as one man. Their instructors marched beside them, admonishing them not to look like that heap of shit—us—and to hold their heads up, shoulders back, stomachs in, asses in.

Under the cover of all the noise I muttered to the boy next to me: "Where are we going?"

"To the barbers, I think."

"But I had my hair cut yesterday, damn it!" I said.

I had indeed. I knew that the Army insisted on short hair, and so the day before I had gone to my local barber, explained that I was going into the Army the next day, and asked him to cut it really short. At the barbershop our squad was halted and given the order to fall out and form a line: eighty men for five barbers. I walked diffidently over to the corporal—Dolan was his name, I remember.

"Excuse me," I said politely. He returned a look of concentrated fury on me.

"You talking to me? Stand to attention! What is it?"

"Excuse me, but . . ."

"Excuse me, corporal!" he roared.

"Excuse me, corporal, but I had my hair cut yesterday."

He looked at me with contempt.

"Well?"

"Well, I thought . . ."

"Thought! Thought! What do you think this is? A bleeding circus? You aren't paid to think. You're paid to do what you're bloody well told! Get back in that line!"

The barbers managed to take off quite a lot more. Five barbers cut eighty men's hair in about an hour. At the time, it made no sense at all.

1965: Uluguru, Tanzania. I was doing research for my dissertation in an area where I had worked, years before, on soil conservation. Now I was trying to be part of the Luguru culture, trying to understand as much as I could by taking part in everything. I was attending the tenth of a series of "coming-out" ceremonies for girls in the vicinity.

The drums pounded, an unchanging rhythm that gradually invaded the body and mind after several hours. The crowd of dancers circled round and round, dust sticking to the sweat that poured off them. The drum rhythm persisted like an endless mantra, inducing an almost trancelike state in which everyday reality was suspended. Every part of the body responded with an inner tremor like a powerful pulse beat.

Robin, the young English VSO (Voluntary Service Overseas) volunteer, nudged me, and as I turned to him, shouted in my ear over the tumult, "But where's the girl then? The—what do you call her—the *mwali?*"

"Not yet. Around sunset," I shouted back.

Time passed in a haze of heat and dust. Great earthenware pots of beer were brought out and women passed round woven raffia drinking vessels—hideously unhygienic but very cleverly constructed. Quarrels broke out and were as quickly ended. The shadows began to lengthen and the dust to look golden as the sun's rays came sideways through the mango trees. Through the crowd one sensed a heightened excitement, and on all sides I caught the word *"Mwali—mwali—mwali—*the *mwali*'s coming——mwali."*

And then suddenly there she was. A nearly naked girl, seated on a man's shoulders as he held her legs firmly. She was jerking and twitching her head, her neck, her shoulders, her breasts, moving her head as though seeking a way out, for her eyes were tightly shut. Her face and body shone with oil and were spattered with seeds. Her right hand held a fly switch made from an animal's tail which she shook and twitched to the new fierce rhythm that the drums had taken up. The circle of dancers broke up into a surging crowd, all moving to the drum beat, the man carrying the *mwali* moving among them, wild-eyed men before him waving branches to clear a way. From a distance the man was invisible, only the shaking, shimmying girl could be seen, displaying her body publicly for once in her lifetime. Everyone was shouting, screaming, ululating, praising her plumpness, her leaping breasts, her round face, fattened and made lasciviously pale by months of lying curled up on a tiny bed in a dark hut and fed everything she could eat.

From the day of her first menstruation until today—perhaps six months, perhaps three years—she had never seen the light, never been outside her prison except for an occasional moment, never spoken above a whisper, never seen a man. After this dance, the high point of her young life, she would go back into a hut again, to be joined by the husband chosen for her.

"Why do they do it?" asked Robin.

I gave him the stock anthropological answers about how rites of passage dramatized a change in status, reaffirmed values, and so on. At the same time, I was dissatisfied. Why such a horrendous mode of doing this? Six months to three years in the dark! Of course it dramatized her move to womanhood, but there had to be some reason why the rites took this particular form. A resolve formed at the back of my mind to find out more.

1976: Soho, London. Soho is a curious mixture of superb restaurants, theaters, and what is called "vice." Vice is the opposite of virtue. Since virtue is often held to be synonymous with chastity and celibacy, then logically vice must mean a concern with nonchastity. Curious that, in English, the adjective from "vice" is "vicious," which has connotations of cruelty, unnecessary harshness, and brutality.

As a teen-ager I remember Soho as a place intriguingly filled with provocatively dressed women standing at doorways. Public morality drove them off the streets by the 1960s, but could not check the notices on the doors: "Judy—model, 2nd Floor," "French model, 3rd Floor," and the plethora of little bulletin boards at stationers' shops and outside subway stations: "Colored girl, 22, seeks driving post, 2 p.m.–midnight," "Maisie, voluptuous model, always ready for clients," etc.

By the late sixties London was called a "swinging" city, a term that has come to be associated with promiscuity: an interesting example of euphemism to which I shall return. The people who used the term would probably be disgusted if one said, "You mean, people fuck a lot?" In reality Soho has become like New York's Forty-second Street: a seemingly endless collection of "sex shops," strip-tease shows, and pornographic movies. It was one of these establishments that caught my eye as I was strolling through Soho in 1970, marveling at the terrible hunger for sexual satisfaction that must exist in our society. The name of the little movie house was "The Filthiest Show in Town." Outside were photographs of women with mammoth breasts or bottoms accentuated by high heels and frilly panties. Other slogans proclaimed "Nothing hidden—explicit—Swedish lust—lesbian lovers—young studs at work—teenage frenzy."

I walked on down the street. On all sides other movie houses advertised: *Curious Newlyweds; Model's First Assignment; Secretaries at Play; The Private Life of a Nurse.* But it was the name of the theater that stuck in my mind. Why "filthy"? Plainly the show was concerned with sex. An "X" rating prevented children from entering, though a few blocks away films depicting war, violence, torture, and physical cruelty were freely available for them. Why should we call sex "dirty"? Why is a dirty joke, a smutty joke, a filthy story, always one concerned with sex? Why is an old man who likes sex called a "dirty old man"?

This is the question I want to explore. I also want to know why a girl should be shut in the dark for years. Why the Army insists on cutting one's hair. And why long hair is so threatening to some men and women.

2

Being in Limbo

The word "liminal" is not something you commonly hear at the supermarket, in the office, or at the tennis club. "Liminal" means things, places, persons, words that don't fit. That is, they do not fit into the normal categories that we are used to. And if this is the case, humans everywhere feel a sense of unease, embarrassment, or even threat. What is liminal is often marginal, nameless, shapeless, betwixt-and-between. Supposing you were in a clothing store looking for a new shirt. You pass by trousers, jeans, socks, underclothes, and suddenly between the T-shirts and sweaters you come on a display stand of chicken livers and veal kidneys. In that situation the liver and kidneys would be liminal, out of place.

When I first went to Tanganyika we did most of our shopping at the rather chaotic store of a dear old Greek man. It was always a local joke that you might well find parts for a pickup-truck differential among the cans of fruit or the cheese. The parts were liminal in that position, though not liminal in another part of the store. Another more dramatic example occurred recently in the faculty dining room of the college where I teach. Someone went to get salad from the salad bar. She dug vigorously into the large bowl of lettuce, then gave a piercing shriek, dropped the servers, and leaped back white as a sheet. Some practical joker had put a large garter snake in the lettuce. Lettuce in a snake pit might be marginal and liminal, but not very. Snakes in a salad bowl are, however, distinctly liminal! The car parts among the cans of fruit were merely funny; the snake was threatening, and some people plainly considered, judging by their subsequent attitude toward lettuce, even polluting.

The concept of being out of place, not fitting the standard categories of a culture, is a very important one. It is one that has been of great interest to me because the research and article which formed the basis for this book grew out of a concern with initiation rites at puberty.[1] These help people to pass from one status to another. They fall into three stages: separation from the old status and community; a transition stage; and, finally, a reincorporation back into the community in one's new status. The transition stage was first called "liminal" by a Frenchman named Arnold van Gennep, one of a brilliant collection of young sociologists known by the name of their journal, L'Année Sociologique. Working about the time of World War I, their group included Émile Durkheim, Marcel Mauss, Lucien Lévy-Bruhl, and Robert Hertz.

Van Gennep's investigation of rites of passage, first published in 1908, proved to be an enduringly important work. These rites take place in three stages in both simple, small-scale societies (sometimes called "primitive") and in large complex ones like our own. Even if one is joining a club, a sorority, a business, a military organization, a jail community—any time that one changes status fairly radically—there is some kind of separation from one's old state, if only by filling out forms, having an interview, or being frisked. There is always a transition phase when one is "in limbo," in neither the old nor the new status. Finally one is fully accepted, becomes a member, gets tenure, etc.

At a wedding one can see the phases quite well. The groom and bride with their attendants are prepared separately from each other and the community. The rite of marriage itself creates a new status, and until the following morning the pair are somewhat sacrosanct. If there is a honeymoon, this extends the liminal period. The return, often marked with a meal, is the reincorporation into the community.

When people carried out formal mourning, the funeral marked the separation, the mourning period marked the transition when people wore special clothes and eschewed social functions, and the end of mourning marked the incorporation of the dead person into the world of spirits and, at the same time, emphasized the adjustment of those who remained to their new roles.

In "primitive" societies the most dramatic events take place at puberty rites, which can involve physical mutilations to the genitals and even the head.

In America today we have little in the way of a formal rite that transfers a child into adulthood—a bar mitzvah, a confirmation are in the tradition, but certainly do not confer full adult status. Perhaps we have other ways of dealing with, or trying to solve, the problems that initiation rites attempt to deal with.

Americans do not emphasize puberty rites, but lay greater stress on rites at birth, marriage, and death.

Van Gennep was struck by the universal nature of rites of passage. However, many scholars, confronted with the bewildering range of variation in human cultures, concluded by the 1950s and 1960s that any search for universal human laws of conduct was doomed to failure. Yet psychologists, and particularly psychoanalysts, persisted, their efforts evoking criticism from anthropologists.

First, like Freud and Durkheim, some latter-day psychologists have persisted in equating early humans with modern primitive peoples like the Australian Aborigines. This *may* be accurate, but we have no way of knowing. All humans have been around for the same length of time; after all, we are all one species. Thus, while the *material* culture of the Australians may have been much the same as that of stone-age Europeans, we have no idea at all about the changes in social, political, and religious beliefs and practices that may have taken place over the past thousands of years.

Second, some psychoanalysts have continued to equate Western infantile behavior with that of "primitive" peoples. This raises an extremely difficult question. No human group is inherently inferior to any other group. In any group there will be highly intelligent and rather stupid people in about the same proportions. If one group happens to be politically or economically dominant over another, then inevitably it will stress the stupid members of the other group and the intelligent members of its own as being typical.

If some of the rituals of peoples in so-called primitive cultures ("simple," "nonindustrial," or "nonliterate" are perhaps better terms) appear to be similar to what children do in the West, this does not make the members of those cultures infantile.

The third reason why anthropologists have criticized psychological theories about human societies is summed up by the great British anthropologist Mary Douglas. Psychology, she tells us, "turns its face away from society, and back towards the individual."[2] But why not? Surely to consider a society as other than a collection of individuals is to think of it as though it existed as a concrete thing—to reify it. True, anthropologists are concerned with the group nature of society, but they also use individual cases to illustrate what seems to be the norm. And if there are problems, fears, anxieties which are common to *all* individuals, then there must be an effect on the whole societies in which they live. Obviously, idiosyncratic, personal, individual problems have no bearing on a society as a whole, but they are not my concern. I am concerned with fears and anxieties common to all humans.

If, despite all kinds of exceptions, we find similar patterns of behavior in societies that are totally separate geographically, linguistically, and ethnically, we only have a limited number of alternative explanations. We can postulate that the patterns arose among the aboriginal human group and that they are genetically transmitted or that they diffused as the group spread over the world. We can postulate that particular environmental circumstances (which might include the way in which the society is organized) generate particular forms of behavior. We could also suggest a combination of these factors.

In the 1960s it was also fashionable to deny that any form of behavior could be genetically transmitted—everything had to be learned. As a reaction to the cruder assertions of racism or to the subtleties of its modern proponents (such as Arthur R. Jensen, William Schockley, and Hans Eysenck), this was fair enough, but some had a nagging conviction that perhaps certain forms of behavior *might* be genetically transmitted. This conviction had nothing to do with race. All humans possess certain similar social institutions. It is as though all societies were issued, for recording, a wax disk which has on it a number of cuts. We all have the same disk which has the same cuts. Each society, however, puts different songs on each cut, the songs being the details of the culture. But they can only be different within the confines of the particular cut and disk. Look at it this way: all societies have a large desk with numbers of drawers and pigeonholes. We all have the same desk with the very same drawers, etc., but what gets put in the drawers is the culture—the ethnographic detail.

The ability to acquire a language—not any particular language —is a genetically inherited trait. The linguistic scholar Noam Chomsky said that we should regard language as part of the physiological make-up of humans in the same way that ears and eyes are. Whatever language is spoken around us before the age of about twelve or thirteen we can pick up like a tape recorder. After that age, we can learn other languages but never as native speakers. (Ironically, it is usually at that age that foreign language instruction *starts* in schools.) The same thing goes for most basic cultural items. The well-known anthropologist Clyde Kluckhohn once said that culture is like a map—one can be very good at map reading and can find one's way around, but one never knows the country like the people born and brought up there.

So, if all cultures do possess the same basic "desk" with its parts, of what do the parts consist? Perhaps the most important genetically inherited trait, and one which affects the rest of us profoundly, is the human need to set up norms of conduct—not any particular norms, except ones that fall within the acceptable range of human conduct. Take a college classroom. After the first few lectures, students tend to sit in the same seats and resent any interlopers. Or take a long sea voyage. The first day no one knows quite how to behave. What should one wear at breakfast? Is a bathing suit acceptable at lunch? What about dinner? What should one tip a steward? Yet within a few days a quite rigid code of conduct will develop, the contravening of which will lead to group disapproval, if not ostracism. This trait once had a great evolutionary advantage. A collection of people who conform to the standards of a group have a much better survival chance in harsh conditions than a bunch of raging individualists.

Humans have culture; culture is only possible in its fullest flowering through speech and language.* Speech and language-learning ability are genetically inherited, but culture is not. However, institutionalization of behavior, or rather, the need to do so, is genetically inherited. Thus, once a pattern of learned behavior develops in a particular society because it proves to be useful or satisfying in some way, then the genetically inherited need for norms, aided by the genetically inherited speech and language capacity, will perpetuate that cultural trait. The trait itself, of course, is *not* genetically inherited. One characteristic of humans, plainly connected to and part of their language capacity, is the use of symbols. All words are symbols: arbitrary sounds used by one society to represent things and concepts. Part of this symbolizing ability is devoted to another human universal: the need to classify and categorize. Presented with a new object or word, our minds immediately test and compare it with previously acquired knowledge, sifting and sifting at great speed until we are able to store it in its correct place. Arising out of this we have tendency to condense and subsume a lot of concepts under one symbol. No doubt this can be useful; it can also prove dangerous and the foe of rational human thought. National flags, sovereigns, particular colors, words for other groups—all these are examples of the result of categorization and the condensation of symbols. Any symbol evokes some kind of emotion; condensed symbols are highly charged with emotion.

A culture has its particular set of symbolic categories which serve to classify the world in which its people live. Because symbols are such a basic part of our existence, we react emotionally

* Many writers still refer to "man" as the species to which we belong. I used to do the same until I read Elaine Morgan's delightful *The Descent of Woman*. I shall write, perhaps ad nauseam, about the extent to which linguistic categorization affects our thoughts and deeds. If we use "man" rather than "humans" to describe ourselves, we tend to get a very warped picture. It is the same with "girl" to describe a woman. Oddly, some of those who pointed out that the use of "boy" for a man of African descent (and see all the stories with room boys, houseboys, kitchen boys, safari boys, etc.) showed that the speaker perceived the person referred to as less than adult, still have not grasped that when they use "girl" for a woman they are doing exactly the same thing. Colleges still refer to "men" and "girls." "woman Friday" might sound particularly absurd, but then the very term "gal Friday" is curiously condescending. Daniel Defoe did at least not use "boy Friday."

when something does not fit our normal way of classifying the
things with which we come into contact. Our reaction varies from
amusement to a feeling of danger or outrage. (Recently I was
delighted when grading an exam. A student was asked to explain
the difference between the pelvis of a monkey and that of an ape.
She answered that a monkey's was quite different because it was
very "svelte." She meant that it is much more narrow than an
ape's, but the use of the word "svelte" in this context conjured up
the immediate mental vision of a slinky simian in a satin skirt.)

When someone is passing from one status to another, as in the
transition phase of a rite of passage, one "does not fit." When one
is in this stage, one is often believed to be in a condition of ritual
danger, open to malign spiritual influences, and often a source of
spiritual danger to others. In all cultures that which does not fit in
the normal established categories may be perceived as funny or
embarrassing, but to many peoples it may go much further: it may
be dangerous-in danger; threatening-threatened; ritually polluting-
polluted.

Any culture sets up its own world view, its cosmology, its own
set of cultural categories. This is based on the language of the culture. Mary Douglas, in her book *Purity and Danger,* takes as one
example the "abominations" of Leviticus and shows that those
things labeled as "abominations" are always those that do not fit
the established classifications of the culture. If there is a category
of animals permitted to be eaten that have four legs, cloven
hoofs and chew the cud, then logically pigs and camels cannot
be eaten. Pigs have cloven hoofs but do not chew the cud and
camels chew the cud but do not have cloven hoofs. Similarly, fish
permitted to be eaten must have scales and fins. If there is a fish
that does not have scales or fins, then it cannot be eaten. The anthropologist Marvin Harris recently explained that pigs are taboo
to Jews and Muslims because pigs do not sweat, cannot stand
much direct heat, and are unsuited to nomadic pastoralism.[3] This
is all true, but the system of categorization adopted by Leviticus
(which, remember, is part of the word of God handed down to
Moses for orthodox believers) gives linguistic backing to what
may have been a pragmatic consideration.

The primacy of the Word—language—is absolute. In Jewish
belief one can never know the true name of God; indeed, even

today orthodox Jews write God "G–d" just to be on the safe
side. The whole mystical movement of Kabbalism was based on
the power of words. One story is told of an old rabbi who asked a
young man what he did and, when told that he wrote out copies of
the Torah, told the young man to be very careful. A letter too
many or too few could destroy the world. The German philosopher Ernst Cassirer wrote of the widespread belief in the Word.
He noted that "thousands of years before the Christian era, God
is conceived as a spiritual being who *thought* the world before he
created it, and who used the Word as a means of expression and
an instrument of creation.[4] He tells us that the Witota Indians, of
Colombia, say, "In the beginning the Word gave the Father his origin." And, in sum, the Word "becomes a sort of primary force, in
which all being and all doing originate."[5] This mystical power attaching to language is not fortuitous. It is the possession of language and speech that radically differentiates humans from all
other animals. This basic uniqueness, which makes possible so
much else that is uniquely human, imparts a sacred quality to language. Small wonder, then, that our systems of classifying and categorizing the world in which we live (and die) themselves
achieve a sacred quality which conditions not merely our thoughts
but our actions. Because of the sacred nature ascribed to them,
criticisms or attacks on the systems for irrationality are resisted
with enormous emotion.

   Not fitting into a category frequently involves ritual impurity, or
pollution. Douglas gives us a good example in our thinking about
dirt. Most of us today when thinking of dirt also start thinking
about germs. Yet it is only a century since Louis Pasteur introduced us to the idea of the existence of micro-organisms, and
there is no doubt that long before Pasteur, people in Europe had
clear ideas about what was or was not dirty. Douglas suggests that
most of what we categorize as "dirty" really is something "out of
place" as we conceive correctness. People would label as "dirty"
shoes on a table, underclothes in a closet for outer garments,
kitchen utensils in the bedroom. People of my generation were so
obsessed about "germs" that we were hesitant to use a spoon or
glass previously used by a parent or sibling and recoiled with
revulsion from an apple bitten by someone else. Sigmund Freud

gives an example of this kind of idea when he observes how bizarre it is that lovers who explore each others mouths with their
tongues are often disgusted by the idea of using the lover's tooth-
brush! Between family members or lovers plainly these reservations have little to do with the reality of shared bacteria and are
much more the result of symbolic associations.

Van Gennep noted, and hundreds of ethnographers have observed the same, that the transition phase placed a person in a
liminal, betwixt-and-between condition and that in this state, the
person does not exist or is considered either dangerous to others
or in danger from all kinds of external causes. I recall in 1957
seeing a group of boys in northern Tanganyika who were wearing
a mixture of male and female clothing and carrying bows and
arrows. Wishing to be polite, I greeted them in the customary
manner but there was no response. I might not have existed,
though in this culture it is unthinkable to pass anyone at any time
without a greeting appropriate to the age and sex of the person
and the time of day. I watched them in astonishment (I had not
studied anthropology then) and saw them pass men, women,
elders without a word passing on either side. It was as though the
boys were invisible. In a society where one greets a person by first
enunciating his or her status (e.g., elder, father, mother, child),
one can hardly greet someone who has (for the moment, at least)
no recognizable status. For everyday purposes, the boys *were* invisible, for they were in the transition phase of their initiation ritual and as such, in a liminal condition.

When something or someone is liminal, then, to a member of
the society concerned, it, he, or she is imbued with danger. Why?
Because the object concerned does not fall into the known categories of the culture. That which is part of our concept of order is
safe and nonthreatening. That which is disordered or does not fall
into the cultural categories of what is ordered is liminal and therefore dangerous. Probably the origin of this idea lies in the dualis-
tic vision of the world that the French anthropologist Claude Lévi-
Strauss has pointed out—the basic opposition between nature and
culture. What is part of culture is safe, known, categorized, part
of our system of order. What is not part of culture is then automatically assigned by our categorizing minds to the realm of dis-

order. Douglas puts it dramatically when she speaks of dirt. "Reflection on dirt involves reflection on the relation of order to disorder, being to non-being, form to formlessness, life to death."

To people in simple cultures, where one lives in a small settlement often surrounded by the bush, the forest, the jungle, the boundaries between what is brought under control—culture—and what is not—nature—are plain to see. Those things or persons who are considered dangerous are thought to be connected with or close to nature. Women are often thought to be closer to nature than men because of menstruation, childbirth, and lactation. Popular belief often imagines that "primitive" peoples feel a great closeness to and affinity with "nature." This may be true of some hunting and gathering peoples whose lives do not seek to alter and control nature, to impose order on it; but for agricultural peoples everywhere nature is seen as the enemy, the realm of disorder, of danger, and of death.

But what about our rational, agnostic, intellectual humanist? Surely he or she is not likely to be influenced by such transparently foolish notions. Perhaps. How do people in our society respond when confronted with a person who does not fit the standardized categories of the culture? Take, for example, a respectable family out for a walk who comes upon a blatant transvestite male decked out in country-western-style blond wig, high heels, and heavy make-up. Or a female prostitute in white boots and microskirt (in the 1960s, of course, this would have been acceptable normal dress and not a source of embarrassment). Neither of these persons fits into the standard categories of the culture and therefore they seem very threatening to order. At the very least, embarrassment is caused which may be covered by laughter.

How do average people respond to a drunk or mentally deranged person? Unless they are personally and intimately connected, they will respond either by trying to pretend that the person concerned does not exist—by ignoring the person—or by acute embarrassment. If they are insensitive, they may find it funny. But supposing you *are* involved? Supposing it is your brother or sister or parent who is behaving in a way that labels him or her as drunk or crazy? Won't your impulse be to try and persuade the person to act as "normally" as possible, to spare

theirs long, the transsexual medium long. Men comb their hair backward away from the face, women comb theirs diagonally forward
from a central parting, transsexuals comb theirs forward from a side
parting, and they oil it heavily in the style of women. Both men and
women cover their head, transsexuals go bareheaded. Perfume is used
by both sexes, especially at festive occasions and during intercourse.
The transsexual is generally heavily perfumed, and uses much makeup
to draw attention to himself. This is also achieved by his affected
swaying gait, emphasised by the close-fitting garments. His sweet fal-
setto voice and facial expression and movements also closely mimic
those of women.

In Omani society, where women are never allowed out without
their menfolk's permission and then only wearing an all-envelop-
ing *burqa* and face mask and are under no circumstances allowed
to speak to any man, they can freely talk to the transsexuals on
the street, admit them to their quarters, take part in singing and
dancing with them, and in general behave with them exactly as
though they were women. Aha, you might say, the transsexuals
are probably eunuchs. But this is not the case at all, for some of
them, when they have earned enough money, "become" men,
wear male dress, and get married to women. It is generally assumed that as *xanīth* they are utterly incapable of taking the male
part in sexual intercourse, and given the astounding effect of the
mind on the body, this may well be the case. However, once they
have become men, they then are able to have intercourse. In other
societies these persons would be liminal, dangerous, and threatening. In Oman, however, by having a special classification which
assigns them largely to the female category, they reinforce the established categories and provide no threat to anyone.

One of the questions posed by Mary Douglas is, What is it that
"makes primitive cultures pollution-prone [while] ours is not?" I
have already shown that while not prone to concepts of ritual purity and pollution to the extent that many simple societies are, we
nevertheless are affected if not infected by the same ideas. Moreover, the idea that only primitives are affected by real concerns
about ritual purity falls apart if we consider certain groups in
complex societies. Douglas, as a Catholic, is herself a member of
such a group. In Catholic belief, the terms "purity" and "pollution" are not used, but surely "state of grace" and "state of sin"

yourself shame and humiliation? In other words, to persuade t
person to be as "like everyone else" as possible?

One could compile an interesting list of persons who don't 1
and who therefore cause a feeling of embarrassment or eve
threat to others. Of course, there is a scale of threat involved
from mildly odd to acutely threatening. Consider how funny o1
sometimes quite terrifying the effect of a mask can be. There is a
paradox here, for if everyone in the world were to be exactly the
same, how dull a world it would be. Yet difference from what is
thought of as the norm can only be tolerated up to certain limits.
This passionate adherence to the normal, the regular, the
nonthreatening probably had its origin in human evolution, and
while the idea of norms is universal, what is considered abnormal
is purely learned cultural behavior.

Let me add one or two variants from the norm from my list:
the deformed and, similarly, lepers (where leprosy occurs) and
victims of poliomyelitis and other wasting diseases. And what
about university students as viewed by the public at large if they
behave in a manner which is not thought acceptable? Consider the
case of "bluestockings." Observe how many apparently intelligent
men feel instantly threatened by a woman scholar. Or note how
often male judges are prone to blame juvenile delinquency on
working mothers, who do not fill the role expectations of the
judge. Why not blame the fathers?

An extremely dramatic example of the effect of verbal categorization has recently been provided by a Norwegian woman
anthropologist, Unni Wikan.[6] Prostitutes and transvestites in
Western society are likely to cause embarrassment to a majority
of people. The same is true of Oman, a rigidly orthodox Muslim
state. However, the problem of liminality is very neatly solved
there by a category called in Arabic *xanīth:* male homosexual
prostitutes who dress in a manner different from men or women
but look much more feminine than masculine. Wikan describes
their appearance thus:

The transsexual . . . is not allowed to wear the mask or other female
clothing. His clothes are intermediate between male and female: he
wears the ankle-length tunic of the male, but with the tight waist of
the female dress. Male clothing is white, females wear patterned cloth
in bright coloured clothes. Men cut their hair short, women wear

are virtually the same. In Catholic belief, a person who has not attended weekly mass, for instance, is liable to be condemned to an eternity of punishment should he or she die before confession. Non-Catholics may wonder about the kindly and merciful deity allegedly presiding over such a brutal and merciless judgment, but the fact remains that a person in a state of sin (or ritual pollution) is liable to such punishment for failing to take the necessary steps to achieve a state of grace (or ritual purity).

The Catholics are not the only people in complex heterogeneous societies who still believe in what humanists would think of as barbarous ideas of this nature. Many orthodox Jews, otherwise totally assimilated into and part of American society, still follow practices based on the avoidance of ritual pollution. The same is probably true of many of the other multitude of religious groups in America.

Elsewhere in the world, the concept of purity and pollution is certainly not confined to "primitive" societies. The populations of the Arab countries, as well as those of Turkey, Iran, Pakistan, Afghanistan, Bangladesh, and Indonesia are in the main Muslim. The Islamic faith is replete with injunctions about pollution. Contact with a dog, for instance, involves one in ceremonial cleansing before one can engage in religious activity. Much more to the point for our present purpose, contact with the dead and with bodily emissions, particularly those concerned with sex, is considered extremely polluting. Perhaps worst of all is contact with a menstruating woman. I shall consider this again later.

In India, in spite of three centuries of contact with the West, in spite of Western-type education and fairly large-scale industrialization, the Hindu religion is all adhered to by a majority. Perhaps no religion in the world is so obsessed with pollution. To a high-caste Hindu, contact with a person from a lower caste is defilement. If a lower-caste person's shadow falls on one's food it may not be eaten. A cup used by a lower-caste person must be smashed lest one should be polluted. Really strict adherents will only drink by pouring a stream of liquid from the vessel to the mouth to prevent the contact of their own lips on the rim from polluting them back again. The traditional treatment of women, based on the concept of the evil and defiling nature of the female sex, is oppressive in the extreme. Hindu men suffer agonies of guilt for engaging in sex, which, they believe, pollutes them and depletes their virility from loss of semen, which is believed to be irreplaceable. In the West athletic coaches still hold a similar belief and it is certainly part of the folk belief of the West that sex for a man is highly debilitating. If one believes anything strongly enough, it usually comes to be so. Thus men who believe this, find sex makes them mentally and physically exhausted. Others, of course, believe the reverse, with highly satisfactory results.

Why is it that people like the Jews, Muslims, Hindus, and Catholics, who have produced so much great art, literature, philosophy, and music, should be so obsessively afraid of what are either perfectly natural and objectively harmless activities or of foods and drinks which are in use by other similar humans who do not suffer from the same concerns? Can it really be that by attaching a particular semantic label to something we thereby can render it dangerous or harmless? Are we really so daft? It seems we are.

Take food. All humans need food, and the range of what we can eat is enormous. At the same time, every culture has its own concept of what is the main food—meat, rice, corn porridge, fish —and also of what is and is not edible. Sometimes the basis for the classification is based on palatability or whether something is poisonous or not, but most often it is purely cultural. The idea of eating shellfish or pork to a strict Jew or Muslim is repulsive. Absurd, some of us say. True, but what about eating a slug or a grasshopper? Good sources of protein both of them and eaten by peoples in some cultures. Snails are considered excellent food by some people, but the same people would probably vomit over a dish of cooked earthworms. If we are taught early enough that certain things are classified as "food," then we eat them, and if not, we may be revolted by the very idea.

Something out of place, something that does not fit our established categories, something liminal, in other words—that is the key to many human ideas.

People like transvestites, prostitutes, drunks, and so on are seen by some to be threatening or embarrassing. But suppose we remove the threat by placing them in a different subcategory? A male transvestite may cause alarm or embarrassment on a village street, but put him on the stage and many people are highly amused. In England at Christmas a curious form of stage show occurs called a "pantomime," which has today little if anything to do with mime and is a genre of musical play based on a fairy tale such as "Little Red Ridinghood," "Puss in Boots," etc., intended ostensibly for children, but usually filled with sexual *double-entendres* only understood by adults. The most bizarre feature of the genre is that there are always three stock characters: the "principal boy," the "principal girl," and some form of old woman. While the principal girl is always an attractive young woman, the principal boy is not played by a man but invariably by a pretty young woman apparently chosen for the beauty and length of her legs. Always wearing minute shorts or tights and relatively high heels, she is dressed in such a way as to excite male sexual interest. She is identified as a male by the wearing of a male-type jacket and hat. Her association with the principal girl is always one of romantic attraction. Objectively, the relationship portrayed is emphatically a lesbian one, but apparently none of the audience consciously perceives it this way. Indeed, the irony is that for the average pantomime audience a lesbian relationship would be abhorrent and threatening in the extreme.†

The old woman, portrayed by a man, is always a grotesquely comic caricature. Were a man to do this in everyday life the theater audience would be horrified and disgusted, yet in this context it is considered excruciatingly funny. A recent extension of the same form of wit is often seen in the British television series called "Monty Python's Flying Circus." There seem to be two underlying themes to this kind of permitted transvestism which in "normal" life would lead to reactions of horror. One is that of male envy of females. The other is the placing of something or someone into a sort of controlled liminality. Because it is safe and under control, humans find it funny. The lesbian theme of the principal boy and girl is plainly sexually titillating, but once more, under strict control, it is considered safe and nonthreatening, rather as the risqué jokes are acceptable if clothed in the restricting limits of the *double-entendre*.

Another example of controlled liminality is a college classroom. In that setting it is possible to discuss freely all kinds of matters—sex, incest, defecation—which would prove difficult or embarrass-

† Both in the United States and Britain the part of Peter Pan is customarily played by a young woman.

ing to many of the audience in private conversation on a one-to-one basis.

Just after writing the above I visited the bathroom at a college library. Two graffiti on the walls demanded that one should "kill all faggots." I recently heard a kind woman of sixty-five remark that she would like to take a gun and shoot everyone on a nude bathing beach. Yet one could guarantee that the graffiti writers and the woman would think jokes about homosexuals or nudists highly diverting. Evidently we laugh at what we find most threatening. But why on earth do we find these things so threatening?

Initiation rites illustrate in a highly dramatic way some of the anxieties shared by all humans about sexuality. The problem that human societies attempt to solve in a variety of ways and with varying degrees of success is how to transfer children from what is perceived as the asexual world of childhood to the sexual world of adulthood. Two problems arise. One is the universal human fear and embarrassment about sex except in prescribed contexts. The other is brought about by the ritualized nature of the metamorphosis and its consequent liminal period. All liminal periods in all rites of passage are somewhat anomalous. As we have seen, anomalousness, or the lack of a "normal" category, is always odd, often rather threatening. If we are dealing with a transfer from inactivity to an activity—sex—which in and of itself is extremely threatening to humans, then inevitably the transition period in the rites is bound to be perceived as unusually threatening and dangerous.

3

Death and Sex

What man is he that liveth and shall not see death?

Psalms 89:48

Being alive and human is to face the inevitability of death. For us, carrying our inescapable mental burden, "Every attempt to get at the meaning of life must inevitably face the question of death."[1]

The story of the creation from Genesis is an allegory of the human condition. Forgetting (if we can) for the present the portrayal of woman as the tempter, the weak, the foolish, what *is* the "tree of the knowledge of good and evil," the eating of the fruit of which had such momentous and tragic consequences? God tells Adam, "[In] the day that thou eatest thereof thou shalt surely die." One might take the view that this sounds like the threatening parent who tells its child, "I'll call a policeman to take you away if you aren't good!" since when Adam does eat the fruit, he does not die the same day. On the other hand, he knows that he *will* die. That is the knowledge of the greatest evil—death. Or perhaps one should say that the greatest evil is not death, but rather the knowledge that death awaits us all.

But what is the first thing that does happen to Adam and Eve after they eat the fruit? "And the eyes of them both were opened,

and they knew that they were naked." This is the great truth
revealed to them. Then, we are told, God said (to himself,
presumably), "Behold, the man is become as one of us, to know
good and evil; and now, lest he put forth his hand, and take also
of the tree of life, and eat, and live forever: Therefore God sent
him forth from the garden of Eden . . ." There are a number of
interesting points here. One I do not wish to pursue but worthy of
mention is the implication that God is one of many deities, for He
says "one of us." What about the knowledge that Adam has
acquired?

He knows about sex and is ashamed of it. He knows that he
will die. Why is it that humans know about death and animals do
not? The knowledge is passed on through language and speech. It
is conceivable that an animal might pass on to its young through
mime to be modest about sex (and we should remember that the
higher mammals have to learn to copulate; they do not know how
to instinctively). Without language and speech, however, the full
range of human fears, anxieties, beliefs, and practices concerning
sexuality would be impossible to inculcate.

If we turn to the mythology of another world religion we find
an interesting parallel to Adam's acquisition of knowledge. In
Buddhism the great emphasis is on the "middle way" in all things,
a sound precept for all of us. Excessive sexuality is strongly dis-
couraged. It is told of the young Buddha that he was a prince. His
parents were anxious not only that he should live in the utmost
luxury, but that he should be screened from all knowledge of the
pain and unhappiness of the real world. However, despite their
great solicitude, he escaped four times from his luxurious palace
and went into the outside world. On his first excursion he met an
old man, on his second a sick one, on the third a dead one. Thus,
he became aware of sickness, old age, and of the inevitability of
the death of the body. His fourth escape from the palace brought
him into contact with a religious person and, it is said, thus initiated his career as a spiritual leader, since he now realized that one
could cope with the problems of pain and death. He had found
the great solution.

The humanist would say, of course, that he had in reality discovered the greatest of all human illusions and self-deceptions:
the same denial of the reality and finality of death claimed by the

adherents of Christianity. I was taken by a character in a recent novel of Paul Theroux's who would not hire an Irish chauffeur because "I would never hire a man who believed in an afterlife to do a dangerous job."[2] Students of mine are often highly amused that some tribes in Oceania still believe that males have nothing to do with the procreation of children. "How can they be so dumb?" they ask regarding those who cannot perceive the reality of the beginnings of life. Yet many of these same students take on faith, and without a shred of evidence that would be admissible in a court of law, the assertion that death brings one to an afterlife. One can almost hear the observing Martians saying to one another: "How can they be so dumb?"

Does a belief in an afterlife negate the fear of death? Is the void that faces the humanist more horrifying than the assurance of an afterlife with which the religious person claims to be endowed? Christians allegedly face death with confidence in a better life to come (though presumably they might have terrible anxieties about the possibility of hell), but Herman Feifel, a professor of psychiatry, tells us: "The religious person, when compared to the nonreligious person, is personally more afraid of death [and] even the belief that one is going to heaven is not sufficient to do away with the personal fear of death in some religious persons."[3]

What about those cultures where a heroic death was ardently desired? Where a cowardly death was more feared than death itself? I was a member of the Household Cavalry during World War II, the senior and most prestigious group of troops in the British Army. Among us, certainly death with dishonor was more feared than death—an example of how effective authority and group disapproval can be. Apart from the berserk phenomenon when the temporarily insane fighter rushes into the fray so assured of his invincibility that he rarely gets killed, there is no doubt in my mind that one continues to fear death. One can conquer and live with the fear, but like the native population of a conquered territory, it is always there, always a threat, always ready to rise again. The fear of being seen to be afraid is probably the most worrisome one to the soldier new to action. And what is it we fear if not the verbal contempt of our fellows, the verbal categorization of coward? But the real fear, the nagging, deep-seated, gut fear, is the terror of mutilation and a death too soon.

Myra Bluebond-Langner, an anthropologist who has concerned herself with the terminally ill, has claimed that terminally ill patients were not afraid of death *per se*—rather that "fear of pain and loss of self-control are more common than fear of death itself. Still more so is fear of dying alone."[4] Surely it is precisely these—particularly the latter—that we mean when we say we fear death. The inevitability not merely of death itself, but of its stark and chilling aloneness, the impossibility of companionship—it is this that compels our worst terror. It was probably this aspect of dying that led important people in ancient times to have wives, slaves, and warriors slain and buried with them, so that they might not go alone into "the undiscovered country from whose bourn no traveller returns."

Once more we return to the primacy of language. In ancient Egypt it was believed that the soul of the dead person needed not only food and clothing for its journey, but also had to know the names "of the gatekeepers in the other world, for only the knowledge of these names can unlock the doors of Death's Kingdom."[5] Only humans know they will die; they know because of language. St. John prefaces his gospel with another recognition of the basic fact that makes humans human: "In the beginning was the Word. And the Word was with God and the Word was God." Without words we cannot be human: that is to say, without words we cannot know about death; we cannot discuss sex; we cannot comprehend the concept of incest. And unless we grasp that fact, we shall not understand a whole connected area of our humanity which is rooted in the basic prohibition on incest. Without the idea of incest and its prohibition, the whole concept of kin makes no sense. Monkeys, apes, and indeed dogs and cats have mothers, fathers, uncles, aunts, and cousins. With the possible exception of mothers (to which we shall return), there is no recognition of any of these relatives except in terms of older-younger, bigger-smaller, our group-other group. Humans do not constantly talk about death, sex, and incest. If we did, we should be accused of being morbid or prurient. We do, however, constantly remind ourselves of all three by implication every time we use kinship terms. We may partially repress our fears of death or joke about it to cover our terror. Freud first pointed out that we laugh most at those things we fear most. If you want to get people's attention at a party or the interest of students at a lecture, just mention death, sex, or incest. Not only have you got their attention but also the audience will never entirely forget what you said.

If we all eventually know about death, when does this awareness first come to us? In our Western society today many people may be in their twenties before they have physical contact with a human death. But for the inhabitant of a small rural village in Africa or Mexico, hardly a month passes without a death occurring in which one is in some sense involved. Of course, deaths take place every day in our society too, but we do everything we can to minimize the fact. "Sickness as the symptom of perishability is largely banished to the hospital [and] in public secular life death plays practically no role at all," writes Helmut Thielicke. We may be delayed occasionally by a string of cars with their headlights on in the daytime, but, as Thielicke reminds us, "in our cities, our genuinely public places, no longer do funeral processions pass ominously through the streets, at least not the major streets, the expressways . . ." This attempt to banish the presence of disease and death, about which I shall have more to say, is, however, as unsuccessful as the attempt of the parents of the young Buddha to insulate him from reality.

A Boston psychiatrist, Gregory Rochlin, in his book *Man's Aggression,* deals with this topic in an unusual manner.[6] Children become aware of death, he suggests, at a very early age and, in an impulse of self-defense against the possibility of their own death or that of those who care for them, respond in an aggressive manner. As we grow older, the well-adjusted person gains control over these aggressive impulses. The less well-adjusted never do and may constitute the violent members of our society. Some of us go too far the other way: we overcompensate and turn the anger resulting from a perceived threat to the self inwards. The result is inevitable: intense depression.

But to return to the child. Even if the child is fortunate enough to grow up in a home where there is no television to make death seem part of every entertainment, whether in cartoons or the never-ending stream of video-sludge that encourages the notion that every problem that afflicts society is cured with a gun, it cannot escape the fact of death almost as soon as speech is comprehended. Does not meat come from dead animals or, for that matter, vegetables from dead plants? Some of our country roads are littered with the corpses of the squirrels, woodchucks, rabbits, skunks, cat, and dogs that we slaughter with our monster automobiles. Bug-sprays kill mosquitoes, ants, roaches (maybe). Unless a child is blind or singularly unobservant, it can hardly fail to be aware of mortality by the age of two or three years, and probably far earlier.

Rochlin has his moments of optimism. It is, he suggests, "the knowledge of death which gives man his zeal for living." Perhaps. Yet Feifel turns this upside down when he says: "I believe that the frenetic accent on, and continual search for, the 'fountain of youth' in many segments of our society reflects. . . . anxieties concerning death."[7]

Let us turn to the fear of sex. We have seen that animals have no knowledge of death. Similarly, they presumably do not reflect on sex. Humans, on the other hand, probably think about, fantasize about, and in fact probably engage in, more sexual activity than any other animal. Just as having to die does not resign us to death, so sexual activity does not lessen our fear of it. A French writer, Georges Bataille, makes this extremely interesting observation: "Man is the only animal who stands abashed in front of death or sexual union. He may be more or less abashed, but in any case his reaction differs from that of other animals."[8] We may have knowledge about sex but it is a knowledge that we hedge about with endless restrictions. Anthropologists have long concentrated and continued to speculate on the prohibition against incest (to which we shall return). Bataille acknowledges its importance. "Is there," he asks, "anything more firmly rooted in us than the horror of incest? We look on physical union with the mother or father or with a brother or sister *as inhuman* [my emphasis]." He is quite right. To be human as we know humanity depends on an honoring of the incest taboo, so that breaking it makes us inhuman. But it is not merely incest we fear, Bataille insists, it is sexuality itself. "The human spirit is prey to the most astounding impulses. Man goes constantly in fear of himself. His erotic urges terrify him."

There is tremendous cultural variation in human attitudes to sex, as I shall describe in a moment, but it is my contention that in every culture we find anxiety surrounding sexuality. One might say, looking at the American scene of today with "swingers" advertising services, "adult" books, magazines, and movie shows, "massage parlors," and so on, that we at least have shed our worries. Not a bit of it. I am bombarded by literature from a variety of craziness. At the very same time as I receive brochures from California advertising grotesque means of satisfying sexual appetites, I also receive the righteous polemics of the so-called Right to Life movement, who would apparently prefer to see the backstreet butchers and coat-hanger abortions that proliferate in those barbarous countries that forbid legal abortion and let the thousands of unwanted children live an abused life. Observe the furious opposition to plans for sex education in schools. I have before me a letter soliciting funds and support from something called the "American Christian Cause" which calls on me to turn back "the tide of corruption, immorality and indecency that is sweeping our nation down the gutter toward total collapse."[9] In a subsequent letter I am urged to nominate other "conservative Christians" to join the fight. Why me? But this kind of thing is an indication of the strength of the reaction to sexual permissiveness that is likely to appear in next few years. Not only will it sweep away the really awful aspects of the "sexual revolution"—the mass of pornography encouraging child abuse, rape, and other forms of sexual violence—but it is likely that we may be stampeded into a hysterical puritanism that will take us back to a darker age. Sometimes it is hard to know which is more nauseating—the leering, elbow-nudging, winking prurience of TV's "Three's Company" and similar shows or the pietistic puritanism of the sexual cripples.

At the time of writing there is great public debate over sex on television. Aljean Harmetz writes in the *TV Guide* of May 6–12, 1978:

A girl runs along the beach on ABC, her breasts bouncing like white balloons in the twilight. On NBC a different girl bends down so the camera can linger on her buttocks. Neither girl was an actress a year ago. Both are beneficiaries of the fact that television is buying "butts and bosoms," "girls that jiggle."

The reporter goes on, however, to note that:

Most of the men who are buying and selling bodies say—quite seriously—that there is no sex on television. They point to the lack of nudity, intercourse and four-letter words. . . . In no way are the joys of adult sex being celebrated on prime-time television. What are bouncing across the screen in tank tops and hot pants, in wet T-shirts and towels, are adolescent sexual fantasies.

We come again to controlled liminality. Providing the frame is established to delimit what is acceptable at that time and in that culture, the people who would otherwise feel threatened, feel secure.

Because of its immense complexity, it is hard to generalize about American society. When one is dealing with small simple societies, generalizations are far easier. Everyone is engaged in cultivation or herding, most hold the same beliefs, likes and dislikes, prejudices. In the United States we have so many different divisions: economic class, religion, ethnicity, occupation, region. And within each of these divisions are dozens of subdivisions. The nearest we can get in our nation to the situation one finds in a tribe is in the small rural village, the sort of place that William Faulkner wrote about in the past or John Gardner writes about today. Yet even there the poulation is split and not homogeneous.

I recently obtained a copy of a book called *Sex Research: Studies from the Kinsey Institute*.[10] It contains brief synopses by Martin Weinberg of the famous sex studies on the American male (1948) and female (1953). In some ways, those studies read today like ancient history, but many of the reported attitudes shed light on our discussion. Consider the following from Weinberg:

Many a college male will have kissed dozens of girls, although he has had intercourse with none of them. On the other hand the lower level male is likely to have had intercourse with hundreds of girls, but he may have kissed few of them. (P. 69)

And on the subject of nudity:

Some of the older men and women in this [lower] group take pride in the fact that they have never seen their spouses nude. . . . There are cases of lower level males who have been highly promiscuous, who have had intercourse with several hundred females, and who emphasize the fact that they have never turned down an opportunity to have intercourse except "on one occasion when the girl started to remove her clothing before coitus. She was too indecent to have intercourse with!" (P. 70)

Let us look at two extremes of sexual behavior to demonstrate the extraordinary range of human sexual behavior and the fact that there is no standard to which all humans conform. The first comes from western Ireland. John C. Messenger says of the community to which he gives the fictitious name of Inis Beag: "Both lack of sexual knowledge and misconceptions about sex among adults combine to brand Inis Beag as one of the most sexually naive of the world's societies."[11] Elsewhere, in a short essay humorously entitled "The Lack of the Irish," published with a companion piece by Donald S. Marshall called "Too Much in Mangaia," Messenger describes the fanatical prudishness of the people in this Irish village.[12] Sex is a "sphere of activity which arouses much anxiety and fear." Men are believed to be much more "sexually disposed than women." Women are taught to "endure" sex with their husbands because to refuse would be a mortal sin. The idea that women might have orgasms was said to be unknown alike to men and women. Sex in Inis Beag is thought to be debilitating and a menstruating woman to be dangerous to a man. The average age for marriage there was thirty-six for a man and twenty-five for a woman, but 29 per cent of those eligible for marriage remained celibate, and premarital sex was quite unknown. Even marital sex was "limited as to foreplay and the manner of consummation," and both partners always wore underclothes. This terror of nakedness was carried to extraordinary limits. Many of the men were fishermen, but none knew how to swim because they "have never dared to bare their bodies in order to learn the skill." Thus, many of them drown at sea, while others "who were unwilling to face the nurse when ill, because it might have meant baring their bodies to her" die because they left treatment too late. Masturbation, body exploration, any words referring to sex, open urination or defecation—all are "severely punished by word and deed." Doubtless the sexual mores of these sad people would be extolled by my friends of the American Christian Cause, but to read Messenger's account of Inis Beag is to read of an unhappy, gossip-obsessed, repressed community. Plainly, human joy and a mutual respect among human beings does not lie here.

The other extreme is described by Marshall, writing of the Pacific island of Mangaia, where, he tells us: "A flick of the eye, a raised eyebrow in a crowd, can lead to copulation—without a word. There is no social contact between the sexes that does not lead directly to coitus—copulation is the only imaginable outcome of heterosexual contact." Of course, this excludes those prohibited by incest regulations—indeed, he tells us that "six-year-old Mangaian brother and sister would not think of walking hand-in-hand in town." A boy undergoes a painful "superincision" at puberty, which involves cutting "through the cartilaginous tissue for almost the full length of the [penis]." Once he is realed, however, the boy undergoes explicit instruction for giving his sexual partners total satisfaction. A man who could not give his partners several orgasms was poorly regarded. A New Zealand administrator who was stationed there and, although married, took every advantage of the opportunities constantly afforded was liked but thought an ineffective performer since he "always laughed before the joke was over"—one of the more delightful euphemisms I have met. Mangaian boys and girls are expected to have had extensive and active premarital sex.

Here then we have extreme promiscuity—very active sex lives by males and females. Happiness? Probably a great deal more than in Inis Beag. Anxiety about sex? Fear of sexuality? Superficially, the idea apears laughable, but in fact it seems that even the Mangaians are victims of the same sorts of fears, though differently expressed, as the people in western Ireland. Marshall tells us that "there is a unique modesty about exposure of adult sex organs; Mangaians are horrified at the casualness with which a European exposes his penis to other men when he urinates."

It seems, too, that because of the very high value placed on adequate male performance, men suffer great anxiety about the possibility of impotence as they grow older—a sure recipe for that very condition. It is odd that the author of the article, published in a psychological journal, should apparently be unaware of the self-fulfilling prophecy aspect of such concerns, since he plainly subscribes to the unfounded American (and British) folk belief that much sexual activity in youth will lead to impotence in middle age. After telling us about the sexual athleticism of the Mangaian male, who "copulates far more frequently and much more vigorously in his youth than does the average European or the average American," he suddenly shows his true puritan colors ("if something is pleasurable, it must be bad for you") and remarks that the activity in youth has its consequence with the Mangaians who "apparently pay a biological penalty for this activity rate." Very odd reading in a psychological journal, one would think, but then, many psychologists are extremely puritanical.

Even so, with the promiscuous Mangaians there are areas of extreme anxiety concerning sex.

The Nuer of the southern Sudan are also nonprudish about sex. Probably few people in the world wear fewer clothes—E. E. Evans-Pritchard speaks of "the stark nakedness of Nuer amid their cattle," for apart from a string of beads round their loins, young people of neither sex wear anything.[13] Older married women who have children wear some clothing but many men wear nothing. The Nuer are also very relaxed in their attitudes to premarital sex, which is expected of boys and girls, though girls should not get pregnant. However, even here we find that a man must always cover his genitals in the presence of his parents-in-law, and though there is great promiscuity among young people, the act of sex itself must always take place in privacy.[14] There is little if any correspondence between the wearing of clothes and strict sexual morality—indeed, clothes in our Western society are frequently used to enhance sexual interest. But whatever society one may mention, there are always some restrictions concerning sexual behavior, and particularly the act of sex itself.

Returning for a moment to Mangaia and the question of privacy, one might challenge my point when we read in Marshall that a man "may copulate at any age in the single room of a hut that contains five to fifteen family members of all ages. . . . His daughter may receive and make love with a series of nightly visitors in the same room." What is made clear, however, is that the Mangaians enjoy "an extraordinary sense of 'public privacy.'" Even though everyone concerned knows what is going on, it is as though the couple concerned were surrounded by an impenetrable wall. I shall return to this in connection with defecation.

But what about "swingers" parties? What about the group sex that is allegedly taking place in major cities today? Does this not cast doubt on the idea that humans are anxious about and private in their sexual activities? I don't think so. Although there has been a "sexual revolution" and examination of any magazine stand will make clear that many people are much more open and frank, they still tend to be inhibited about the *act* of sex being done publicly. It may be true that, group sex takes place, but it only does so as a very self-conscious rebellion, and it in no way represents any kind of norm.

If sex does take place in public it is usually for a particular ritual purpose believed to generate power in a mystical way *because* it is the very antithesis of normal human behavior. A good example of this is found in a very powerful secret society in western Tanzania called the Bacwezi who believe that under ritually induced trance they become possessed by the spirits of bygone heroes.

A German anthropologist, Hans Cory, claimed that he was initiated into the society.[15] He described how during the period of the initiation rites, the initiands are identified as children and grandchildren of the previous initiates, and how, on the fourth day of the rites, there is a rite called *kumala muziro,* meaning "to end the taboo," which includes two normally unthinkable forms of behavior. The rite involves the leaders performing a public act of sexual congress before the assembled members and initiands; the new initiand doing the same; and all the people present being paired off and also doing the same after being blindfolded and partnered with an unknown person. Sex performed by couples other than in private is one of the normally tabooed actions. The other is that the members and initiands have been fictitiously named mothers, fathers, grandparents, and children for the rites, and the pairing off with unknown partners therefore constitutes a ritualized breaking of the prohibition on incest. I suggest that the intention is the same—namely, to carry out an act normally utterly prohibited to members of a society, but in a controlled setting. The parallel to transvestism and lesbianism in the Western theater is clear. But in the case of Bacwezi the actors go much further. The intention is to generate mystical power. There is, too, a clear parallel with the so-called Black Mass, when the latter-day seekers after sensation reverse the order of the mass, invert a cross, say the Lord's Prayer backward, and so on, in the (objectively) vain hope that by so doing they will obtain power from the devil. Later I shall discuss witchcraft and we shall see the same idea at work. Once more, however, we can see how powerful is the hold over the human mind exerted by the need to classify and categorize.

We take it absolutely for granted that there are always separate changing rooms and bathrooms at a swimming pool for males and females. Of course. But why? Because we are decent, modest, respectable, one could answer. True, but that does not explain why we seem frightened of being otherwise. The moment we cover our genitals, and women their breasts too, we feel safe. Like Adam and Eve, we feel safe behind our fig leaves.

The fear of death hardly needs emphasis. I hope to show that these two sources of anxiety are linked.

4

Oestrus and Incest

Most historical and anthropological accounts of our human past hardly refer to women at all, a fact which it is easy to document. In effect, 50 per cent of the population did not rate a mention. One could make a parallel between this amazing fact and another —that until quite recently, except for books sold covertly, there was little mention of sex in literature except in a veiled, euphemistic, or allusory way. Even now, when respectable authors use perhaps .01 per cent of a novel to describe sexual activity in a relatively explicit way, there are plenty of people ready to say that the work is a "dirty book." When one considers that only through sexual activity did any of us get here and the extent to which most people think about sex, this deletion from public mention of such an overwhelmingly important part of human life is truly astounding. It is certainly an indication of the extent of the fear we feel. There seems little doubt that part, at least, of our fear of sex comes from something which at first examination seems a paradox. Human females no longer come into heat.

Somewhere in human evolution we stopped having an oestrous cycle. Apes have both a menstrual and an oestrous cycle, humans only the former. Precisely when this took place we shall never know, unless we invent a time machine. The word "oestrous" comes from the Latin word for a gadfly, which is also the word for "frenzy."

Since most Americans are today urban dwellers, they have little or no experience of the phenomenon. For people who live in the country, it is commonplace, though a matter of great embarrassment to those who find sex disgusting. A bitch in heat stays that way for three weeks every six months, during which time she will be followed (if she is allowed free range) by every male dog for miles around, from dachshunds to St. Bernards. The luckier or stronger males will copulate with the bitch. It is not unusual to see a bitch followed by twenty or more dogs.

Cows usually come into heat for one day at a time every three weeks. Once the animal becomes pregnant her oestrous cycle ceases. Since most male cattle are castrated to become steers, the cow is surrounded only by other females, unless a bull is allowed to range with the cows. The other cows will often follow their excited fellow around, licking her and occasionally mounting her in simulated copulation. Nowadays few cows have sex at all, since it is considered wasteful to allow the millions of sperm cells contained in one ejaculation to inseminate only one cow, when they could be used for dozens of cows. Therefore bulls only get masturbated by the breeder to ejaculate semen and each cow only gets injected with a tiny shot of it into the cervix when she is in heat. All very efficient but dull for the cows—perhaps, someone once wittily suggested, why cows have long faces.

When an animal is in heat, she is possessed of a frantic and cerebrally quite uncontrollable urge to engage in sex with any male of the same species. The idea that all nonhuman animals have an oestrous cycle was well known to our ancestors, who, until the early twentieth century, mostly lived in the country. The idea that the human female might also act in a comparable way therefore became part of folk beliefs everywhere. When we speak of people "behaving like animals" we usually mean either in their eating or their sexual habits. This comes out in poetic language where Shakespeare describes Venus' seduction of Adonis when

> With blindfold fury she begins to forage;
> Her face doth reek and smoke, her blood doth boil,
> And careless lust stirs up a desperate courage,
> Planting oblivion, beating reason back. . . .

The impression we gain is of a female unable to control her sexual desire—like a bitch in heat, some might say.

Of course, much popular literature ascribes uncontrollable sexuality to males rather than females, perhaps with good reason. One wholly desirable result of the "sexual revolution" has been to bring home to Western people what the Mangaians always knew —that both men and women have sexual desires. Our panhuman problem has always been and no doubt always will be how these desires can be met without disrupting other aspects of human society.

However, the great difference between human females and other mammalian females lies in the cessation of the oestrous cycle. There are two immediate and important co-related points which also differentiate the human female from the nonhuman. First, a human female is physically capable of engaging in voluntary sexual intercourse from the moment she becomes sufficiently mature until the day she dies, except when sickness or very advanced pregnancy prevents her. Second, a human female has cortical control over her sexual activity, whereas a nonhuman mammalian female can only engage in sex when she is in heat. Only in oestrus do her genitals become sufficiently enlarged and lubricated to allow penetration to take place. When not in heat, she is neither interested in sex, nor is she physically capable of having it. Once she becomes pregnant and until she finishes breast-feeding her infant, she will not come into heat again—a gap of nine months plus at least another year in apes and monkeys. In some monkey troops in India it has been observed that males who manage to expel other males after they come into a strange troop thereupon kill all the infants, which brings all the nursing females back into their oestrous cycles, thereby making them sexually available to the immigrant males. When an ape or monkey female is in heat she may be somewhat selective about those males with whom she mates, but essentially her body really is her destiny. Not so the human female. The fact that humans are *potentially* sexually receptive at all times makes it on the one hand possible for the human female to be totally discriminating in her mate selection, since she is not driven by the uncontrollable, genetically determined frenzy found in oestrus. On the other hand, and this is a point to which I shall return, it does make her vulnerable to a uniquely human horror through which some men express their hatred and contempt for women. I refer to rape.

It is worth considering for a moment what life in the suburbs would be like if humans still had an oestrous cycle of one month. For about three quarters of each month a wife would permit her husband a momentary embrace and a kiss or two, but any sexual activity would not only not interest her but would be physically impossible. Then for eight days or so, career, housework, child care—any activity but sex would be of minimal interest. Her husband would be totally unable to satisfy her potential sexual needs. Thus, we could picture driving through a neighborhood and seeing groups of men jostling each other round the front doors of a particular house. Other more crafty ones might be trying to get in through the back door or climbing through the windows.

The door opens and a man comes out. Immediately a fight breaks out as several of the stronger men struggle with each other to get in the door. Finally, one makes it inside and the rest continue to mill around on the lawn. For a week or so each month the husband would have sex every day—if he were strong enough to fight off the other contenders. For the rest of the month there would be no sex at all, though of course he could join the jostling, fighting little crowds at other houses in the neighborhood.

If his wife became pregnant, there would be no sex at home for the entire period of the pregnancy and nursing—perhaps two to three years. If all the females in the neighborhood became pregnant there would be peace, if "no sex" is peace. But then, given the greater social awareness of today, most intelligent women, conscious of diminishing world resources, would consider it near criminal to have more than two children and take some sort of contraceptive precautions. Thus, they would not get pregnant, though they would continue to come into heat monthly. All economic activity would plainly come to a standstill, unless some imaginative person were to segregate groups of men in barracks as workers and arrange a work schedule for women of three weeks a month.

Bizarre and ridiculous fantasy! Of course it is, but it does bring home rather dramatically how society as we know it just could not function if the human female still went into oestrus. We assume that most children are born of known parents united in a legal marriage. We assume as a generality that the biological father and social father of a child are one and the same person, even if in fact the mother was impregnated by a lover. Many societies, reflecting the possessive, property aspects of marriage, have proverbs that say something to the effect that the child belongs to the man to whom the bed belongs. In other words, no matter who the physical father, the genitor, may be, the man to whom the woman is married is assumed to be the father. And if it is so assumed, he is effectively the social father, the pater, in terms of rights, duties, and responsibilities. True, in every society illegitimate children are born, who are often regarded by those who are terrified of sex and therefore call themselves the guardians of morality as a punishment for transgression of the rules about sex and marriage. Illegitimate children, however, provide the exception that proves the rule.

All these notions about the legitimacy of children would appear absurd if human females had an oestrous cycle. Of course, there could be other kinds of societies. Apes and monkeys have societies which are arranged and ordered on comprehensible lines. What it would mean for us, in effect, might be a greater stress on mother-child link, none on father-child link (since he is unknown), and an expectation that all males have obligations toward all infants. Apes and monkeys do have societies, but they do not have relatives as we reckon relatives. Biologically they have second cousins once removed, but socially they do not and cannot. They cannot have such categories because they lack the language capacity to explain such an idea. Moreover, even if they had speech and language and could explain such ideas as kinship, their societies would have to be different from ours because they lack the basic concept on which all human societies are founded: the prohibition on incest. The concepts of incest and marriage would make no sense at all in a group where the females come into heat; where sexual access to a female is limited to a few days a month or, more probably, a few days in two or three years; and where the major criterion for access to females is the male's physical capacity to fight off every other male who for the moment is not sexually sated.

The basis for all human societies, the foundation on which they are erected, no matter how differently they may be structured, lies in the incest taboo. The rules about which particular relatives are outlawed vary considerably from society to society and reflect concepts of biology which have little to do with objective reality and more to do with how descent is traced and authority allocated. A marvelous illustration of this comes from Maxine Hong Kingston's *The Warrior Woman,* that extremely moving, angry, and fascinating collection of fantasy, fiction, and autobiography.[1] Writing of a village in mainland China she says:

All the village were kinsmen, and the titles shouted in loud country voices never let kinship be forgotten. Any man within visiting distance would have been neutralized as a lover—"brother", "younger brother", "older brother"—one hundred and fifteen relationship titles. Parents researched birth charts probably not so much to assure good fortune as to circumvent incest in a population that has but one hundred surnames. Everybody has eight million relatives.

There may be societies in which a girl's father deflowers her before she gets married to another man, but he does not *marry* her. There have been instances in history where in certain royal families—the ancient Egyptian, the Inca, the Hawaiian, the Nyoro of Uganda—the king actually married his sister. The usual rationalization for this was that the royal blood must be kept pure, that there was no one else of equal rank. These ideas are certainly still current, as one can observe in countries where royalty is still to be found, where there is great speculation about royal persons marrying what are called "commoners," though the question of marrying an actual sibling does not arise. What seems to be a much better real explanation of brother-sister royal marriages is that it was the exception that proves the rule for everyone else: royalty was allowed to do the one thing forbidden to everyone else. Once more, the importance of categorization appears. As in the case of the Bacwezi reported by Hans Cory, the carrying out of a ritualized form of controlled incest doubtless carried with it the concept of the consequent generation of great spiritual power. It should constantly be remembered when thinking about the whole curious idea of royalty that there must always be efforts made to make them appear to be superhuman—different from and superior to ordinary mortals, not subject to the laws that constrain those over whom they have been able to impose their rule. "Mortal" is an apt word here as it implies mortality—death. Kings have often been made to appear as gods and hence immortal.[2] When some modern royalty go on tour, special toilet seats are used so that souvenir hunters (and profit-loving entrepreneurs) should not steal or sell the one in normal use which has thereby achieved a special distinction.

Every society has some form of marriage and prohibits incest within the immediate family (mother-son, father-daughter, brother-sister). Outside this circle the rules vary enormously. In some states of the United States one may marry a first cousin, in others one may not marry a first or second cousin. Until recently in England a man could not marry his deceased wife's sister. In most African societies and many others in the world, any one of hundreds if not thousands of persons in one's clan may be classified as a "sister" or "brother" and thus outlawed for sex or marriage. I recall vividly in 1961 sitting on the front porch of the house of a young chief in Africa at sundown, drinking a beer with him. As we sat there we watched all the women and girls of the village go past on their evening trip to the river to fetch water. They returned with heavy pots on their heads, their tightly draped clothes clinging wetly to their bodies. As we watched the hundredth pair of swaying buttocks go by, he heaved a deep sigh and said: "You know, there's not one woman in this village I could go to bed with—they're all my 'sisters.' "

If we look at the universally forbidden unions (mother-son, father-daughter, brother-sister), we find that there is something of a hierarchy of disgust accorded to the three. This seems to reflect the degree of frequency with which incest occurs; the authority structure of society; the evolutionary background. In terms of statistical frequency (though accurate data are hard to come by), far the most common form of incest is father-daughter, then brother-sister, and—a poor third—mother-son. Let us consider the three possibilities in greater detail.

There are no societies of which we have knowledge in which males are not dominant in terms of authority (not power, note). Since authority implies the ability to exact obedience, not only is it difficult for a girl to refuse but it is also almost impossible for her to complain if she is propositioned by her father. The recent trend encouraged by the growing strength of the women's movement has been for revelation of how frequently this has occurred in American society. The occurrence is linked to a number of factors, authority and the universal "double standard," by which

many actions frowned on or forbidden for women are permitted
to or condoned in men. One dramatic example of this is in the relative ages of the partners in a sexual or marital relationship.
Whereas it is considered quite "normal" for a young woman to
have a relationship with an older man, often as old as her father,
the reverse—a young man with an older woman—is often considered "abnormal," revolting, or, at the least, comic. Why this injustice? And does this not take place anywhere within what some
societies consider "normal"?

Two examples occur in Western society, neither particularly
edifying. In Germany before World War II it was considered normal for an urban young man's first sexual experiences to take
place with an older woman prostitute who would be able to guide
him in a motherly way with gentle kindness, so that he would not
feel afraid or humiliated by failure to perform adequately after
marriage. However, this was really seen as a first step in sexuality,
before the young man graduated to having sex with women of his
own age or younger than himself, which would thenceforth be
the acceptable pattern, and there was no expectation of a permanent young man-older woman liaison.

The other Western phenomenon is that of the gigolo, when an
older, wealthy woman hires a young man to accompany her,
dance with her, or have sex with her. The nature of this relationship is often seen by some as being far more disgusting than
the reverse, for both the nature of the relationship and the person
of the young man are considered contemptible. The relationship
of a pretty young mistress of a physically repellent rich old man
may be deplored, but it is the relationship which is deplored
rather than she.

One unusual case of men marrying women much older than
themselves occurs among an aboriginal Australian people, the
Tiwi. C. W. M. Hart and A. R. Pilling, who jointly wrote an eth-
nography of this hunting and gathering group, note that the general marriage pattern was for men to begin marrying the first of
several wives at about age thirty.[3] The first marriage a man would
make was almost invariably to a widow considerably older than
he. The arrangements of marriage among the Tiwi are part of a
total career and influence pattern which the authors describe as "a
sort of nonstop bridge game wherein the scores were never to-

talled up nor a new game ever started on a clean slate." The marriage to an older woman was part of this game, but also had pragmatic practical ends in that an old woman was an expert in
gathering food from the bush. Later marriages might be to other
older women, but ultimately a man would hope to marry nubile
girls. Hardly an inspiring example to the women's movement. In a
way, it is comparable to the phenomenon of the American graduate student who is kept by his secretary-wife, who types his papers
and dissertation and then is abandoned in favor of a more intellectually stimulating and physically exciting young woman. At
least the Tiwi old wives remain part of the family and are not
shed along the way.

A related phenomenon is the difference which has emerged in
what attracts men in women and vice versa. What comes through
very clearly from the Kinsey studies is that men are much more
easily aroused sexually by visual stimuli. It is difficult for some
women to comprehend (though some cash in on it) the extent to
which virtually all men are aroused by women's bodies and clothing which accentuates or draws attention to those areas—breasts,
legs, buttocks—commonly associated with sexual activity.
Women, on the other hand, seem to be much more aroused by intellectual, verbal activity. Similarly, most men are much more
rapidly aroused than women.[4] This is in no sense to claim that
men are more in need of sex or enjoy it more than women, but
only that it is extremely easy to arouse the average man. Thus, the
Kinsey study of sex offenders, considering the difficulties that
arise when a man marries a woman who has a sexually mature
daughter, notes that:

The man may find himself sharing a home with a female with whom
he could have a socially acceptable sexual relationship were it not for
the fact that he married her mother. To view this female, whom he
can scarcely look upon as a true daughter, in provocative dishabille
without any thought of sex entering his mind is a virtual impossibility.

And, the report goes on:

Many a father who would rather commit suicide than have sexual contact with his daughter has guiltily repressed incestuous thoughts that
come unbidden to his mind. It is hard to recognize sexual attrac-
tiveness without being sexually attracted.

It is recognition of this rapid arousal which has, it would seem, caused male judges to deny that rape occurred.

Wisconsin Judge Archie Simonson, in sentencing a high school boy charged with rape, declared that rape was a "normal" reaction to the way young women dressed.[5]

Rape can never be condoned, excused, or justified. On the other hand, woman should realize the powerful effect that their clothes have in stimulating male sexual interest. If this were not the case, Frederick's of Hollywood would be out of business.

Let us return more specifically to father-daughter incest as a more common phenomenon than others and, related to that, the double standard that encourages older male-younger female relationships rather than the reverse. Culturally and aesthetically father-daughter incest makes no sense. In biological and evolutionary terms, however, it is at least explicable, though whether it is ethically defensible in modern circumstances is a totally different matter.

Studies of primates show that there is a strong attachment between mothers and their infants, which persists over two or more generations and leads to what sociologists call a "matrifocal subunit," that is, a group of animals who are not only attached to the entire community, but also relate to each other in a special way. This seems to be true of rhesus monkeys, Japanese and Puerto Rican macaques, and the primate closest to humans in genetic make-up—the chimpanzee.[6] Moreover, sexual relations between mother and son do not occur. If this was the case for the ancestors of humans, as seems highly probable, it certainly provides a reason for the strength of the human prejudice against mother-son incest, and since under comparable historical circumstances the father of any child born would be unknown, the less strong prohibition against father-daughter and, by extension, older male-younger female becomes explicable.

Another evolutionary explanation which fits with rather than excludes the previous one is this. A woman can go on having sex until old age, but she cannot have children after menopause. A man, on the other hand, can go on producing sperm into his eighties. Evolution always follows the path that most favors the maximum production of offspring. Thus, the old man-young woman or father-daughter union has a biological, evolutionary backing to it, whereas the reverse does not.[7] Since the development of culture has consistently removed more and more of the environmental pressures for human evolution, and since, moreover, the slightest application of common sense tells us that it is madness to produce an ever-greater population, it must be obvious that in cultural terms there is no further reason to continue the sanction against associations between older women and younger men. The abolition of millennia of prejudice is no easy matter, however.[8]

Also, the idea that mother-infant bonds are common among all primates enhances the notion of the sanctity of motherhood. A recent case came to my attention through one of my students who has been observing macaques in captivity.[9] A high-status and a low-status female both gave birth at about the same time. The latter's infant was healthy, but the infant of the high-status female was stillborn. The high-status female thereupon stole the infant of the low-status female and adopted it, without protest from its biological mother. The bond which develops will, therefore, be based on association rather than true maternal links. Many think that this could not be true of humans and that there is some kind of mystical link of blood and genes between mothers and their children, an idea that seems to be in line with the thinking of some sociobiologists. The fallacy of this idea can be shown in cases of adoption and, just as dramatically, with many upper-class families in America and Europe, where children are consigned to the care of nursemaids or nannies.

In the same way that women can act as mothers or not according to their inclination and social status, so they can engage in sexual activity through their own understanding and preferences rather than being driven by an oestrus-dominated anatomical destiny. Since women, unlike apes and monkeys, are physically capable of engaging in sex at all stages of their menstrual cycle, and even during pregnancy and lactation, there *could* be total promiscuity all the time. The evident popularity of erotic and pornographic books, magazines, and films shows that in fantasy at least this would be a male ideal. Nowhere, however, even in Mangaia, is this fantasy realized. Sexuality is feared everywhere. It is as though humans (and men in particular) recognize that were there not barriers to promiscuity, except within controlled limits, they would not be able to control their urges. Put otherwise, if full advantage were taken of the potential sexual receptivity of human females, as is the case with animals that have an oestrous cycle, there would be little time for anything else.

Ironically, we are far more scared of sex than we are of violence; we consider it healthy for children to see shows like "Hawaii Five-O" or John Wayne movies but forbid them to see human bodies or sexual activity. The arbiters of public morality who make these decisions are the same people who declare it acceptable for blatantly sexual women to go "bouncing across the screen in tank tops and hot pants, in wet T-shirts and towels," as Harmetz writes. They also encourage sexually titillating drum majorettes and cheerleaders. Surely, one would think, such displays would encourage promiscuity. Not so. As in the case of the principal boy and the female impersonator of the English pantomime, the activity is felt to be controlled and so safe.

We can now link together a number of points. One is the universal prohibition on incest, the adoption of which seems to be tied in to the cessation of oestrus and the change to a purely menstrual cycle. The prohibition of incest was momentous. If we have mating by rules rather than by brute strength, we can have the concept of marriage as a relatively durable relationship which allows for two results: first, sex relations are regulated and therefore potential quarreling and fighting among males are reduced; second, the enormously long dependency period of the human infant is provided for. A foal or calf is on its feet within moments of birth and sexually mature within one to two years. A human child could hardly function alone before, at the very earliest, seven years of age. It does not become sexually mature for about another seven years (though the age for the onset of puberty in many countries has dropped dramatically in the past century as a result of diet). Whether we ever become emotionally mature is open to debate, but one of the problems with which humans have to grapple is that boys and girls commonly become physically capable of sexual activity long before they are fully physically and mentally mature.

Jane Beckman Lancaster, a primatologist, has made some fascinating speculations about the origins of human behavior, which reinforce the ideas I have been suggesting.[10] She has been concerned, as I have, with the cessation of oestrus, the prohibition of incest, and the institution of marriage. Although she believes that the adoption of hunting was crucial to human development, she does not think this means that the male of the species was responsible for all our cultural and intellectual developments.

Most primates, though operating as a group, forage for food as individuals. Each feeds himself or herself, rarely sharing anything. Even a mother does not share any of the food she has obtained with her infant unless the latter importunes her. There is no question of one's putting food aside for a mate or children. Human behavior is quite different: mothers share with their children, wives with their husbands, husbands with their wives and children. There has been, in fact, an evolutionary pressure against groups "with overly aggressive individuals who could not control their own emotions and need to dominate others."

Food sharing, then, is an important stage in human development. Whereas most primates all forage for the same things, often together, human males hunt and human females gather fruits, nuts, roots, and so on. If there were no sharing, men would lack vegetable foods, and women and small children would lack meat. In strictly accurate terms, this is not quite true because men do gather some fruits, and women and children do collect some small animals, grubs, termites, and similar things. Over-all, however, in hunting and gathering societies, women get vegetable foods and men get meat. Each sex shares with the other the products of its labor.

Why did men hunt and not women? Because of the long dependency of the human infant. Of crucial importance is the helplessness of the human infant and its absolute dependence on its mother's milk for its sustenance. There are no formula or weaning foods in the bush, and women customarily go on breast-feeding children for two to three years, a fact which has great relevance for boys to the Oedipal crisis and initiation rites. Hunters, Lancaster says, "cannot be burdened by children." Three-day hunting trips on foot of a hundred miles or more would be totally impractical for a woman with a nursing child and perhaps a four- or five-year-old trailing along as well. It is not that women are incapable of hunting—it is just that their attachment to their small children would make only short trips feasible. Why could the husbands not take care of the children? the feminist might ask. Because they don't lactate and have no other foods to give. In addition, once humans start doing something in a particular way, it becomes hard to change, and often becomes sacrosanct. If humans adopted, as they did, the division of labor which has had such tremendous consequences for our cultural development and for the institutionalization of sex roles right up to the present day, then "there was no other way for the division to have evolved except between males and females." Of course, one could argue, but what about athletic fourteen-year-old girls? I have two answers. One, because of fears of incest, they would not be allowed to hunt with their fathers and brothers. Two, because it has become the custom for men to hunt. Establish categories—men-hunters and women-gatherers—and, as we have seen, humans find deviation from them dangerous and threatening. That may well seem objectively foolish, but then one might say that so is the taboo on eating pork for Jews and Muslims and the revulsion that many of us have to slugs and grasshoppers as potential food. We establish symbolic categories.

Not being dependent solely on hunting or solely on gathering gave humans a fantastic degree of flexibility and a capability to survive almost anywhere in the world, from the Kalahari Desert to the Arctic wastes. Apes are only found in tropical forests.

Now we come to one of Lancaster's most important and illuminating points. If males hunt and females gather, they have to share with one another. This means that a band of hunters and gatherers has to be virtually balanced in numbers between males and females, because only a superhunter could get enough meat for more than one woman, her offspring, and perhaps elderly parents; and only a supergatherer could collect enough vegetable material for more than one male, her offspring, and perhaps elderly parents. All right, one might say, but why not just live as a group sharing everything together? After all, material on the Hadza of East Africa, who live by gathering and hunting, shows that all food is largely shared by the whole group. True, says Lancaster, but the whole system of division of labor would be disrupted if human females came into oestrus. As she puts it, "Who is going to go hunting if there is an irresistible female in camp?"

If this had been the case, it would have been evolutionarily adaptive for females to suppress the oestrous cycle. Not only would oestrus have had to be brought under control, but a female would have had to keep a male relatively permanently attached to her to assure a supply of meat for herself and her children. To do this females would have had to be sexually receptive at all times and also develop visual stimuli that would have had the effect of "turning on" males at any time in order to retain their emotional attachment. These stimuli, she suggests, are the unique human breast, hip, and buttock development. Television and strip-show producers may not live by hunting and gathering, but they seem to be aware of the signaling that produces male interest.

Thus, Lancaster claims, human males have had an almost inevitable push toward the role of husband-father, and indeed toward monogamy. Today, a handful of hunting and gathering groups remain in the world, and among them monogamy does seem to be the norm. It is only with the development of farming that we see polygamy—when it becomes advantageous for a man to have, in effect, a larger agricultural work force for whom he is not obliged to provide a regular supply of meat through hunting. Her explanation makes economic sense; it also provides a reason for the reaction of men to visual stimuli from females.

Sexual attraction may be the basis for the bonding of a male husband-father to a female wife-mother, but there has to be rather more to it than this. Sharing constitutes an important trait which helps society to function. Another is the notion of contract. The idea that human society was based on contractual obligations was one raised by Jean Jacques Rousseau long before the concept of human evolution from earlier hominid forms was thought of. It has recently been interestingly resurrected by an anthropologist in New Zealand, Peter Wilson. He entitled his article, in a classic piece of British punning, "The Promising Primate"—promising in the sense that it was this particular one rather than another, and promising in that what gave one particular hominid promise as a human precursor was the trait of giving promises.[11] Apes do not customarily share, with any degree of exactitude, quotas or predictability. Humans do. It is the expectation of contractual type of obligations based on promises which also differentiates humans from nonhumans. The ability to do this, however, is dependent on the other crucial traits that make humans unique among animals —speech and language. One cannot have the notions of promise, contract, rights, duties, obligations, etc., without the precondition of being able to speak.

Among humans everywhere another basic component of the structure of human society is physical strength. According to Lancaster, "Differences in muscularity between men and women is greatly exaggerated in modern society because of the relative inactivity of women." True enough, but one could make the same observation criticizing American men, most of whom are overfed and underexercised to a degree probably unparalleled in history. However, even where women are physically active and in good physical shape, it is still possible for an overwhelming majority of men physically to subdue a majority of women. While contracts and promises are doubtless major components of the structure of all societies, this physically coercive quality is crucial.

I have spoken at length of how and why we find sexual activity frightening or threatening at a mental level, and, therefore, why we are so disturbed by our erotic urges. In a prehuman condition the only constraint on the satisfaction of those urges lay in inferior physical strength and fighting ability for males; for females it was largely a question of waiting to see who would win the fight. In most human societies today we deplore the idea of men fighting over a woman, even though the concept is considered rather romantic and titillating to some. Instead, we have set up rules constraining access to females, which constitute ideals for every society, no matter that in reality there are always some breaches of the rules. Everywhere these rules tend to favor male control of females.

We have seen that not only are women potentially sexually receptive at all times, but that their sexuality is largely under their intellectual control. Thus, a woman's body is not her destiny. It might be possible, one might think, that in consequence one might find as many societies controlled by women as by men. In reality this seems nowhere to be or to have been the case, in spite of the myths of ancient matriarchies so beloved of some ardent feminists. Robin Morgan, Barbara Ehrenreich, and Elaine Morgan, among others, all believe in the myth. Serious women anthropologists on the other hand, like Michelle Rosaldo, Louise Lamphere, Ernestine Friedl, and others, take the view espoused by Dorothy Hammond and Alta Jablow in the opening lines of their book *Women in Cultures of the World:*

It is ironic that we should begin our study of women's roles with a discussion of an outmoded theory. The theory of the matriarchy is a relic of Victorian thought completely disavowed by modern anthropologists.[12]

The problem with proponents of the ancient-matriarchies theories is that they have not yet grasped the difference between myth and history. Sometimes the line is thin, but one usually finds that myths not only incorporate supernatural elements, but customarily provide justification for the status quo. The anthropologist Bronislaw Malinowski gave us the famous phrase that "myth provides a charter for social action." If we look at the matriarchy stories, what we find is that they prove, not that women ruled, but rather that women were incompetent to rule and that therefore it was necessary for men to be in charge. It matters little that the alleged seizure of power by males took place by brute force or chicanery. After all, both these qualities are often admired by the politically successful. Thus, the myths everywhere, in fact, explain and rationalize male monopoly of all the important authority roles and in fact probably represent childish fantasies of overthrowing mother which elsewhere come out as the defeat of the wicked witch. In a world in which intellect is really much more important than brute force, women certainly should be the equals of men in all activities. That they are not recognized as such needs further explanation.

One of the key points for the matriarchy believers is the idea of the great female deity who was later supplanted by the male gods like Apollo, Zeus, and Jehovah. The snag to this line of reasoning is that we still have female deities around, of which Kali in India and the Virgin Mary are good examples. It only takes a moment's rueful thought to realize that the primacy of Kali as mother of all the gods and Mary as the mother of God have little if any effect on the status of Hindu or Catholic women. Woman on a pedestal is anathema to a feminist; why is a deity different? Did the Taj Mahal show the high status of women in Mogul society? If it is claimed it did, then one could picture a future archaeologist deducing an overwhelmingly important position for women in twentieth-century Western society based on the extent to which women are used to advertise products, from cars to clothing.

5

"The Filthiest Show in Town"

Perhaps by now, part of the source of our fear about sexuality is plain: it is the feeling that because of our physical qualities, promiscuity could overtake us unless sexuality were rigorously controlled. Because human females no longer have an oestrous cycle but at the same time have had to establish a permanent attachment to a male, women's bodies paradoxically can seem to be signaling their readiness for sex at any time—a problem to which no one has any totally adequate answer, unless one considers the orthodox Muslim solution of completely covering a woman from head to foot in enveloping black garments to be one. E. O. Wilson, in his controversial work *Sociobiology,* takes seriously the British zoologist Desmond Morris' suggestion that loss of body hair, particularly in the female, was brought about to allow for the visual signaling to take place. Morris, he says,

drawing on the data of [William] Masters and [Virginia] Johnson (1966) and others, has enumerated the unique features that he considers to be associated with the loss of body hair: the rounded and protuberant breasts of the young woman, the flushing of areas of skin during coition, the vaso-dilation and increased erogenous sensitivity of lips, soft portions of the nose, ear, nipples, areolae, and genitals . . .[1]

It is fairly obvious that the Bible is a male oriented and written document, but were the Garden of Eden story written by a

woman, the knowledge of nakedness might only have necessitated
the adoption of fig leaves by the woman. According to Weinberg,
the Kinsey report on females observes:

> It is difficult for most males to comprehend that females are not
> aroused by seeing male genitalia. . . . On the contrary, many females
> feel that their husbands are vulgar, or perverted, or mentally disturbed,
> because they want to display their genitalia.[2]

Males *are* aroused by the sight of the female body. They therefore
assume—incorrectly, it seems, for most women—that the reverse
is true. Thus, Adam and Eve both put on fig leaves. Only Eve, we
may assume, really needed one.

Perhaps one could accept that the points I have already
brought out are sufficient to account for the universal human anxiety about sex. One could argue though that what I have covered
is only a source of anxiety to males. If this is so, then one might
say that since males universally occupy most authority roles, they
have been able to impose their viewpoint on everyone. On the
other hand, women too have a real source of anxiety arising out
of their permanent potential receptivity—and hence, the possibility of rape. Yet there is more to it than this, something more
sinister and menacing, something that could give rise to William
Shakespeare's agonized:

> But to the girdle do the gods inherit,
> Beneath is all the fiends';
> There's hell, there's darkness, there's the
>   sulphurous pit,

Burning, scalding, stench, consumption; fie, fie, fie! pah, pah! Give me
an ounce of civet, good apothecary, to sweeten my imagination . . .

> *King Lear* (Act IV, Scene 6)

And something, too, that could bring religious fanatics everywhere to denounce sexuality and even to demand that their initiated devotees eschew and abjure sex. I think the answer lies in a
physical fact resulting from our evolution.

Consider other primates. Monkeys leap from tree to tree using
all their limbs and, on the ground, go on all fours like a dog,
though they can stand temporarily erect. Most apes have two
modes of locomotion: one, most perfected in the gibbon, is called

"brachiating" and consists of swinging by the arms like a super trapeze artist; the other is knuckle walking. An ape can stand erect for a time, but it is not comfortable with the posture. Proportionately its arms are very long and its legs very short compared to a human's. The human's stance is, or should be, totally erect, with the spine curved like a flattened S to insure this. Our legs are much longer than an ape's in relation to our body, and our arms much shorter. Knuckle walking is not practical for humans, nor is brachiating. The only practical mode of human locomotion is the striding gait which, in its fullest flowering, gives us the beauty of ballet and the excitement of athletics.

However, our upright stance has presented us with a unique problem far more momentous in its consequences than the varicose veins which are also its by-product. By standing erect and developing the kind of fleshy buttocks characteristic of humans we have done more than call attention to the features demanded for *A Chorus Line*—"tits and ass." What has happened is that we have covered the anus with fleshy flanks except when we bend over or squat. The result is that we have to do something that no other animal does regularly: we have to wipe or wash ourselves clean after defecation.

With other animals the more exposed nature of the anus and the nonupright posture mean that rarely are feces left around the anus after defecation. If any should be left, the residue will soon dry off with sun and air and become innocuous. Humans, like pigs, are omnivorous. In consequence, our excrement tends to be, like pigs', far more fetid than that of a total herbivore like a cow or horse. There is a close parallel between the problem of humans and that found among our artificially bred woolly sheep. Careful selection and breeding for the maximum fleeciness were not able to prevent the wooliness occurring on the tail and bottom too. Therefore, lambs customarily have their tails docked. If they did not, there would soon be an accumulation of feces in the wool under and around the tail, kept moist by its protection. Flies take advantage of this and lay eggs, which hatch into a mass of maggots within a few days. This mess, irritation, and subsequent secondary infection of the raw tissue could certainly result in, at the least, loss of fitness and, at the worst, death.

Humanity seems to have had its origins in the tropical regions of Africa, and our nearest relatives, chimpanzees and gorillas, are only found in the tropical rain-forest regions. In these areas, flies and bacteria proliferate; indeed even, in the drier regions of Africa flies are found by the million whenever there is any organic material in which they can breed. Under these circumstances, unless humans learned to clean the anus and perineal area after defecation, maggots and bacterial infection would inevitably have followed. Further, when living in the tropics it is impossible to avoid relatively frequent attacks of diarrhea. The upright posture and striding gait, and the development of the sexually attractive buttocks are all crucial to this requirement. If we went on all fours or knuckle-walked, no problem would arise.

It is clear then that humans standing erect must cleanse themselves; they also have to control their excretion of feces and urine to be human as we understand the word. Most importantly of all, they have to be *taught* to do these things. There is little doubt that this is where humans universally acquire the idea that sex is "dirty." The penis and vagina are at one and the same time the organs of sex and of urination; the anus is situated nearby. In the case of females, the gap of perineum between vulva and anus is very small—in coarse British usage is called "the narrowest bridge in the world." With the common parental reaction to feces and urine as dirty, it is very hard for children not to make an association between the organs of sex and filth. This is exacerbated by those parents who react to a child's touching its genitals with sharp admonitions "not to be dirty." It seems speculative in the extreme, but the simple fact of the necessity to control urination and defecation and to cleanse after defecation may quite easily be the basis of all human ideas about ritual pollution. Once more, the whole question of language and categorization comes in with immense force. The notion that feces and urine are dirty cannot adequately be expressed in full strength without the tool of language. And once we categorize something or some place as "dirty," "filthy," "disgusting," "revolting"—we have plenty of adjectives—then it is labeled, pigeonholed, and classified.

If we have classified feces and urine as "dirty" and something for which we feel some horror, then the association is not hard to make between sex and filth. As W. B. Yeats so aptly put it,

> . . . Love has pitched his mansion in
> The place of excrement.

Today we rationalize our fear of and disgust at feces and urine by associating them with germs and other forms of infection, and it is undoubtedly true that indiscriminate disposal of feces, in the tropics particularly, is responsible for the spread of a whole range of sicknesses: typhoid, dysentery, poliomyelitis, and hepatitis, as well as hookworm, roundworm, and tapeworm. However, we must realize that our revulsion goes back far beyond Pasteur. Moreover, we feel the same kind of revulsion toward urine, which is comparatively sterile and harmless, though it can spread typhoid. What particularly revolts us is the smell. Yet no animal is so revolted. Why is it that humans respond to what we call "bad" smells sometimes with a sense of shock that will induce vomiting? Before we consider that question let us look at two other points.

First, the position adopted in sexual intercourse. Food, drink, sleep, and sex are all needs of the human organism in a purely physiological way, yet the way in which these needs are gratified varies enormously in different cultures. Food and drink we already touched on briefly. The mode of sleeping, too, is culturally conditioned: it may be taken on a bed, a hammock, a mat, in short naps or long stretches. Similarly, the modes of having sex vary enormously. In Western society, what came to be called the "missionary position"—both partners lying down and the man above—is often accepted as normal. With a greater openness current today, it has been realized by many couples that the missionary position is only one of many potential positions. Many find much more satisfactory the mode commonly used in Greece and Rome, with the man lying on his back and the woman squatting, kneeling, or lying above him. Some people, including (one is ashamed to say) some psychologists, feel that the man-dominant position should be the normal one. This odd assumption is based on a pseudo theory of correct sex roles; it would be hard, for instance, to think of Roman society as female dominated. One of the many modern popular positions is for the woman to kneel and the man to enter from the rear, a mode which allows for little clitoral stimulation but which is satisfying to some after an initial face-to-face encounter. This is the mode always adopted by other animals and therefore rejected by many humans as being animal-like and inhuman.

There have been many speculations on this subject. One suggests that the greater emotional attachment of humans to each other, with no oestrus and with fidelity as an ideal, may have led to a greater desire to see the face of the beloved and thus a face-to-face position in sexual intercourse. This is aesthetically pleasing but not really in line with evolutionary probability. If we want a cultural explanation, we could suggest a desire consciously to stress one's human rather than one's animal nature. Certainly that would be in correspondence with the practice found throughout Africa and the Arab world of men and women removing all pubic hair as being bestial. A very persuasive evolutionary explanation, however, could be that those human ancestors who adopted a face-to-face position might have had a better chance of producing healthy offspring. With the recent experimentation in modes of sexual behavior, many different ways of intercourse have become common. The practice of oral sex has nowadays become normal for many couples, whereas to many of a previous generation it was regarded as a perversion. Much more controversial is the practice of anal sex. Its first advocacy in modern literature is presumably by D. H. Lawrence in *Lady Chatterley's Lover*. Many reject the practice with downright disgust. It seems that their aesthetic and associational repulsion may have a pragmatic basis: many micro-organisms present in the anal tract are not normally found in the vaginal tract, and if introduced there, may set up infections. Both oral and anal sex are still against the law in some states.

Here may be our reason for the face-to-face position. As the early humans became more erect and as the buttocks developed, it may have been some time before the absolute necessity for anal cleansing was appreciated. Under these circumstances, entry from the rear in the customary apelike manner could have proved to be dangerous because it tended to introduce fecal material into the vagina. Thus, those that practiced face-to-face sex would have a slight adaptive advantage in the production of healthy offspring. A final reason, related to the modern repulsion that many feel, could be that because of the associations we make with the smell of feces, the presence of any fecal material in the perineal region would be so anaphrodisiac as to preclude the possibility of satisfactory sex.

Just as an erect posture and the necessity for anal cleansing differentiates humans from other animals, something besides the presence of oestrus differentiates females from males: the menstrual flow. Let us consider its effect on human behavior in a direct physical way. E. O. Wilson, in his book *Sociobiology*, writes of the much greater human menstrual flow than that found in other animals and explains that what he calls the "disappointed womb" sloughs off its lining each month. A wrathful feminist critic recently wrote an amusing satire on this point referring to her grief for all the disappointed and frustrated sperms in the world. However, the fact remains that for most women there is a relatively heavy flow, at least for a day or two, and this has to be dealt with in some way. The way varies from culture to culture. In the modern Western world there are many things we take for granted. This was brought home to me very forcibly by an article on China in *The Guardian* (Manchester) of December 14, 1975, by Anna Coote. She entitled her article "Cloth Captives?"

Most of us are familiar with the contemporary image of Chinese womanhood: a stalwart, smiling figure in blue overalls and a cloth cap, grappling confidently with a large piece of machinery, shoulder to shoulder with her male comrades. She and her rural sisters, engaged in the agricultural equivalent, appear so uniformly in magazines, posters, films and books that it is hard to believe they are real. They seem to suffer no discrimination, to be unencumbered by household chores or child-caring duties, unconcerned with her effect on the opposite sex, more liberated than most women in the West. Yet 26 years ago they were little more than chattels in a semi-feudal society. Can they really have travelled so far so fast?

After describing many of the work places she visited and the allocation of jobs by sex, she goes on:

Whenever we had discussions about working women, the Chinese displayed much concern about their physical condition and the need to take special care of them because of it. I found this perplexing. Chinese women were clearly no weaklings and some of the work they did (on building sites and in the fields, for instance) showed they were equal to most tasks. Wasn't the emphasis on physiology unnecessary? Didn't it perpetuate myths about feminine frailties? Light was shed on the situation when I learned that Chinese women have no modern sanitary protection. They use cloth, which they wash and re-use, like our grandmothers did. In some factories there are special "hygiene stations" for menstruating women. Apparently, female interpreters rarely accompany tours which last as long as three weeks: it would be too inconvenient for them to travel at the wrong time of the month.

Four hundred million women and not a single tampon? China had made such great strides in industry and agriculture, it seemed a shame that this small but vital detail had been overlooked. Was it too much to expect of a developing country? It might do more to liberate women and increase their productivity than any amount of criticising Confucius.

In many simple societies the menstruation problem is solved by segregating the woman in a special house. She is often not allowed to cook or undertake certain tasks. She is, after all, liminal at this time. One friend of mine observed that preventing a woman from cooking and so on was very much to her advantage and that she wished she got a week off from housework every time she got her period. One can look at it that way. I suspect most intelligent women would prefer to be "liberated" by sanitary napkins or tampons.

In a totally natural state, the human female would have the same problem I mentioned for feces: unless she kept clean she would become flyblown. Also, her presence during hunting would be undesirable because the scent of her blood might frighten game or attract carnivores. We shall consider this matter in greater detail later. For now, let's consider why it is that humans are disgusted by what we call bad smells when animals are not.

6

"Our Vile Body"

Knowledge about our mortality is only possible to humans because of the Word—that is to say, we have language and speech, so that from a very early age the awareness that we or our guardians could die is there in our brains. It is always there nibbling and gnawing away at our minds. We joke about it, even when its possibility may be imminent as in war. Our first contact with a human death is distressing. If it happens to be a violent death, the shock is much greater in that it provides a sharp reminder of the very thin line between death and life and how easily the line is traversed. I recall quite vividly even today seeing a man's head crushed under a truck when I was about eleven. I went home feeling stunned and presently vomited violently. Even for an adult who has seen violent death in war, the shock remains; I still have nightmare memories of particular deaths in World War II that nothing can exorcize.

Poets have ceaselessly reflected on death, artists have portrayed it in a hundred forms. Perhaps it is the very awareness of the irreversible finality of death that gives humans their obsessive desire to have heirs, to have lineages that will carry names into the future, to create works of art that will survive us. There is an irony that paintings, drawings, and poems about death remind the artist of his or her death, and so remind the audience and, at the same time, serve to insure the artist's immortality. Tombstones or pyramids have the same effect, yet, as Thomas Gray wrote,

> Can storied urn, or animated bust
> Back to its mansion call the fleeting breath?
> Can Honour's voice provoke the silent dust,
> Or Flatt'ry soothe the dull cold ear of death?

The "dull cold ear of death" assumes a sentient being. In our inmost hearts we know there is no such being, nor anything but an end.

In spite of this, religions the world over claim that their adherents should have no fear. In the words of the Anglican *Book of Common Prayer,* regarding the burial of the dead:

. . . we therefore commit his body to the ground; earth to earth, ashes to ashes, dust to dust; in sure and certain hope of the Resurrection to eternal life, through Our Lord Jesus Christ; who shall change our vile body, that it may be like unto his glorious body. . . .

As one would expect of Freud and his followers, his one-time associate in Vienna Otto Rank suggests that doctrines like the one above represent human beings' attempts to master the terror of death and in their way to try to deal with the "seemingly unavoidable projection of life before birth into the future after death," a projection which, he claims, accounts for "mistaken religious superstitions . . . crowned by the doctrine of immortality."[1]

The idea that everyone shall die is daunting enough. Unfortunately, the survivors have another problem, and one which has momentous consequences for humans far beyond its immediate requirements. The problem is how to dispose of the body, a problem that some assume belongs only to murderers, but which in fact is universal. Humans solve it in a variety of ways. The Masai, nomadic pastoralists of East Africa, let hyenas dispose of their corpses, a very pragmatic and ecologically sound solution, though hardly practical for New York City. (The notion has a certain grimly comic appeal to which the cartoonist Charles Addams might do justice.) Rather similarly, Zoroastrians place bodies on "Towers of Silence" to be eaten by vultures. Christians, Jews, and Muslims, as well as many other peoples, bury the dead in what may well be a symbolic return to the womb, from which it is hoped that the person will be reborn after a rather unclearly defined gestation period. Many peoples actually place corpses in fetal positions in their graves. Hindus cremate their dead, an idea which is anathema to those who believe firmly in the resurrection of the body. My grandfather told of how he found a man in Wales early one morning on the railway track with a severed leg. He rendered first aid and got the man to a hospital where he recovered. The man was, however, in a condition of great anxiety until the missing leg was returned to him to be kept in a box and buried ultimately with him, so that on the day of resurrection he would not have to hop before the seat of judgment.

For this corruptible must put on incorruption, and this mortal must put on immortality. So when this corruptible shall have put on incorruption, and this mortal shall have put on immortality; then shall be brought to pass the saying that is written, Death is swallowed up in victory. O death where is thy sting?[2]

All these methods of disposing of the dead are based on a human notion of fulfilling some ritual. Even the rationalist atheist can hardly dump a family corpse out with the garbage. However, the real basis of these methods lies in the fact so stressed by "The Burial Service" quoted above—the corruption of the body. In reality, they are a means of getting rid of something too horrifying for people to contemplate. It is no accident that Judaism and Islam, both originating in a hot climate, bury their dead if possible the same day that death takes place. Death in itself is awful; it is doubly awful to find that a body very soon starts to putrefy. Many urban dwellers today have never experienced even the smell of a putrefying woodchuck or rabbit, though perhaps they have had some meat go bad. Few things smell worse than decaying flesh; the decay of an entire body filled with fermenting juices is almost beyond imagination for those who have not encountered it. The putrescent body of a stranger is shocking enough; when the body is of someone whom one had loved and perhaps physically desired, the horror is enough to break the mind.

I wrote that many urban dwellers may not have experienced the smell of death in any major way. True, but everyone has some idea of the smell of decay, so well described in John Gardner's *The Sunlight Dialogues*. The "Sunlight Man," returned figuratively from the dead, is throughout described as carrying with him an appalling odor, which it seems he can turn on and off. To the blind wife of the chief of police:

He had a sickening smell. It was like hoofrot, she said, or like burning flesh. It was like a cancer smell and like a sewer on a hot, wet day. He smelled like a goat, like an outhouse, like fire and brimstone.[3]

Those of us who have had the misfortune to be involved in wars, earthquakes, or comparable catastrophes, react to the imagery of the description like a computer that has received the correct instructions for the retrieval of certain information—and probably wish that we had not.

There are plenty of other reminders of the reality of putrefaction. Edgar Allan Poe's tales continue to be popular, particularly with teen-agers who are beginning to come consciously to grips with the fact of death, which hitherto they had skated around. William Faulkner, in his story "A Rose for Emily," tells a macabre tale of a woman who lived with the corpse of her fiancé, who was thought to have disappeared and was finally found after her death in old age, merged into the bed in which she slept. In the early days of her fiancé's disappearance it was assumed by the sympathetic neighbors that he had run off and left his bride-to-be. They were disturbed by the terrible smell that surrounded the woman's house, but charitably ascribed it to dead rats and secretly sprinkled chloride of lime round the house at night.

For early humans there were no "funeral homes," nor are there in most "Third World" countries today. In these circumstances humans have attempted to reduce the horror by having someone else take care of the preparation of the corpse and the burial or cremation. In many parts of Africa arrangements exist whereby members of one clan perform the service for another clan with whom they have a special relationship and, in turn, receive the same service on a reciprocal basis. In the Western world we have undertakers.

In India, the castes are different from classes, in that one is born into a caste and can only marry within that caste (though as an illustration of the double standard, women but not men may practice hypergamy—marry into a higher subcaste than their own; thus a man may marry beneath him, but a woman cannot). Many people have assumed that the castes are based on occupation, and indeed castes may be called by such terms. However, examination on the ground will show that persons of a particular caste may undertake all kinds of occupations other than the one ascribed to their caste.

According to A. M. Hocart, one of the real reasons for the arrangement of the castes was concern about the pollution of death.[4] The three "excellent castes" must not come into contact either with death or decay, because, it is believed, the purity of these castes in this sense is responsible for the health of the entire community. However, if one section of society may not have anything to do with death, someone has to take care of the disposal of corpses. Therefore we find that there are a number of inferior castes whose responsibility it is to deal with those activities that might pollute the upper castes as "vehicles of the immortal gods." Drummers, for example, do not perform at auspicious occasions like weddings for they are members of the pariah caste—weddings are taken care of by a musician caste. Drummers are for funerals and for services at temples when animals are sacrificed. Similarly, Hocart tells us, barbers and washermen are not so much technical experts at those trades, but, like the drummers, are "priests of a low grade, performing rites which the high-caste priest will not touch." The "barbers" and "washermen" are involved in "the extreme pollution of the cremation ground," and by a feedback mechanism, he says, "Because of the pollution involved, the two are low caste." There is a great concern among high-caste Hindus: not to have to touch the dead—more particularly, one's own dead.

This concern, not confined to India, is of great antiquity. In a nineteenth-century study, *A History of Mourning,* Richard Davey writes extensively of the practices of ancient Egypt.[5] The Egyptians were motivated by two concerns: one manifest and the ideal, one unacknowledged but doubtless the real. The manifest reason was a belief in the resurrection of the body in an afterlife and hence a need to keep the body physically intact as far as possible. The real reason was probably the need to deal with the brutal fact of putrefaction and the consequent smell. The person responsible for the initial incision required for draining and removal of the viscera was always a "person of low class," and after he made the incision, it is reported, he "was then pelted by those around with stones and pursued with curses." The Greek historian Herodotus related that all Egyptians, and even animals, were embalmed in some way to prevent corruption, though he noted (shades of today's practitioners) that there were three modes: expensive, medium price, and cheap. The cheap method meant that the body was "simply washed in myrrh and salted for seventy days." Davey mentions that not only the Egyptians but many other peoples of the area used embalming techniques, though only for their important persons. The Persians used wax, the Assyrians honey, the Jews spices. Alexander the Great was said to have been preserved in wax and honey mixed. One wonders whether it worked, how long it lasted, and where his body ended up.

As we know, so-called primitive societies often put the greatest and most dramatic stress on the life crisis of puberty, whereas in American society we tend to de-emphasize this and lay greater stress on marriage and death. The answer to this difference is not far to seek. In the New York *Times* of Sunday, April 23, 1978, we find the following headline:

THE $4 BILLION-A-YEAR FUNERAL INDUSTRY:
ALL TOO OFTEN GRIEF IS EXPLOITED FOR GAIN

The articles describes how the cost of "typical funerals" in New York City exceeds $2,500 and notes that the "study found business practices common to the funeral industry that were curious if not illegal." It says that it is nearly two decades since writers began critically to examine American funerals. The best known of these books, Jessica Mitford's *The American Way of Death*,[6] the New York *Times* noted, "depicted undertakers as little more than a secret society of predators who had foisted elaborate funerals on an unwitting public."

Mitford's book is a damning indictment of the whole funeral business in the United States, most of its data culled from the pages of the journals of the undertaking profession. She found there had been a complete takeover of Madison-Avenue selling techniques, resulting in, for example, coffin linings of "more than 60 color matched shades" and a product called "Nature-Glo—the ultimate in cosmetic embalming." She found absurd the tenet that the present types of funeral are rooted in the American tradition, which more properly, she asserted, was "simplicity to the point of starkness . . ." There is a sympathetic echo of the three-price embalming system of the ancient Egyptians in a statement she quotes from a funeral director in San Francisco: "If a person drives a Cadillac, why should he have a Pontiac funeral?" To the funeral director in America today, she says, "the bereaved person who enters his establishment is a bundle of guilt feelings, a snob, and a status-seeker." Can we doubt that some of the ancient Egyptians, whom John Fowles in a recent novel excoriates as plainly having been greedy, tasteless, and vulgar, were much the same?[7] It does not need much stretch of the imagination to hear the Egyptian embalmer murmuring gently to his client: "Surely you would only want the best for your loved one?"

The explanation for the increasing elaboration of funeral customs can be found then in the manipulation by others of our feelings of guilt and snobbery for their financial gain. If anyone doubts this, he need only look at the ski industry. Fifteen years ago skiing was an enjoyable sport. No longer. Today life on the slopes is only partly skill and pleasure in the sport. Mainly it is a style competition demonstrating that one has been blackmailed by fear of ridicule into buying the latest skis, bindings, ski-stoppers, poles, boots, and even electric boot-warmers.

So much for the elaboration and expense side of funerals. What is more important is the staggering effort of the funeral industry to deny the fact of death, to apply consumer-society techniques to that most ancient of fears incurred by the taste of an apple. Jessica Mitford sums it up by using a quotation from a book by an undertaker named J. Sheridan Mayer:

Our customs require the presentation of our dead in the semblance of normality . . . unmarred by the ravages of illness, disease or mutilation.

The ultimate result of this obsession, one might call it, with the denial of the reality of death and corruption is expressed graphically by Mitford as follows:

Alas poor Yorick! How surprised he would be to see how his counterpart of today is whisked off to a funeral parlor, and is in short order, sprayed, sliced, pierced, pickled, trussed, trimmed, creamed, waxed, painted, rouged and neatly dressed—transformed from a common corpse into a beautiful memory picture.

The people concerned with this billion-dollar business have, she tells us, "managed to delete the word death and all its associations from their vocabulary." In a later chapter I shall consider the question of euphemism and obscenity, but what she is referring to are such gems as the cost of the funeral being referred to as "the amount of investment in the service," corpses becoming "loved ones," and so on.

But the real technical skill of the industry lies in the attempt to remove that aspect of death which I maintain is most intimidating —the smell of corruption. To this end, enormous pressures are exerted on the relatives of the dead person to agree to have the body embalmed. Indeed, it was my conviction until recently that it was a legal requirement of most states that this be carried out, a conviction which, Mitford shows, is fostered by the funeral industry without any reality in law. The idea that embalming prevents the spread of infection, she shows with medical evidence, is complete nonsense. We have somehow managed to graft the germ theory of disease into our horror of the smell of death. After a major disaster like an earthquake, one hears again and again that the authorities have decided to use mass graves, bulldozers, quicklime, flamethrowers, and the like "to prevent the danger of epidemics." The reality is that the smell of decay becomes insupportable. The other contention that embalming preserves the body she also shows is a travesty of the truth. It prevents the immediate onset of decay for the period of the funeral and thus saves the mourners from the additional shock of having to cope with a smell of dissolution emanating from the body of one who was perhaps loved and admired. But, she says, "in no state is embalming required by law except in special circumstances."

Even though the funeral business may be a gigantic money machine, the aura of deathly pollution still clings to its practitioners. This is well expressed in Saul Bellow's novel *Humboldt's Gift*.[8] The hero's woman friend wants to marry him, she claims, but is tempted to marry instead an extremely rich businessman who owns a chain of funeral parlors. The hero says of him, "Flonzaley had a ton of money, but his degree from the state university, it couldn't be denied, was in embalming." On another occasion the manipulative mother of the woman, Renata, says:

"Flonzaley belongs to the past. Renata is very sensitive to pain and when the man was in agony what could you expect her to do? She cried the entire night he was there. He is in a vulgar business and there is no comparison between you. She simply felt she owed him a consideration. And as you are an *homme de lettres* and he is an undertaker, the higher person must be more tolerant."

Again, Renata says of Flonzaley: "As president he doesn't have to handle corpses any more but I can never help remembering his embalming background."

The fear of contact with death is not, as many people assume, solely a product of an elaborate complex industrial society. I have shown how Hindus deal with it by allocating the task to lower castes; how many African peoples have reciprocal obligations with other groups to handle the dead so that one will not oneself be polluted. Let me take a final example from the Nuer of the southern Sudan, whom I mentioned before as going almost totally without clothes. "Death," Evans-Pritchard tells us, "is a subject the Nuer do not care to speak about."[9] And "they regard it as the most dreadful of all dreadful things." A man who has died is shaved and all his ornaments are removed for he "goes to the grave as naked as the day he was born." All who are not concerned with preparation of the grave, especially children and young people, keep away from the homestead, "even those nearest to the dead, such as his sons and younger brothers, however grieved they may be at the loss. . . . death is an evil thing and only those who must get rid of the corpse should go near the grave." The grave is dug on the left-hand side of the hut, "the side of evil." When the grave has been dug, the body is placed in it and the participants stand with their backs to it pushing the earth in on top of it as quickly as possible with their hands behind them. After the burial the senior person present sprinkles them with wild rice dipped in water and then all wash in the stream to purify themselves from the polluting contact.

It has already been noted that there is great Christian concern with the idea of the resurrection of the body so that "our vile body" may become like the "glorious body" of Jesus—the glory being that Jesus is alleged to have overcome death and to have returned on the third day after his apparent death with no signs of corruption on his body. An interesting, indeed radically shocking, view of this event is held by M. J. Field.[10] She suggests that Jesus, like the Ghanaian prophets she studied and the Old Testament prophets, was probably able to go into trances; that when he was taken down from the cross he was probably not dead at all but in a trance. Being wrapped in spices and cloths he was laid in the tomb and a rock placed before it, to prevent the entry of scavengers. However, those in a condition of trance frequently perform feats of physical strength of which they would under ordinary circumstances be quite incapable, and thus the bursting of the winding sheets and removal of the rock would pose no problem for Jesus. Her suggestion is, therefore, that when Jesus reappeared to his astonished followers, it was indeed he in the flesh and of course his body was not in the tomb. He showed his wounds, ate, and went off, reappearing again twice and then disappearing finally. His final disappearance, she suggests, was when he went out alone into the desert and died of his wounds. Of course, we shall never know which account is the correct one. To many humanists it all seems very irrelevant, but for the committed Christian of the more orthodox sects the return from the dead without trace of decay is the very core of belief. To others in the world who believe in an afterlife the body is of no consequence and what matters is the spirit, and indeed this is probably the feeling of many Christians today.

The idea of the conquest of the dissolution and decay of the body is, however, still very much with us and appears as an aspect of beliefs about two opposites: saints and vampires. In many parts of the Roman Catholic and Greek Orthodox world, the apparently intact and undecayed bodies of saints are often exhibited to the public as evidence of their holiness. If one should think that this is only an example of the poor, ignorant peasants of Europe, we must think again. *The New Yorker* of June 27, 1977, reported on the astounding case of St. John Nepomucene Neumann, Roman Catholic Bishop of Philadelphia, who was recently canonized by Pope Paul VI. It was said that when he died, in 1860, many of his congregation claimed that such a saintly man could only be a saint and should be nominated for that title. The clergy, however, trained in modern times to be skeptical of matters which long ago would have been held to be miraculous, were not convinced. The agitation of the public went on, however, and finally some of the clergy secretly exhumed the good bishop a month after he had been buried. To their amazement, so the story goes, the body was without a trace of decay. Whatever the scientific explanation for the curious phenomenon may be—embalming, extreme dryness, very cold conditions—is really irrelevant. What *is* relevant is that the absence of bodily decay was more convincing evidence of sainthood than all the spiritual qualities and good works of the bishop. Ordinary mortals decay until the resurrection of the body when "this corruptible shall have put on incorruption," but saints, closely associated with God, who has conquered death, do not. Presumably, while the rest of us are renewing our fleshy envelopes like chrysalids, the saints will be up there at the head of the line with no unnecessary delay.

This ability to defy corruption is not confined to saints. Again and again we find that humans are so convinced of the power of the Word and of the effect of categorization that reversal of what is said to be the normal, correct, pure, or holy is held to generate enormous spiritual power. Thus, vampires, allied to the devil rather than to God, are alleged to have precisely the same non-decaying qualities as saints. You identify a vampire in the same way as a saint. If it is a vampire, there will be no decay and the face will appear delicately flushed. I don't suppose too many people do this nowadays, but if "Nature-Glo—the ultimate in cosmetic embalming" really does its stuff, we could have a lot of vampire suspects around.

I have, I hope, thoroughly established that humans everywhere have a horror not merely of dying, but of the dead body. The aspect which we find most horrifying is the corruption of the flesh and its accompanying smell. We go to great lengths to avoid having to deal with this. Why is it that humans everywhere are so appalled by putrefaction and the accompanying smell? Indeed why is it that we automatically categorize every smell we meet into two basic types, good and bad? Animals often have a more acute olfactory sense than we do, yet, so far as one can see, appear not to make this kind of distinction (though it is true that a nervous horse may shy at a strange smell). Dogs certainly do not mind what we call bad smells in the least and often seem to take pleasure in them to the extent of rolling in what we describe as filth such as feces or decaying flesh so that they can carry the smell around with them like Old Spice or L'Air du Temps. The difference between humans and other animals once more lies in the knowledge we carry in our minds of our own inevitable mortality. All humans, since first we developed language and speech, must have developed a sense of past, present, and future. We also become aware of death and pass that knowledge on, at first perhaps unwittingly to a child, later by conscious explanation. Being aware of death, we respond to the stimulus of the smell of corruption with horror. To an animal, unaware of its future, its death, its decay, lacking speech and language, a smell is just a smell. To humans it is a reminder of what is in store.

What else smells terrible—in fact, very like a putrescent corpse? Feces, of course. The Nyakyusa of southwestern Tanzania recognize this very explicitly, and directly equate feces and a decaying body. They say "the corpse is filth, it is excrement."[11] Is this the isolated reaction of one small people remote from the outside world? Not at all. Consider a recent novel of John Gardner's, *October Light*.[12] One of the main characters discovers that his now dead wife had concealed from him the secret which had led to his son's suicide because she had promised the son that she would. Reflecting on the validity of his wife's loyalty to the promise given to their son so long ago, he considers how pointless it seems that she should cling to a promise given to what is now only a "manure pile": the very same image used by the Nyakyusa. In the same book Gardner also expresses very vividly our attitude to feces. The old man's sister, shut in her bedroom in a feud between the two of them, uses a bedpan and dumps it out of the window. Her niece and husband, coming to reason with her brother, the niece's father, discover this. The husband sees what has happened at once and remarks, "She been throwin' her shit out the window, looks like." The niece does not take this in at first and goes for a closer look, seeing bits of paper like blossom on the withered leaves of a lilac bush. As she gets near to it he describes her as being "suddenly assaulted by the stench" and how she had to fight not to vomit.

An interesting illustration of our attitude toward feces (and an awareness of death) comes from small children, who frequently play with their own feces without shame or disgust. The same is true when some people have shed what we regard as their humanity and retreated into insanity. In both cases, most people respond with total revulsion or even nausea. Although today, in Western society, people neither come into contact often with decaying corpses nor equate feces and corpses, yet Gardner uses just that image. There is also a general awareness from literature, newspapers, and television reports that the stench of death is awesome. Some people say of a smelly or stuffy room that "it smells like a battlefield on the third day," never having experienced such a gruesome phenomenon, but clearly indicating that they know what is involved. We may not today, in our society, have to deal very frequently with rotting corpses, but we carry a cultural memory of thousands of years that knows of the facts of decay and its attributes. And no one can avoid evacuating the bowels.

Let us look a little more at the question of defecation. However toilet training is accomplished, at some point the child has to undergo it. Clyde Kluckhohn, a social psychologist and anthropologist, was at one time critical of the weight given to toilet training by the psychoanalysts. The people he knew best and with whom he worked, the Navaho, were, he claimed, very relaxed about the matter, and therefore it was of no consequence in their upbringing. Geza Roheim, however, an anthropologically oriented psychoanalyst, with the tendency of that profession to adopt a heads-I-win-tails-you-lose attitude to the interpretation of phenomena, writes critically of the effect of Navaho toilet training and says: "Whatever the mother may do or not do, the child on account of its own *oral aggressions* (Melanie Klein, Bergler, etc.) will project mother (and later the father) as a cannibal demon."[13] Perhaps. But was Kluckhohn right about the relaxed attitude of the Navaho? It may be that the Navaho are not strict about toilet training per se, but in his account of Navaho witchcraft beliefs he describes how a child becomes aware that feces might be collected by an evil-intentioned person for magical purposes (we shall return to this idea again):

When the toddler goes with mother or older sister to defecate or urinate, a certain uneasiness which they manifest . . . about the concealment of the waste matter can hardly fail to be communicated to the child. The mother, who has been seen not only as a prime source of gratification but also as an almost omnipotent person, is now revealed as herself afraid, at the mercy of threatening forces.[14]

We approve of animals that are, as we put it, "clean in their habits"—that is to say, they defecate outside and away from a house. We strongly disapprove of what seems to be an atavistic tendency in dogs that I mentioned earlier to rub themselves in feces or in decomposing animal carcasses. Why do they do it and why do we disapprove? Plainly we disapprove because we find the smell disgusting. As to why they do it, my guess is that dogs make part of the very same mental linkage that we do: decaying flesh equals feces, and feces equal sex. But since dogs lack speech, they make no equation between decay-feces-death. Thus, to them, feces and decay have no frightening connotation of death and the association is purely pleasurable. It is, of course, only a guess, but it fits my theory.

Is the human disgust at the secretiveness about defecation universal? Certainly many peoples view foul-smelling latrines with more equanimity than we do after a century of flush toilets. Mary Douglas, considering the idea that there is a universal urge for privacy in defecation, discounts that notion as Western ethnocentricity, using as her evidence V. S. Naipaul's account of his first visit to India.[15] Naipaul, though of Indian parentage, was born in Trinidad. As I have previously noted, there are probably few people more obsessed by ideas of ritual pollution than the Hindus, yet Naipaul returning to his ancestral land was astounded to see that

Indians defecate everywhere. They defecate mostly beside the railway tracks. But they also defecate on the beaches; they defecate on streets; they never look for cover . . . these squatting figures—to the visitor, after a time, as eternal and emblematic as Rodin's Thinker—are never spoken of; they are never written about; they are not mentioned in novels and stories; they do not appear in feature films or documentaries. This might be regarded as part of a permissible prettifying intention. But the truth is that Indians do not see these squatters and might even, with complete sincerity, deny that they exist.

The same phenomenon is remarked on by Naipaul's friend Paul Theroux in 'The Great Railway Bazaar in an account of the early morning in southern India.[16]

Does this evidence, then, deny the universality of shame and disgust? Not in the least, in my view. I saw the same phenomenon on open ground in Addis Ababa right across from Ethiopia's splendid parliament building a few years ago. Given the appalling conditions of poverty, overcrowding, and squalor in India's cities and in Addis Ababa, it is understandable that some human inhibitions break down, but the important point is touched on when Naipaul writes that "the truth is that Indians do not see these squatters and might, with complete sincerity, deny that they exist." Though the action may occur in public, it is as though it were in private; it is as though the person were invisible—like the boys in the middle of their initiation whom I saw in Tanganyika.

In an earlier chapter I mentioned of the Mangaians that they have sex in a room filled with other members of their family as though they were completely alone. Here we have precisely the same phenomenon of "public privacy." All cultures have a concept of personal space which is comparable to and related to the same idea. This personal space surrounds each person like an invisible plastic bubble which can only be breached through permitted intimate contact or for attack. The amount of space involved varies from culture to culture. For instance, Latin peoples stand much more closely to one another when talking than do the English or North Americans, who step back if someone stands too near. Even in the crowded situation of a subway train in the rush hour this idea still holds good, even though one is physically in contact with people on all sides. Under these circumstances people tend to allow only certain parts of their bodies—usually their upper arms and shoulders—to touch the surrounding strangers. Contact with the hand, wrist, foot, or leg would, unless it is plainly fortuitous because of the train's movement, be perceived as a sexual advance. Of course, there are those who get their sexual thrills out of just such a situation and will rub themselves against fellow passengers.

Returning to the public privacy concept, in Western society one may observe couples embracing and kissing in public parks or on beaches, though this is more blatant in England than elsewhere, sometimes to the acute embarrassment of overseas visitors, who respond to couples copulating in English parks as Naipaul did to the "squatters" in India: it all depends on what one calls public. Take urination. The average Briton or American is amused, disgusted, or embarrassed by the type of men's urinal that used to be common in France. This consisted of an iron trough attached to a metal screen which hid the middle of the man but allowed his head and shoulders, legs and feet, to be seen by passers-by and which was situated right on the sidewalk in major cities. But everything is relative—in British or American usage, a men's urinal is in a closed room but each individual man is visible to every other man. The public-privacy convention is for each person to stare straight to his front, glancing peripherally at his own genitals and not at all at those of the men flanking him on either side. It will be recalled that the Mangaians, promiscuous to an extraordinary degree sexually, found the Western custom of men urinating "publicly"—that is, in front of other men—quite horrifying.

The convention of not seeing what is before one's eyes appears in an extreme form at a nudist camp, according to a Kinsey Institute report:

As the publisher of one nudist magazine said, "They all look up to the heavens and never look below." Such studied inattention is most exaggerated among women, who usually show no recognition that the male is unclothed. Women also recount that they had expected men to look at their nude bodies, only to find, when they finally did get up the courage to undress, that no one seemed to notice.[17]

In line with nudist thinking that no aspect of the body should be shameful (though there was fanatical avoidance of any overt sexuality whatever), some nudist camps, according to the report, had communal latrines. Some members felt this was going too far. Why? "There are niceties of life we often like to maintain, and for some people this is embarrassing . . . you know, in a bowel movement it isn't always silent."

Think, too, of how embarrassed most of us are in a hospital when presented with a bedpan for the first time or given an enema.

In Naipaul's second book about his ancestral land, *India: A Wounded Civilization,* he once more mentions the ubiquitous excrement. In a description of a visit to a rebuilt squatters' village (no pun intended), he says:

. . . we walked . . . picking our way between squirts and butts and twists of human excrement. It was unclean to clean; it was unclean even to notice.[18]

Unclean to notice: that is the crux of the matter. Moreover, cleaning would be done: "It was the business of the sweepers to remove excrement, and until the sweepers came, people were content to live in the midst of their own excrement." The sweepers were the untouchables, outcastes, what Naipaul calls "the pariahs of pariahs." In Hindu culture it is possible for the higher castes to ignore filth in the comforting security that it is the duty of the sweepers to remove it. Sweepers are beyond pollution since their contact with feces and corpses makes them pollution themselves —"walking carrion." (After independence, in 1947, India officially "abolished" caste; one might as well try to abolish kinship.) But whether fortuitously or not, we see once more an equation made between the corpse and excrement.

Humans everywhere know about death. It is a matter of concern at the back of our minds from early childhood. For instance, a random opening of the *Oxford Book of English Verse* can show thirty-four mentions of death in only thirty pages. Death as death we can mention. The details of death and particularly the facts of decomposition we find more difficult to deal with. Sex, similarly, is acceptable to mention in a very general way, but once again the details are like the term our forebears used to describe underclothes—"unmentionables." Defecation and urination may be mentioned in a very clinical way, but here particularly we find the device of euphemism used, which I want to consider further in the next chapter.

Only a minute proportion of our literature is devoted to so overwhelmingly an important aspect of life as sex. Similarly, I used to find it odd as a child that in none of the adventure stories did anyone apparently have to urinate or defecate. I am suggesting that subconsciously we link the smell of feces and any other "bad" smelling substance with the decay of the body—death. We also, I believe, link such smells with sex because of the proximity of the genitalia to the organs that excrete body wastes. These ideas are sometimes carried to extremes, for there are fetishists who can only achieve sexual satisfaction by being urinated on, defecated on, or by having sex with a dead body—necrophilia. Sex we find threatening then for two reasons: because it reminds us of our mortality; because it reminds us of the possibility of the dissolution of the security conferred on us by ordered society were we not to have very strict rules about how we have sex. By suppressing oestrus and allowing permanent sexual receptivity, our remote ancestors opened the way to emotional links culminating in the supreme achievement of love. They also gave us the possibility of the supreme pain and grinding misery of rejected love.

The linking between death and sex appears in the doctrine of "original sin"—surely one of the most strange notions ever to emerge from the human imagination. It appears first from the pen of St. Paul, who, from his writings, seems to have been both obsessed with and terrified of sex. In Romans 5:12 et seq. we find the idea that Adam, by his sin of disobedience, brought death to the world, finally to be redeemed by the person born without sin, that is, without sex, through the Virgin Birth—Jesus. St. Augustine of Hippo, another person drawn to and repelled by sex, carried on the idea: in effect saying that since Adam disobeyed God's command and all his descendants could only be perpetuated by sex-sin, therefore original sin is part of us all. The position of St. Thomas Aquinas, yet another person who saw the perfectly natural urges of the human body as evidence of original sin, is as follows:

In this view original sin is not a positive evil added to human nature, but the deprivation of a supernatural good originally bestowed upon the race in the headship of Adam. Following this original loss, as a penalty of Adam's transgression, came the direful consequences of death, the confusion and disorders of all the human faculties, and the sting of concupiscence. This is the accepted teaching of the Roman Catholic Church, and the Council of Trent defines as of faith, that Adam lost original justice, not only for himself but also for us; that he poured sin, which is the death of the soul, into the whole human race, and that this sin comes, not by imitation of Adam's transgression, but by propagation from him.[19]

Luther "held that it consisted in concupiscence." To the religiously neutral rational humanist, these doctrines cannot but appear as evidence of the human fear of sex and death. One wonders too how a rational person could respect a deity so apparently petty. From this doctrine we must deduce that Adam may be blamed for all our misfortunes and that he, poor fellow, was led astray by that cursed female, Eve.

The ambiguities and ambivalences which inevitably accompany such a strange teaching are still with us. They are well expressed by Mary Gordon in her novel *Final Payments*.[20] Her heroine, Isabel, released by his death from the bondage of caring for her invalid father after eleven years, comes out into the world again at age thirty and finds herself, like poor Eve, beset by the sexual needs of her body. Her attitudes, however, have been molded, bent, and twisted by the doctrines of original sin. One of her closest friends calls her but she cannot tell her in detail about her doings, involved as these doings have been with sex, which, as she puts it, "separates us from everyone but our partner." At least she was joying in the pleasure of her body and the mutual fulfillment to be achieved with a loved person. But later, under the denunciation of her lover's terrible wife, the burden of sin settles on her like an unbearable weight. She can only achieve restitution for her terrible "sin" by caring for a woman so utterly unlovable that even Isabel finally comes to realize the fact. But before this, her mind tortured by the teachings of her childhood, she can only be obsessed by the ideas that all her troubles had stemmed from giving in to the desires of her body.

Tragically, humans have tortured themselves because their consciences have been imbued with the obsessive hatred of their bodies, of sex, of love between men and women, arising out of their fears which do not arise from any sin, any failing of Eve or Adam, but rather from a knowledge of our own mortality and a terror lest our erotic urges should fragment our carefully erected edifice of society. As Swinburne put it:

> In his heart is a blind desire,
> In his eyes foreknowledge of death . . .[21]

7

Obscenity and Euphemism:
A Two-sided Coin

Today when one is reading novels, it is fairly common to find words that fifteen or twenty years ago would never have occurred in print. For instance, in the British writer Nevil Shute's tales of the 1940s and 1950s, his working-class characters refer to "muggers" when clearly they mean "buggers," and "muckers" when they mean "fuckers." One would look in vain in the earlier novels of Margaret Drabble, another British novelist, for what are called "obscenities," but they occur realistically in her later ones. The same is true of the fiction of Edna O'Brien, Margaret Atwood, John Gardner, John Updike, Saul Bellow, Bernard Malamud, and others. I find the more realistic trend commendable.

There has been a great rise in the use of obscenity by the middle classes over the past two decades, and the past ten years has seen a great increase in the use of obscenity by educated women. There was a comparable increase among men between 1939 and 1945. In part this can be traced to World War II. Further increases may be due to the Korean and Vietnam wars. In wartime situations there is great mixing of social classes, and both in America and Britain many working-class men (not all) use obscenity as a form of adjectival and abverbial emphasis, sometimes to an extent which robs it of all drama and reduces it to a dull banality. After all, obscenity is only what is defined by the culture as obscenity.

If we turn to the dictionary meaning of "obscene," we find that it is given as "disgusting," "filthy," and "grotesque"; "grossly repugnant to the generally accepted notions of what is appropriate"; "marked by violations of accepted language inhibitions and by the use of words regarded as taboo in polite usage." It is also referred to as "stressing or reveling in the lewd or lustful." Moreover, an example is given of "death under the stars is obscene somehow." Thus we have filth, sex, and death all bracketed together.[1]

Plainly, obscenity is defined by a culture, though the boundaries of what is considered obscene move in response to social and class pressures. As a child, I recall being shocked by my friend saying "bloody" and telling my mother, who in turn went to see his mother. By the time of World War II, it had become acceptable for middle-class English people to use "bloody" occasionally to dramatize an utterance, a fashion started much earlier, of course, by Eliza Doolittle in G. B. Shaw's *Pygmalion*. When used by middle-class people, and particularly by women, it was said as though in quotes, rather as English people will mimic Cockney or other working-class dialects with a very self-conscious affectation. Today in America and in Britain, it has become acceptable and fashionable even to use the word "fuck" in the same manner, though this is by no means standard practice among the middle classes: a lesson that many a student going on vacation or taking a job may suddenly realize with a jolt.

Let me go back to my experience as a child, since it brings out one of the fascinating and essential characteristics of obscenity: I *told* my mother that my friend had said "bloody." The point is not so much that he used a term which at one time was assumed to be a version of "by our lady," though now thought to refer to menstrual blood. No, the important point is that I *knew* it was a "rude" word, a "dirty" word. Sometimes people have been horrified by intensely respectable elderly maiden ladies who have had a nervous breakdown and who utter obscenities in "a stream of filth." Onlookers have often been mystified by this phenomenon, saying, How could a woman like her, who has lived such an impeccably pure life, possibly know such words? She must be possessed of an evil spirit, would be the diagnosis in certain places and times. First, we might consider whether the very impeccability of her life, starved of natural sexual satisfaction, might not be the reason for her breakdown: when the sum of years of loneliness, unhappiness, restraint, respectability, and adherence to the prescribed conduct for an unmarried woman suddenly becomes beyond bearing. Second, there is no mystery to her using the words. All adults know the words that are outlawed as obscene, but they do not use them.

There may be considerable variation within a language area as to usage or even meaning for some words. For instance, "bastard" is used as a term of affectionate abuse in southern England, as in "You're a crafty bastard!" In northern England, in some circles, it was considered fighting talk as being an insult to the mother—and that imputation is very widespread in many cultures. This probably takes us back to the primacy of the mother-infant bond found even among primates, but in the human case it may be viewed as a direct attack on one's mother's adherence to the rules about mating. Words in common English use such as "sod" for "sodomite" (that is, a man who engages in anal sex), or "bugger" also for "sodomite" have little impact in the United States. Similarly to be "pissed" in England means to be drunk as in "I was pissed as a newt," whereas in America it means to be annoyed. I recall in my first contact with American teachers in East Africa in 1961 being somewhat shocked by a woman who said, "Oh shit!" in annoyance. Certainly it was used in English circles, but never by women.

This raises another interesting point. Obscenity is intended to be shocking; it becomes doubly shocking from someone assumed to be "pure." This has been recognized by feminists who have come to realize that men's chivalry, gallantry, and the imputation of maidenly purity are devices used to discriminate against women. Thus, many feminists have adopted the formerly exclusively male usage of incorporating obscenity into their speech.

Some terms in use in America are readily understood in England but not used, such as "mother-fucker" and "cock-sucker," and as such have a far greater and more dramatic impact in Britain.

This brings us to a closer consideration of what is most commonly thought of as an obscenity. Apart from oaths which break the Third Commandment—"God," "Jesus," "Christ," "Jeez," "God Almighty," which might better be termed "profanities"—the majority of obscenities are concerned either with sex, incest, or elimination of body wastes. Perhaps the commonest expletive in American usage is "shit." This has parallels in England and in France. In the United States persons are referred to as "assholes" or "farts." But now we come to a fascinating example of euphemism. No one ever uses the precise terms of "vagina," "penis," "anus" as obscenities. On the contrary, they use terms for them many (not all) of which (1) are derived from animal terms, (2) are in effect euphemisms, and (3) though euphemisms, have themselves become obscenities so that we have to have further euphemisms to avoid "the use of words regarded as taboo in polite usage." The fact that we use animal terms has been commented on by Edmund Leach in a fascinating essay.[2] His essay has recently come under strong criticism, but this does not detract from the points I wish to use.[3]

Thus, we have vagina becoming "pussy," in itself a quasi euphemism for what seems more coarse and brutal, "cunt." Yet "cunt" is probably derived from the same source as "coney"— rabbit. Leach observes amusingly that there seem to be mental links between a Bunny Club in New York and an eighteenth-century London institution called a "cunny house." In American but not British usage we also have "beaver" for vulva. The penis too achieves an animal character with "cock," the use of which for male chickens is now almost outlawed in polite American usage in favor of the neutral "rooster." A real Anglo-American difference is in the word "pecker." In American usage it means the penis, but in English, nose. Hence, the common English exhortation not to be downhearted, "Keep your pecker up!" has often caused Americans in Britain acute embarrassment. Another difference which has caused embarrassment in the word "fanny," which in American usage is a fairly acceptable euphemism for the buttocks, but in England means the vagina: hence the *double-entendre* of the title of John Cleland's immortal work *Fanny Hill*. The buttocks or anus is sometimes thought to have an animal attribution in "ass," which, in fact, derives from the English "arse" and has nothing to do with donkeys; but because ass-anus and ass-donkey in American usage are homonymous leads some Americans to avoid "ass" for donkey. It seems, therefore, that people are accepting what they perceive as animal terms for parts of the body concerned with sex and defecation.

Why animals? Could it be that at some level we perceive sexuality generally as part of our animal nature? We refer to a man behaving "like a goat" or a "ram" and a woman "like a bitch," in disapprobation of their sexual looseness. Many other terms of abuse in many languages are put in animal terms: a "dirty dog," a "real swine," a "pig of a person," a "snake," a "son-of-a-bitch," "pig-headed," "bull-headed," "sheeplike," a "dirty rat," a "real skunk," "toadying." True, we do have a few approving animal terms like "lion-hearted," "he's a lamb," "she's a duck" (in Britain), but they are scarce compared to the disapproving terms.

Returning to the genitalia, sex, and elimination, we use the terms for them in abuse: "he's a real prick"; "what a stupid asshole"; "don't talk balls"; "blow it out your ass"; "stick/shave/push/work it up your ass"; "I was really screwed"; "he was shit on badly"; "you fucked it all up." An interesting piece of sexual discrimination comes out in the fact that it is said of a man that he is a "prick" or a "cunt." A woman may be called a "cunt" but rarely a "prick."

Animals, then, perhaps because we are concerned with the nature-culture dichotomy. Why sex and elimination? We find sex threatening because it reminds us of defecation, which reminds us of decomposition and death. Sex we also find threatening because of our fears of promiscuity as being destructive to the social fabric. Perhaps we have an echo of death in the use of the adjective "rotten" in a phrase like "you rotten bastard" or even more in "you stinking rotten bastard." Curiously, this has its exact parallel in Swahili, where the phrase "you're a rotten person" (*wewe mtu mbovu*) occurs. The use of obscenity is relatively rare in Swahili usage, but occasionally a man when goaded will shout, "Your mother's cunt!"—*Kuma nyoko*.

This last expression has relevance to a very widespread phenomenon called the genital curse. In many cultures, if a parent wishes to curse a child, she or he in effect exposes her/himself to the child. Among a people I worked with in East Africa, the Luguru, the parent would say, "If this is not what gave you birth, may you die!" This is the explanation of why Ham, the son of Noah, was cursed. Genesis 9:20–25 has it thus:

And Noah began to be an husbandman, and he planted a vineyard: and he drank of the wine and was drunken; and he was uncovered

within his tent. And Ham, the father of Canaan, saw the nakedness of
his father, and told his two brethren without. And Shem and Japheth
took a garment, and laid it upon both their shoulders, and went backward, and covered the nakedness of their father; and their faces were
backward, and they saw not their father's nakedness. And Noah
awoke from his wine, and knew what his younger son had done unto
him. And he said, Cursed be Canaan; a servant of servants shall he be
unto his brethren.

It is this passage that is used by the Afrikaners in South Africa to
justify the inhuman government policy of apartheid. Presumably
the logic goes that since the white people are served by the black
and since everything is ordained by God, then the blacks must be
descended from Ham, since otherwise they would not find themselves in this subservient position. The irony of this is that the
whites must therefore be descended from Shem and Japheth and
therefore Jewish. How the Afrikaners square this with anti-
Semitism it is rather hard to fathom.

The physical exposure of the genitalia is comparable to verbal
abuse using them for imagery. Presumably the custom of "moon-
ing," or exposing the naked buttocks, is in the same category of
acts. The same people whom I mentioned as cursing by exposing
themselves, the Luguru, also have a related belief. They believe
that an infallible protective magic against witchcraft can be produced if one has the right ingredient. This is some pubic hair
plucked from a parent while the latter is asleep. There are two
snags to this. One is that if you have uncovered your parent's
pubes you have in effect committed incest, which, it is believed,
causes you to *become* a witch. You may now have a remedy for
witchcraft, but you are fighting fire with fire. The second snag is
that in this culture pubic hair is always shaved or plucked out.

Leach, in his essay on animal categories, observes that "whatever is taboo is a focus not only of special interest but also of anxiety. Whatever is taboo is seemed, valuable, important, powerful,
dangerous, untouchable, filthy, unmentionable."

Here we can turn once more to Evans-Pritchard, who in 1929
wrote an interesting essay on uses of obscenity in Africa.[4] Like
Leach, he recognized that making something taboo has the effect
of enhancing interest in it. When that something is the use of obscenity, he found that ·

. . . the main characteristic of obscenity is that a man *may* do what he is normally prohibited from doing.

He was examining the phenomenon that caused great perplexity to European missionaries and administrators in Africa: the fact that on certain specific occasions an institutionalized use of obscenity occurred in songs, riddles, jokes, gestures, and dances that would normally have been unthinkable. The occasions he listed were ceremonies for initiation, funerals, feasts in honor of spirits, rain making, protection of crops, secret societies, birth of twins, marriage, illness of children, sowing of seed, and on the occasion of arduous collective tasks.

His explanations for this puzzle were quite simple. First, he suggested, the withdrawal of the normal prohibition of a particular act emphasized the importance of that act. Second, the effect was to canalize and direct human emotion into specific channels at times of crisis, rather than having it spill in all manner of unexpected directions. Third, he believed, the withdrawal of the taboo acted as a stimulus and reward to the workers if the occasion was one where communal work was involved. All of these make sense to me. There is a parallel in the case of sibling marriage between royalty. The normally outlawed act receives great emphasis and serves to dramatize the norm. Anthropologists have recorded many comparable examples from around the world of rituals of reversal. To the people concerned, the expressed purpose may be to generate spiritual power. To the outside observer, the intentions may seem more concerned with emphasizing the everyday norms and, at the same time, allowing people to get rid of a lot of repressed emotions in controlled circumstances. "Controlled liminality" was how I described the English pantomime transvestism. We have the same phenomenon here. On many of the occasions described by Evans-Pritchard, there is licensed wearing of clothes of the opposite sex, which, if done by individuals in an uncontrolled way, would lead to accusations of that prime belief in reversal of the norm—witchcraft. The transvestism and the question of witchcraft are areas we shall have to explore later. For the moment, let the explanations given so far suffice but add in the one of allowing fantasy full rein, even in the case of the sibling marriages.

Are these strange manifestations merely examples of the behavior of "primitive" peoples? I think not. At weddings in Western societies people often do things normally prohibited, such as the horn blowing by cars in the procession at many American marriages. At wedding parties, highly respectable older ladies often make remarks and jokes that normally would be considered at least risqué, if not obscene. Older people frequently dance in a very uninhibited fashion.

And what about carnivals? The word comes from the removal or putting away of flesh (*carne levare*), according to Webster's Third, and thus the meatless penance of Lent, but since the word antedates Christianity, one could think of other etymologies. Be that as it may, the occasions of carnivals throughout Europe in the past were rituals of reversal when all kinds of behavior normally barred were permitted. The same is still true of Mardi Gras in New Orleans and comparable carnivals in Latin America, Germany, and elsewhere.

In the British Army it is customary to reverse roles on Christmas Day, when the officers and NCOs wait on table for the enlisted men, who shout rude remarks about the service.

During World War II, before joining up, I worked on a big farm in Norfolk. On occasions when there was a need for a large work force for a few days, such as for harvesting potatoes, a gang of about thirty women would be taken on. Working with them as a fairly innocent sixteen-year-old was a revelation. Women who as individuals normally behaved with the utmost propriety shouted obscenities, sang obscene songs, and constantly made sexual suggestions to all the men present.

Sometimes people deduce that the ancient Greeks and Romans were much more relaxed about sex than we are because of the tales of the orgiastic rites of Dionysos and Bacchus. While it is true that we don't have our local church or synagogue organizing anything much more orgiastic than Bingo games in these days, nevertheless I do not think that the Dionysian and Bacchanalian rites prove that the Greeks and Romans were relaxed about sex. On the contrary, the fact that we do not have such rites may prove that it is we who are more relaxed and therefore do not need the safety valve and emphasis of the norm effect implied by such rites.

Obscenity, then, seems to be used to dramatize a situation. Humans everywhere feel fear of sex and the elimination of feces and urine. If we turn the coin over, what do we find? In the English countryside it used to be customary to plant roses round the outhouse to mask the smell. Today, the supermarket shelves are full of deodorizing sprays to be used for the very same purpose. At the verbal level we use euphemisms as a device to pretty up the same kind of thing.

"Euphemism" is defined by Webster's Third as

1: the substitution of an agreeable or inoffensive word or expression for one that is harsh, indelicate, or otherwise unpleasant or taboo. . . . 2: a polite, tactful, or less explicit term used to avoid the direct naming of an unpleasant, painful, or frightening reality . . .

In the anecdote about my childhood and the use of the word "bloody," I remarked that the curious aspect was that I knew the word was bad. Had my friend said "ruddy" or "blinking," it would have worried no one. I recall a seven-year-old cousin once falling over in a courtyard where he thought he was out of everyone's earshot. Looking round to reassure himself that no one was about, he said, "Damn, bugger, bloody, blast!"—a singularly inappropriate combination of obscenities, but indicative of the fact that he knew the words as such, and he also felt that falling and hurting himself was the right occasion to use them. I do not wish here to embark on a neurological discussion for which I am inadequately prepared, but it does seem that emotional shocks provoke responses from the limbic system of the brain rather than from the cerebral cortex. The limbic system is the "old," lower part of the brain which we retain from our animal ancestry, whereas the full growth of the cerebral cortex is what makes humans human. The limbic system would, in Freudian terms, be the home of the Id, whereas the Superego is in the cerebral cortex. I once heard a neurologist describe how some of his antagonistic colleagues responded to his ideas in what appeared to be a cortical (i.e., cerebral) way, but, as he put it, it seemed that the responses were really emotional ones arising in the limbic system and filtered through the cortex to achieve a guise of respectability. My suggestion is, then, that obscenities, especially when uttered in anger or some other violent emotion, are limbic in origin, whereas euphemisms have been filtered by the cortex, which rationally weighs the potentially painful, embarrassing, or frightening aspects of the words to be used and selects the euphemism to avoid them. To many of us the use of euphemism is like an over-compensation involving a reluctance to face reality.

We must grapple with the human tendency to set up categories, which, although created by us, nevertheless come to rule our thinking and even actions in powerful ways. Long ago Émile Durkheim pointed out that religions are expressions of the socie-ties that produced them, mirroring their arms, values, hopes, and fears. Later, the British anthropologist A. R. Radcliffe-Brown claimed that the opposite was the truth—that religions validate society. Yet both are true: humans create religions out of their ex-perience; the religions they created come to dominate and provide a *raison d'être* for the societies. We have a parallel situation here.

By taking a word out of one category which is perceived as dangerous, threatening, frightening, or offensive and putting it in another category, we then find it nonthreatening, even though to the rational observer the tendency may seem self-deluding and puerile. Perhaps one of the most tragic of human behaviors is to utilize the euphemistic tendency in some cases to justify actions that would otherwise be unthinkable. We normally deplore murder. However, by calling the person whom we normally would not dream of killing "enemy," the normally unthinkable becomes thinkable. If "enemy" is not sufficient as a condensed symbol, then we seek for some other appellation that will place the enemy into a nonhuman category, such as "Krauts," "Nips," "Gooks," and so on. Since the verb "to kill" or "to murder" has very nega-tive associations, we make up euphemisms like "to liquidate" or "to waste," which somehow manage to get through the mental screening process to which we subject everything with which we come into contact and reassure ourselves that what we are doing is acceptable.

Let us look briefly at the things for which we use euphemisms. Everything concerned with sex, for example. Today, sexual inter-course is called "making love," which must give naïve young readers very odd ideas about the conduct of the heroines of Vic-torian novels. In many languages people may talk about "playing" together. In Swahili, people say, "Let's converse" (*tuongee*). In English the genitals become the "private parts"; breasts become the "bust" or the "bosom," or people say "she has a good figure." The buttocks become the "butt," "tush," "heinie," "rear end"; in

England the buttocks become the "b.t.m." (or less polite, "bum"), the "sit-upon," and so on. Problems arise for parents who want their children to know the proper terms for body parts when a child talks about his "penis" to some teacher who reacts with acute embarrassment. If we turn to Swahili again to illustrate the phenomenon, we find that among the coastal people of Kenya one has to avoid a number of words that elsewhere are considered perfectly innocent, such as to "put in" (*kutia*); to "split" (*kupasua*); a "hole" (*tundu*); to "wash the hands" (*kunawa*) a "crack" (*ufa*). People also make circumlocutions to avoid combinations that might be ambiguous. For instance, the infinitive form of the verb "to hurt" is never used because it would be *kuuma,* which sounds like *kuma,* cunt. A Malaysian film called *The Story of Kuma* (a person's name) remained unused in a Tanganyikan film library, to the astonishment of the English librarian.

When we turn to defecation and urination, we get into a whole area of astounding euphemism. I have had college students who talk about cows or dogs "going to the bathroom." In America one asks for the "bathroom," the "rest room," and, most awful of all, the "comfort station." In England, as Nancy Mitford so brilliantly described in her book *Noblesse Oblige,* there are sharp class divisions evidenced by the word in use for the room used for defecation and urination, "lavatory" being upper-class usage and "toilet," lower-class (her famous "U" and "Non-U," which have now become part of the English lexicon). But "lavatory" really means a place for washing. So what about "latrine"? That too comes from French and Latin words for "to wash." "Privy" was the old English term, but that really means somewhere private or secret. The performance of the acts, too, is subject to the same sanitizing tendency. Families have their own code of saying "peepee" and "poopie," "No. 1" and "No. 2," "little job" and "big job." In Swahili people say they are going to "the prayerhouse," "to a need," and also "to help themselves." A woman assistant I had who spoke English once left me a note on my table to explain her temporary absence saying, "Please excuse me for a few minutes. I have just gone to help myself." Not knowing the phrase in Swahili at the time, I caused her embarrassment when she returned by asking what she meant.

Menstruation is surrounded by euphemism: "period," "the curse," "those special days." The old English biblical usage was "flowers." A girl reaching puberty in Swahili is said to have "broken the joint."

Other bodily excretions become similarly screened: pus becomes "matter," sweat turns into "perspiration." A very curious convention in English written material in the Victorian period was to put any words or sentences of sexual association into Latin.

In the field of death euphemism becomes rampant—a sure indication of where our greatest anxiety lies. People "pass on," they are "interred" in a "casket." Jessica Mitford's *The American Way of Death,* from which I quoted earlier, chronicles this in repellent detail. "Undertaker," itself a euphemism, becomes "funeral director" or "mortician." Flowers become "floral tributes," corpses "loved ones," though a specific corpse is referred to by name as though alive; the room where the body is laid out becomes the "slumber room" or "reposing room." The funeral becomes "the service," a morgue the "preparation room." Even a death certificate becomes a "vital statistics form" (surely a tongue-in-cheek sexual reference).

In a slightly muted way we see the same tendency toward avoiding references to dirt and decay and also a comparable attitude toward the persons engaged in the disposal of them. Garbage men and sewer men become "sanitation workers." Even charwoman, one who undertakes "chares," or "chores," becomes "cleaning lady." We have rather ambivalent attitudes toward those engaged in the butchering of animals. The great irony is that everywhere cultures have tended to glorify and honor those who engage in the professional butchery of other human beings. As I said before, categorization is all-important. To kill someone in one's own group is usually considered a crime; within one's own familial group a sin as well. Yet to kill someone who is labeled as "the enemy" is laudable. Some are beginning to question this arbitrary classification, and no longer is it quite so easy for government propaganda agencies or religious practitioners to create in our minds the idea that the enemy is not really human and therefore worthy of extermination.

An aspect of obscenity, or profanity, where euphemism is employed is the "taking of God's name in vain." In England children may say "Oh cripes," or "Oh Crippen," or "Christmas," without reproach, though clearly these are euphemisms for "Christ." In earlier times men were constantly saying "Zounds" (God's wounds), "'s blood" (God's blood), "Gad," or "Egad." In one way the rationalist looks at these manifestations and thinks, Do they believe that God is so easily deceived? Put another way, it is an illustration of the idea that man is not made in God's image, but the reverse.

Recently I was talking with someone who counsels terminally ill patients and their relatives. She remarked that it has become much easier to do this in the past few years because of a more open and relaxed attitude that has become current. I suggest that it is no coincidence that we have also seen a great increase in openness about sex and that the two go hand in hand!

8

"Come Lie with Me, My Sister"

If one were to pronounce the above quotation from the Bible (2 Samuel 13:11) or a modern equivalent at a party today, there would probably be a shocked hush. The word "incest" is a condensed symbol which strikes in everyone an immediate emotional chord. Even those federal legislators who think that it is acceptable for a well-off woman to have an abortion but not a poor one agreed in December 1977 not to ban Medicaid-funded abortion in cases of pregnancy resulting from incest, though the final choice is made by the states.

I spoke in the earlier chapters about the importance of the prohibition on incest in the development of human society and suggested that it is partly the fear that incest might take place which produces the more general universal human fear of sexuality. Whether the incest taboo is genetically inherited, as Robin Fox, for instance, would suggest, or whether it is something we learn is still a matter for debate.[1] In the case of the mother-son relationship, the primate studies that show an avoidance here may imply a genetic acquisition. I am personally doubtful that any kind of mystical genetic link prevents mother-son incest. Much more likely are behavioral patterns established in infancy.

Thus a man separated from his mother early in childhood and reunited with her in later life without being aware of their relationship might quite easily be attracted by her sexually without guilt feelings. This situation is, of course, the classic one described in the story of Oedipus, in which he unknowingly slew his father and married his mother. Mythologically, he had to be punished for his sins of parricide and incest, even though he was ignorant of having committed either. The didactic purpose of the story appears to be to show that mother-son incest and parricide are quite possible, particularly if the parties to the acts were unaware of their position, but that because of the utterly socially disruptive nature of either of these actions, divine retribution must nevertheless follow. Freud and his followers have used the term "Oedipus complex" to describe the hostile feelings of a son toward his father, whom he perceives as a rival for the affections of his mother. Many little boys say to their mothers, "I want to marry you when I grow up."

It is behavior patterns established in childhood rather than blood relationship that preclude mother-son incest in most cases, though there are doubtless many exceptions to this in fantasy, if not reality. An interesting example of the strength of the taboo on mother-son incest comes out in the fairly common phenomenon of husbands who had been strongly sexually attracted to their wives and who find that after children are born they feel cool sexually to them. The reason is that the wife has now become a "mother," and mothers are not possible to think about as sexual partners. Absurd? Perhaps, but it certainly often takes place and is indicative once more of the power of words to mold our thought processes and actions. The paradox is that a really satisfactory sexual partner has to have variable attributes, various roles to play. Men may wish their lovers/wives to be variously maternal, sisterly, dominant, submissive, wanton, virtuous, and modest; and my guess is that women have similarly complex bundles of ambivalencies in their attitudes to their lovers/husbands. Perhaps the true test of love and compatibility is to know which role is required when.

The mother-son incestuous link, then, seems rather unlikely, but that it can occur, in fantasy at any rate, is evidenced by the story of Oedipus.

Hamlet, while overtly concerned about the murder of his father and the union of his mother with his father's brother, (a union called incestuous both by Hamlet's father's ghost [Act 1, Scene 5] and be Hamlet himself [Act 1, Scene 2]), appears to be envious of and disgusted by the sexual privileges extended to his uncle when he says:

> . . . Nay, but to live
> In the rank sweat of an enseamed bed,
> Stew'd in corruption, honeying and making love
> Over the nasty stye,

Hamlet, Act II, Scene 4

The modern French writer Simone de Beauvoir considers the phenomenon of mother-son attraction in this way:

Here he is, come to her at last from the depths of the past, the man for whose glorious advent she once scanned the distant horizon . . . He is going to defend her against the domination of her husband, avenge her for the lovers she has had and not had; he will be her liberator, her savior. She resumes toward him the seductive and ostentatious behavior of the young girl keeping an eye out for Prince Charming . . .[2]

Cutting through the torrent of Gallic verbiage—the French tendency, shared by Claude Lévi-Strauss, of never saying in a sentence what could make a chapter, never saying in a short essay what could make a book—we arrive finally at this succinct question: "To what extent can these sentiments be considered incestuous?" This is her answer:

There is no doubt that when she pictures herself with self-satisfaction on her son's arm, the term *elder sister* is but a modest shield for equivocal fancies; when she is asleep, when she is off guard, in her reveries, she sometimes goes rather far; but I have already remarked that dreams and fantasies are by no means invariably the expression of hidden desire for a real act. They are often sufficient in themselves, they are the fulfillment of a desire that demands no more than an imaginary satisfaction. When a mother plays in a more or less disguised manner at seeing a lover in a son, it is only a game. Eroticism in the true sense of the word usually has little place in this couple.

Interesting and probably accurate as this passage may be, it seems to me to exhibit a reverse double standard. In other words, were it the father and his daughter under consideration, the exoneration from real desires in the case of the mother would not be extended to the father. Perhaps Walter Mitty-type fantasies are recognized by those using them as nothing but that, in the same way that some women fantasize being raped, well knowing that the grim reality has nothing to do with their dream; but a fantasy must be generated by a some kind of wish. Perhaps once more we can see the filtering, cortical effect of euphemism shielding us from the harsh reality we are unable to confront.

The Freudian view of feelings about incest is well represented by the following quotation:

Respect for this barrier is essentially a cultural demand made by society. Society must defend itself against the danger that the interests which it needs for the establishment of higher social units may be swallowed up by the family; and for this reason, in the case of every individual, but in particular of adolescent boys, it seeks by all possible means to loosen their connection with the family—a connection which, in their childhood, is the only important one.[3]

And in a footnote to a later portion of this passage, Freud adds:

Psycho-analytic investigation shows, however, how intensely the individual struggles with the temptation to incest during his period of growth and how frequently the barrier is transgressed in phantasies, and even in reality.

Elsewhere, Freud notes that his one-time associate Otto Rank, in his *Das Inzestmotiv in Dichtung und Sage* (The Theme of Incest in Poetry and Myth), "reaches the remarkable conclusion that the selection of subject matter, particularly in dramatic poetry, is limited chiefly by the range of the Oedipus complex."[4] Most people would probably regard this conclusion as greatly exaggerated, though Freud was speaking of epic poetry, sagas, and myths rather than modern theater. The fact remains though that some variant of the theme does appear again and again.

Another example of how humans can order their perceptions of the world in a self-deceiving manner, and one which has some features of mother-son incest, is the ethos of *machismo* (Mexican Spanish for exaggerated maleness). In many ways this ethos must be one of the most dysfunctional and the most productive of marital unhappiness that humans have invented. It is also sadly self-perpetuating and requires a high degree of ambivalence. In effect, it represents the fullest flowering of the double standard.

Under the principles of *machismo,* as found, for example, in Mexico, a man sees himself as the conqueror and seducer of all women, so that the more times he can "score," the greater his status. However, to do this, means that there must be females available to be seduced. Obviously, these must be the sisters, daughters, wives, or mothers of other men. But at the same time as a man is convinced of his own roosterlike success, he also believes in and jealously guards the purity of his own sister, daughter, wife, and mother. If everyone has the same goals and other males are to make their conquests, then something has to give somewhere, inevitably involving male honor and shame. Since a man continues his career of promiscuity after marriage, while protecting his wife's virtue, their marital life is unlikely to be one of love and mutual trust. In consequence, mothers lavish their love and affection on their sons, to whom they are models of all the virtues. Thus, a totally impossibly ambiguous view of male-female relations is built up generation after generation, based on a fierce attachment of mothers to sons and sons to mothers, while the sons are busily pursuing their Don Juanesque conquests of other women, whom at some level they cannot but despise for failing to adhere to the standards of virtue prescribed for them.

Could such a system be changed? It would certainly be very difficult because the women in the system subscribe to its values, too, and enculturate the next generation. Attacks aimed at changing what is thought of as masculinity, virility, toughness, or whatever else the sad value may be called are difficult to mount and sustain. It *is* possible to bring about change. Two examples come to mind. One is that of male dancers, whom many ignorant people used to think of automatically as being homosexual but whose image has been changed radically by the great Russian dancers Rudolf Nureyev and Mikhail Baryshnikov and the film *The Turning Point.* The other is this. The American anthropologist Ralph Linton, writing in 1936, commented that cigarette smoking reached the United States

. . . within the memory of many persons now alive, and there encountered vigorous opposition. Although there seems no proof that the cig-

arette is any more harmful than the virile corn-cob or the chewing tobacco which was the American pioneer's special contribution to the
tobacco complex, laws against its use are still to be found on many
statute books. It was considered not only harmful but also effeminate,
and traces of the latter attitude survive even today.[5]

Today, the image projected for cigarette smoking for men is one
of aggressive masculinity. If such a tragicomic switch can be en-
gineered by Madison Avenue, hope is not dead.

If we turn to the father-daughter aspect of incest, we do not
have far to seek in literature or life. Vladimir Nabokov, for example, exploits the idea in his 1956 novel *Lolita*. While Humbert
Humbert is Lolita's stepfather rather than her father, he poses as
her father at the various motels at which they stay to account for
their sharing a room and the pattern is the same.

A much more ancient example in literature comes from Genesis
19:30–33:

And Lot went up out of Zoär, and dwelt in the mountain, and his
two daughters with him; for he feared to dwell in Zoär: and he dwelt
in a cave, he and his two daughters. And the firstborn said unto the
younger, Our father is old, and there is not a man in the earth to come
in unto us after the manner of all the earth: Come, let us make our father drink wine, and we will lie with him, that we may preserve seed
of our father. And they made their father drink wine that night: and
the firstborn went in, and lay with her father; and he perceived not
when she lay down, nor when she arose.

The following night the second daughter did the same. Both
daughters became pregnant, bearing children who founded famous lines—the Moabites and the Ammonites. The second
daughter called her son Benammi, which seems to mean "son of
father's brother." Is this to make the child less incestuous as being
a child of her paternal uncle? Or was Lot indeed their paternal
uncle, their *amm,* and only a classificatory father?

The didactic point of the story may be to explain a number of
sociological phenomena—how two peoples came into being, how
Lot's line was perpetuated though he had no sons—but the
inclusion of the story in the Bible shows that the possibility of
father-daughter incest was not unthinkable.

A further example from modern literature comes in the British
writer Piers Paul Read's 1971 novel *The Professor's Daughter.* A

Harvard professor, a member of an old Boston family, takes his college-age daughter on a vacation to East Africa. The hotel reservations are messed up and the only place they can get into is a small hotel which has one room available with a double bed. The daughter takes it all in a cheerful spirit, but the father is appalled and disgusted with himself because the touch of her body against his arouses him sexually. All night he lies next to her in mental anguish, and the next day on the beach he finds the sight of her absolute torture, being torn between desire and terrible guilt. The only remedy he can think of is to withdraw from the frequent touchings and hugs in which they had indulged since she was little and to be cold and aloof. She, on her side, is terribly baffled and hurt, thinking that her adored and adoring father is unaccountably rejecting her. She finally feels this sense of rejection so strongly that she joins a revolutionary group.

The story is fictitious, but the painful attraction of father to daughter must be something which has happened millions of times in human experience.

In a recent article in *Ms.* magazine, entitled "Sexual Abuse Begins at Home," Ellen Weber claims regarding father-daughter incest:

Sexual abuse occurs in families of every social, economic, and ethnic background and runs the gamut from "fondling" to fellatio, cunnilingus, sodomy, and ultimately, full intercourse.[6]

Not only is abuse of daughters by fathers very common, she says —"One girl out of every four in the United States will be sexually abused in some way before the age of 18"—but since it often begins early "before a child understands its significance," the child is deceived by the authority of the person abusing her into believing that what they are doing is normal. Then,

According to several psychiatrists, when the victim learns the truth, she may feel both betrayed by the offender, and guilty and ashamed about her own cooperation.

The end results of this kind of victimization can be appalling. A Chicago pediatrician, she tells us,

has found that nearly all the girls at Chapin Hall, a home for disturbed and homeless children, had been sexually abused.

Further, many adolescent runaway children, Weber claims, are often trying to get away from an in-family sexual relationship. If they do not succeed, they frequently turn to drugs. She quotes a family therapist in Minneapolis who found that 70 per cent of five hundred children the therapist treated "were caught in some form of family sexual abuse." A study of adolescent prostitutes in the same area "found that 75 percent of them were victims of incest."

The cover of this particular issue of *Ms.* (April 1977) shows the child actresses Jodie Foster and Tatum O'Neal with the caption: THESE TWO CHILDREN ARE HOLLYWOOD'S NEW SEX SYMBOLS. What are movies trying to tell us? The answer to this question may be had in much more explicit detail from advertisements from another part of Hollywood which have come through my mailbox. The Mailers Service Company of 6255 Sunset Boulevard, Hollywood, offers, among others, these films:

Cathy: Teenie tot takes off her bikini and does a wild dance while straddling the viewer.

Mom and Dad: Brother and sister watch mom and dad through the keyhole.

Abducted: Two little girls are picked up while playing in the park and forced into sex!

Molested Moppet: Man picks up little girl coming home from school.

Another film company, Eros Discounts, of Universal City, California, offers:

Preteen Baby Movies: Baby and dad Sex.

Incest, particularly father-daughter, or its equivalent, is a part of life to an extent we shall probably never be able to gauge. Whether these vile films encourage the tendency or are merely reflective of a more open attitude it is hard to say.

If we turn to the brother-sister link, there is plenty of material in literature both ancient and modern. In 2 Samuel 13:1–39 we have the tragic and bitter story of David's son Amnon and how he became infatuated and obsessed with desire for his half-sister Tamar, the sister of Absalom. Amnon, crazed with lust, listened to the advice of his friend Jonadab, who suggested that Amnon should feign sickness and then ask as a favor that Tamar should come and make cakes for him, a request to which his father acceded:

And when she had brought them unto him to eat, he took hold of her, and said unto her, Come lie with me, my sister. And she answered him, Nay, my brother, do not force me; for no such thing ought to be done in Israel: do not thou this folly. And I, whither shall I cause my shame to go? and as for thee, thou shalt be as one of the fools in Israel. Now therefore, I pray thee, speak unto the king; for he will not withhold me from thee. Howbeit he would not hearken unto her voice: but, being stronger than she, forced her, and lay with her (13:11–14).

So far there are many points of note, one being that Tamar seemed to think that their father would allow them to marry as half-siblings, perhaps an echo of Egyptian practice since Israel had established royalty. However, as though the rape were not enough, Amnon is now overcome with revulsion:

Then Amnon hated her exceedingly; so that the hatred wherewith he hated her was greater than the love wherewith he had loved her. And Amnon said unto her, Arise, be gone (13:15).

Here we have, then, a raped woman, robbed of her precious virginity in a society which put a premium on that, rejected by the brother who had so passionately desired and raped her. Her brother Absalom later took his revenge and had Amnon killed like a dog. But what a story of lust and brutality, of pain and horror! Later in this chapter we shall look at an interesting hypothesis by the psychiatrist Robert Seidenberg, which seems to me to have relevance to this case.

The poet Lord Byron is believed to have had a physical relationship with his half-sister, Augusta, and while it is highly unlikely that incest took place between William Wordsworth and his sister, Dorothy, there is little doubt that he was in love with her. As a literary theme, the brother-sister attachment is used by Nabokov in his 1969 novel *Ada, or Ardor* and by Theroux in his brilliant recent novel *Picture Palace*.

To many people the idea of brother-sister incest is ridiculous: familiarity breeds contempt, they say. Well, if not contempt, at least lack of interest. But anthropologists Pierre Van den Berghe and David Barash think that this lack of interest may be "natural":

Increasingly, it is realized that offspring dispersal on the onset of sexual maturity, far from being a human monopoly, is, in fact, a common strategy of relatively unprolific higher vertebrates to maintain a certain level of heterozygosity and therefore genetic adaptiveness.[7]

How is this lack of interest between siblings produced, though? As we shall see later, the question hardly arises in many human societies where girls are married off the moment they reach puberty—an idea which would doubtless appeal to the promoters of Hollywood "moppets." However, Van den Berghe and Barash, drawing on the material of a number of researchers, tell us that among nonhumans "play patterns, established during infancy, interfere with copulatory behavior" and suggest that the same may be true for humans, so that human brothers and sisters brought up together where they can play during a crucial period thereby establish a sexual antipathy to one another.

But this idea presupposes a neat male-female-male-female pattern of birth order in a family. Supposing there are several females and then a male or vice versa? Supposing there is a gap of several years filled by miscarriage, stillbirths, or just lack of pregnancy? Lastly, one must reckon with the fact that, as we shall see, almost all simple societies impose a long post-partum taboo on sex between husband and wife, so that children are rarely closer than three to four years apart. Thus, by the time the younger child is old enough to play, the older is beginning to do domestic tasks.

Here, perhaps, is a glimmer of explanation of why in some cases siblings may be attracted to one another and in others, not. If the older is a girl, she may well be assigned the role of nursemaid—that is to say, a maternal role—and this could well act as an inhibiting mechanism. Robin Fox alleged long ago that one perfectly good reason for the improbability in early societies of sibling mating or marriage arose from the long post-partum taboo, and that by the time the older sibling of either sex reached sexual maturity, it would be mated off and so unavailable to its younger sibling.[8] Once more we have what looks like a convincing argument which on closer inspection proves to have some difficulties. A major one is that, as noted above, most simple societies marry off girls at puberty, so if the older sibling was female, this separation would work. It would not work, however, if the older sibling was male, since boys in these societies often do not get married until they are nearly thirty. Sexual interest of males in females certainly antedates girls' actual puberty, witness the film material cited earlier in this chapter. The Masai of East Africa customarily allowed girls of nine or so to sleep with adult men in the warrior grade—from about fifteen to twenty-eight. When the girls reached puberty, they were removed from their warrior "playmates" and married off to "elders"—men of thirty and up.

Two pieces of evidence seem to point to a "natural" lack of interest between brothers and sisters. First, evidence from kibbutzim in Israel seems to show that boys and girls reared together, sleeping and showering under the same roof, rarely view each other as sexual partners when they grow up, and tend to seek mates in other settlements.[9] Second, evidence from Taiwan shows that marriages between men and women adopted as, in effect, step-daughters to save the cost of bride payments, were rarely successful.[10] Both these examples seem to give weight to the Van den Berghe-Barash argument that when males and females play together as small children, the association acts as an inhibiting mechanism preventing sexual interest. I remain unconvinced.

To me, what this evidence shows is not that propinquity makes for lack of interest, but rather how extraordinarily successful human societies are at inculcating a sense of shame and guilt about all human sexuality and particularly familial sexuality. Both from a genetic and from a social viewpoint the inculcation is adaptive. The fear of sexuality I have dealt with at length: the fear that incest might take place and fracture the fragility of our social structures, which are all based on an honoring of the incest taboo, feeds into the already existing fears of sex based on fear of death and fear of unbridled promiscuity. Sir James Frazer said long ago, when speaking of incest, that one does not have to forbid in stern terms what one does not want to do: one does not have to forbid people to put their hands in the fire!

If it is natural to avoid incest, why is literature filled with references, hints, suggestions, and examples of it? Why, in Emily Brontë's *Wuthering Heights,* was Heathcliff so passionately obsessed by his stepsister Catherine? Amnon by Tamar? African folk-tales are filled with allusions to the possibility. A modern African novel, David Rubadiri's *No Bride Price,* has the hero falling in love with his unknown illegitimate half-sister and the consequent ruin of his life. In some legends of King Arthur we have Arthur seduced by his half-sister Morgan le Fay, who conceived

and bore Mordred, the evil treacherous knight responsible for
the destruction of Camelot. Jean Cocteau's play *Les Parents terribles* (1938), which outraged the French government, is described
by Nicholas de Jongh in a review of its recent London revival,
who says

. . . its real core of concern lies in the elemental and classic Greek
subject of incest. We are close to the territory of *Oedipus Rex* with
Jocasta in a modern bedroom . . .[11]

But who among us would commit incest? My friends of the
American Christian Cause would doubtless ascribe incest in today's world to the lapse of morality brought about by the
secularization of society. As a sign on a bus I saw said, convinc-
ingly, CHILDREN BROUGHT UP IN SUNDAY SCHOOL ARE NOT
BROUGHT UP IN COURT! What has the careful and painstaking
research of the Kinsey Institute revealed?

One important aspect of the incest offenders [against] adults was obvious during the reading of each case history in our search for varieties
of offenders. This is their ability to be religious, moralistic, intolerant
and sexually inhibited, and at the same time to live a life of disor-
ganization, drunkenness, violence, and sexual activity opposed to their
religious tenets. This incongruence usually occasions no psychological
stress, or at least none that cannot be relieved by periodic open repentance. The incest offenders [against] adults were the "most religious" of
any offenders, nearly half being classed as devout. Nearly all of these
devout men were members of Pentacostal sects or were "hard-shell"
Baptists and Methodists.[12]

Let us look at the incest prohibition in a different manner, one
that might help to explain racism, excessive patriotism, and jin-
goistic chauvinism.

Robert Seidenberg observed that many studies of anti-Semitism,
for example, have failed to consider the reverse phenomenon:
anti-Gentilism, let alone prejudice against blacks, whites, Catholics, or Protestants. As he points out, not only are major groups
prejudiced against minorities, but the minorities are usually highly
prejudiced against the majority group. Since the minorities lack
political power they can do little or nothing to the despised other
group, but should the minorities become the majorities, "history
as well as contemporary events have shown that the persecuted
can soon become the persecutors."[13] One can think of plenty of

historical examples: the Huguenots, persecuted in Europe, went to South Africa, intermarried with Dutch settlers, and subjugated the native blacks; in more recent times, Jews, fleeing from Nazi Germany, went to the same country, and today support apartheid; freed black slaves from America tyrannize indigenous Africans in Liberia, the "Oakies" of the depression era treating the chicanos in much the same fashion that they were.

What is it that creates such a fanatical attachment to one's own group and disparagement, hatred, and contempt for others? Seidenberg's answer fits well with the fictional and historical material we have considered that shows how great a part thought about incest plays at some level of the human mind: some outside group is seen "to constitute a threat to the primal repression of the incestuous drive, and at the same time a source of gratification." Our most ardent denials of this tend to constitute a proof.

As I read him, he is saying that we all have to struggle to repress incestuous ideas about our parents, which leads to a general fear of sexuality. Any person of one's own group who in any way could be seen to resemble one's own mother or father provokes some anxiety. The other group or groups, however, clearly are nothing like the mother or father, so that while the group as a whole appears threatening to one's own group as not being forbidden, they may also be perceived as a source of sexual gratification without anxiety.

Seidenberg cites the example of a white woman who was very prejudiced against blacks. She remarked, "Is it true that negroes have extra long penises and that they are erect all the time? Wouldn't it be disgusting to have intercourse with a negro?" Later he learned that the only way this woman could achieve an orgasm with her husband was to fantasize being raped by a large black man:

This woman had great prejudice against negroes. Prejudice was necessary—negroes made her anxious with their sexual freedom (jeopardizing the repression of the sexual drive toward father), and at the same time finding gratification through the negro in phantasy (the father now completely unrecognizable).

Another story is of a white northern boy who went down South some years ago and tried to erase his accent and become like his peers. They went as a group to have sex with some black prostitutes. The one with whom the boy in question went caused him great chagrin by saying, "You must be from the North." When he asked why, she said because he had kissed her, which no white southern boy would have done.

The phenomenon of wanting sex and yet being repelled by it because of an ingrained fear of incest is widespread. Avoiding those similar to one's siblings and parents may lead people to seek partners from a different racial group; it may also explain why some men only achieve satisfaction by going to a prostitute. Surely sex without some degree of affection must be without joy? Yet that thousands of men go to prostitutes regularly in most countries, who can doubt? Seidenberg, like a true psychoanalyst, sees the incestuous drive rearing its head everywhere. While I am prepared to admit to the importance of it, my own feeling is to ascribe these feelings to a generalized fear of and disgust at sex arising from the ideas I have covered: fear of death, filth, and promiscuity. It is the rigid inculcation of these largely unjustified fears (unjustified, that is, if humans are raised rationally, reasonably, and with understanding) that has given birth to all the doctrines of sin and sex. Instead of understanding how our bodies work, understanding that children are naturally attracted to their parents and siblings, understanding that we are filled with erotic desires and that all of these can be rationally dealt with, what do we do? Religions everywhere perpetuate the idea that sex is evil, sinful, polluting, debilitating, and thus guarantee that their most ardent adherents will be drawn to do what their bodies naturally urge. But instead of doing it in a controlled, reasonable, and joyful manner, they will see sex like some foul drug to which they are addicted and therefore make it that way.

What attracts so many people to sex with another group? Fear of incest; a rigid inculcation of ideas about the dirtiness of our bodies, about sex, about defecation and urination; and a lack of discussion of any of these, together with a euphemistic tendency in all these areas, culminating in the pretense that death does not exist.

The relief (and self-hatred) that people raised in this way get by seeking sexual partners from another group has many facets. The effect may be benign if perhaps the family concerned was rather anxious about incest but not unduly concerned about nakedness or the filth of sex. In this case, persons may achieve the greatest sexual satisfaction with a person of another ethnic, or racial, group. That is to say, because of the obvious physical difference there is no anxiety about parents or siblings, and since the attitude to sex is open and healthy (which does not mean promiscuous, I hasten to add), the experience of sex may be a beautiful one, without the contempt or prejudice Seidenberg describes. The other extreme, characteristic of an authoritarian background, strict religious principles, and a fear and disgust toward sex, is what potentially leads to, at the furthest extreme, Nazis murdering and raping Jews, Klansmen burning crosses and lynching blacks; or, at a more mundane level, poor William Ewart Gladstone flogging himself with a whip after his sex-starved body forced him against his better judgment to go to a prostitute.[14]

It is no coincidence that, because of rigid inculcation of ideas about sex and incest, we have prejudice between groups in our own society and in the wider world. As Seidenberg reminds us, stories against Catholics are often about priests and nuns "having a good time," whereas Catholics "warn against the vice, corruption, and adultery as practised by the infidels around them." Strict Jews often think "that Gentiles are promiscuous and sexually loose." He also reminds us the rich think the poor "breed like flies," while the poor think the rich are sexually perverted. The English and Germans called syphilis the "French disease," the French called it the "Italian disease," and so on. A recent anthropological study of the tragic situation in Northern Ireland showed that "anti-birth control doctrines of the Catholic Church are interpreted by the Orangemen as an insidious attempt to outbreed the Protestants," and both Catholic and Protestant citizens perceived members of the other faith as being sexually loose.[15]

Not only are humans terrified of incest; any form of sexual activity arouses anxiety. There is also a relation between the degree of severity with which the incest taboo is inculcated and a general anxiety about the other factors involved. Where there is a rigid and authoritarian attitude, which is most frequently found with a strick religious morality, there one will find anxiety about and euphemisms for everything concerned with incest, sex, feces, and death. The degree of anxiety will be directly proportionate to the degree of moralistic and pietistic rigidity.

9

Initiation: Authority and Oedipus

When I wrote the article which gave birth to this book my original intent had been to look at initiation rites in simple societies. I had been fascinated and appalled by what was done to girls in the society where I did field research and I wanted to find, for myself at least, an explanation of why humans carried out what appeared at first sight to be punitive actions against young people. Some believe it is to strengthen, uphold, and reinforce the social structure. Thus, today one could look at a party given by a particular person and analyze its functions in terms of emphasizing the solidarity of the group invited, the prestige that the party giver acquires, the obligations fulfilled to others by inviting them and placed upon them by the acceptance of an invitation, and so on. Or one could look at the symbolism involved in customs: the colors used to represent particular concepts, the movements of dancers, the types of clothing worn. However, in line with Malinowski's publicly expressed views, no one in anthropology has been willing to say that a particular custom was good or bad, because that would imply an ethnocentric value judgment. Thus, some have looked at the most agonizingly painful ceremony and made solemn (and accurate) statements about its function in reaffirming the values of the group, providing a symbolic model of the cosmology, without ever even mentioning the physical pain and mental trauma involved. Some of us are so afraid of being accused of value judging that were the Inquisition conducting autos-da-fé today, there would no doubt be some scholar ready to provide an analysis of the rituals of renewal, solidarity, and leadership involved in it, while totally ignoring the fact that people were being brutally put to death. (By extension, we should not criticize the Soviet Russians for persecuting the Jews, since this behavior is, after all, a reaffirmation of the values of Russian culture. Klansmen who burn crosses on the front yards of black people or lynch those who allegedly offend their code of morality are, one could say, upholding their cultural traditions.)

Carrying out research and writing about initiation rites led me to a greater understanding of human behavior in general, so that whereas I originally started with initiation rites and worked out from there, I am now coming the other way round, and looking at initiation rites as one aspect of a more generalized pattern of human behavior. But it was study of the rites themselves that led me to what I have said in the earlier chapters. Let us, then, look with some detail at what is involved.

If we encounter things, persons, or ideas that do not fit our categories, these immediately become liminal—like the persons in the transition stage of a rite of passage—and as such, anomalous and threatening. The etymology of "anomalous" is revealing since it means "without name." That which is without name at some level of reality does not exist: it is the Word that gives shape and form to formlessness. Think how alarming the "horror movie" titles are that speak of some shapeless monster, the faceless horror, the nameless creature. In a rite of passage, and most dramatically in an initiation rite at puberty, when one passes through the transition phase, one is liminal, anomalous, and, like the silent boys I saw in 1957 in Tanganyika, virtually nonexistent.

What is really so astounding about humans and their cultures is not that their songs on the tape record, the contents of the desk drawers are so different; no, what is truly amazing is that these cultural details of one culture are so incomprehensible to other humans from other cultures, who have similarly inexplicable cultural features from the viewpoint of the first culture. But remove a very young child from one culture and bring it up in another and it will come to possess all the cultural facets that are the conventional norms for the new one.

It is these different ways of looking at the world that cause us so much trouble in dealing with people in other cultures. Everything revolves round symbols. There do seem to be some universal symbols which convey the same message, no matter with what culture one may be dealing—a fact which led Carl Jung to believe in what he called a "collective unconscious" for all humans. In the main, though, symbols only work for the culture which has generated them. The most overwhelmingly important use of symbols is in words, speech, language. That is why one can never satisfactorily study another culture though an interpreter. One must have a really strong command of the language so that one can sit in a corner and listen to others talking together, can overhear conversations on buses and at drinking parties. Even then, it is not easy to understand all the implications of a particular sentence, word, or statement. For instance, I lived and worked among a particular people in East Africa for some years before I became a qualified anthropologist; I laughed, joked, and shared experiences with them, but only after I asked the right questions in the right manner did I begin to get a glimmering of how their thought processes went. One can be deceived by our common humanity into believing that other people see the world as we do, though a moment's thought about our own religious scene ought to disabuse us of this.

Checking the "yellow pages" in a small city like Poughkeepsie, New York, I am astounded by the proliferation of Christian sects, all no doubt professing to know *the* truth. The pages list *twenty-five different denominations* of Christianity, three different versions of Judaism, as well as groups of Muslims and Hindus—all within the area of a town and its suburbs of about 70,000 people! The common humanity we share means we use most of the same public facilities, shops, movie theaters, and so on, eat many of the same kinds of foods, are amused by many of the same jokes, and above all, share a common language. But if there can be thirty different belief systems currently operating in Poughkeepsie, there must be areas of thought where different citizens respond to quite different symbols.

Among the Luguru people in East Africa, it was only when I asked the correct questions that I discovered that there were many things no one had told me because it was assumed that "everyone knows that"; in other words, they had been socialized within a system that, to questions about the world, they, like us, gave answers they assumed to be universal ideas. For instance, I found that they believe that unless a person is really old and senile, there is no natural death: every death that takes place is assumed to be by the agency of someone else's malevolence by way of witchcraft or sorcery—a difference in basic world view of staggering implications, since in effect every death must be a homicide.

Sociologically, the purpose or the effect of ritual (or both) is to sustain a particular belief system as part of a particular culture. The symbolism used in any ritual possesses meaning to the members of the society because of their shared assumptions based on shared learning within that particular culture. Some of the symbolism used may be totally meaningless to persons from another culture; some may have an impact because of our common humanity. One has to be cautious though—the same symbol having great dramatic impact may be used by different cultures for slightly or even largely different purposes so that the observer may make wrong deductions.

Yet symbols strike the mind at different levels: they may be manifest and overt, plain to all; they may be latent—that is, perceptible if one points them out; and finally, they may be received at an unconscious level which may be profound but of which we are quite unaware at a conscious level of thought.[1] Thus words, phrases, verses, portions of music, drawings—any or all of these may affect us deeply emotionally, provoking anger, joy, kindness, stubbornness, languor, or any other feeling, without our being able consciously to pinpoint what it was that was the stimulus. The symbolism which occurs in dreams and in many cases does seem to be universal among humans (perhaps because it arises from the "old" brain and is part of our genetic inheritance) is not accessible to us in everyday conscious thinking, but it can hardly be denied that it is of profound significance to our minds. It may come out, as, for instance, in art, without the artist being aware of it.

A ritual expresses social needs, emphasizes authority roles, and dramatizes the event that is being celebrated. Audrey Richards, a distinguished social anthropologist, in her book *Chisungu* (London, 1956), who was one of the first seriously to study girls' initiation rites, even talked of the "expressed" purposes and the "deduced" purposes, the former being what the participants say the ritual is about and the latter what the observer deduces it is about. For example, the people may say an initiation rite is "to make boys into men" or "to test their manhood." The observer may conclude that the real purpose is to dramatize and publicize the change in status from child to adult and to emphasize who has authority over whom.

But initiation rites have an inner meaning as well. Bruno Bettelheim has shown this in his brilliant study of initiation rites, which we will consider in depth in the next chapter. Mary Douglas dismisses his study as being "merely descriptive," and when Bettelheim deduces psychological reasons for carrying out male circumcision, she writes that "what is being carved in flesh is an image of human society." How ironic that a social anthropologist accuses a psychoanalyst of being overly imaginative! If one has to "carve an image of society" on something, why not on a totem pole, a piece of soapstone, a piece of driftwood? Why choose the agonizing alternative of a potentially fatal operation? At a circumcision rite for boys attended by Jean La Fontaine in Uganda, two boys died—one from shock and one from uncontrollable hemorrhage. Yet La Fontaine would ally herself with Douglas and insist that the reason for mangling a boy's genitals is because sex is important in society and the rite makes the occasions more dramatic. Excruciating agony is certainly dramatic, especially when it is required that one shows not a flicker of an eye or a twitch of the face nor make a sound to indicate the degree of pain being undergone.

Dramatic? Certainly. But why the genitals? Or why, in some cultures, the head by means of a haircut or scarification? True, humans do not customarily sit down and construct rituals with any conscious awareness of the significance of the symbols used, except at the very manifest and overt level. At the latent, and still more at the unconscious, level there is no overt intent to involve symbolism that will have a particular psychological impact on the participants; but that this impact occurs is unmistakable. On Madison Avenue, of course, and presumably in the mind of a film director like Alfred Hitchcock, there *is* a conscious choice of symbols used, designed to affect the sensibilities of an audience. It can hardly be in doubt that these are highly effective efforts.

To return: Douglas attacks the notion that rituals are in any way intended to solve the psychological problems of individuals. Certainly I would agree that they are in no way addressed to the problems of any one individual. But what if they address problems that are common to all humans? Or, at the least, common to all the members of that particular society? One might ask why it is, then, that one does not find initiation rites in all societies or even in all small-scale, nonindustrialized societies. Yet they do occur in a very large number of societies—there may well be a correlation between the presence of rites and socioeconomic level, and we may very well have comparable mechanisms—at boarding schools, camps, armies—which achieve the same results.[2]

All humans suffer anxieties over the questions of death, sex, incest, and the elimination of body wastes. That all societies do not have easily identifiable initiation rites, then, is a measure of particular cultural conditions rather than an absence of a universal psychological condition. For instance, "dirty" jokes and pornography do not exist in those societies that have initiation rites and may conceivably act as substitutes, however grievously inadequate, for that portion of initiation rites which involves explicit instruction in sexual conduct. Having abolished oestrus, introduced marriage and the concepts of promiscuity and incest, humans have to have *some* mechanism whereby people learn how to perform sex. Even monkeys do not know naturally how to copulate and learn by observation. There are plenty of examples of couples who went to a doctor after some years of marriage to ask why they had no babies and revealed that they had never had sexual intercourse and did not know what it was.

Because one symbol conveys a particular message to members of a culture does not mean it is not also carrying other messages. At one and the same time, a symbol may convey a message about authority, about sex, and about death.

Do initiation rites differ for each sex? Indeed they do. Rites for girls often "appear to be more a celebration of natural developments than a 'proof' of femininity or a challenge to past ties."[3] But boys frequently endure frightening, painful, or arduous experiences said to prove their manhood. As we shall see, rites frequently express the different statuses of men and women, and although sometimes agonizingly painful rites do occur for girls, there is usually more celebration of the boy's achievement. Where painful rites do take place for either sex, it is probably for some of the same reasons.

Some anthropologists fear being accused of ethnocentrism if they make any kind of judgment about the goodness or badness of particular practices, but the same does not apply to psychoanalysts. For instance, Theodor Reik, a pupil of Freud's, wrote this about initiation rites: "We prefer to take these refined acts of cruelty at their face value, i.e., as cruel and hostile acts of the men against the youths."[4] Very often in rites for boys we find the idea that the boys are going to be devoured by a monster, perhaps die, and be resurrected. As Reik puts it:

It is the adult men of the tribe who drag the youths to the monster, terrify them and perform circumcision upon them; yet these same men ostensibly protect the boys from the monster and even fight for them.

I am irresistibly reminded of the hearty, overweight armed forces veterans who never heard a shot fired in anger and who from the safety of their age and failing vigor raucously encourage young men to be patriotic, to fight the enemy, and yet who wax sentimental and tearful about "our boys" who end up missing in action or dead.

But why should men be cruel and hostile to their sons and their sons' generation? The Freudian explanation, based on the theory of the Oedipus complex, would be that not only does the son perceive his father as a rival for his mother's affections, but that the reverse is also true. Reik accepts this as unquestionable. Not only is this evident in the "refined acts of cruelty" shown by the father's generation to the son's generation, but, Reik points out, it appears in the strange custom called "couvade," which appears in many places in the world, including parts of Europe.

Couvade is a custom by which the husband takes to his bed with simulated labor pains when his wife is about to deliver a baby. His male friends may come to condole with him and he may groan with the pains which, Reik suggests, he may indeed feel as a result of guilt. Why guilt? Because unconsciously he may feel pleasure at the real pain his wife is undergoing. But why on earth should he feel pleasure? He should, and probably at a conscious level is, feeling distress and sympathy for his wife. We have to dig deeper though to find the nasty, selfish old self that is lurking somewhere, probably quite literally deep down in the brain. This unpleasant creature, whose promptings probably gave rise in other cultures to ideas about sin and the devil, is presumably whispering to a part of the mind that could not possibly accept such ideas at a conscious, rational, reasonable—human—level. What it is suggesting are the unpalatable truths that the arrival of the baby is going to render the wife sexually unavailable (especially where a long post-partum taboo is the norm); it is going to focus public attention on the person of his wife, who is more usually recognized as an appendage of the husband; particularly in the case of a first child, it is going to provide a rival for the wife's affections which hitherto might have been exclusively directed toward the husband. Since thoughts of this nature are too mean, too selfish, too gross to be acceptable, the custom is often rationalized as a means of warding off the demons who are waiting to pounce on the wife in her spiritually vulnerable position. The husband is to act as a kind of heroic psychic lightning rod and demonstrate his noble altruism.

Reik makes a comparison with the extreme tenderness and solicitude shown by a neurotic which may mask utter hatred. Among the Eskimos, hostility and anger is expressed with great joviality, smiles, and laughter.[5] Similarly, if we mourn a dead person or relationship for too long or with too much fervor, it is often a sign that we feel some guilt about the death. In Turkey, Reik tells us, it was customary in the rural areas to lay a sword under the woman's bed and to beat her with sticks "to ward off the demons." In other cultures the husband was beaten after the child was born—to make the child strong, the local belief had it; Reik sees it as self-inflicted punishment to relieve the guilt generated by the hidden wish to kill the child. How absurd, you may say. How else can one explain it?

It is worth restating the case for the psychoanalytic interpretations of such events. The psychoanalyst records the fears, thoughts, dreams, and impulses of patients as expressed in their words in analysis. If a number of similar ideas, dreams, fears, anxieties, terrors occur again and again in many different individuals the deduction is made that these are common to all of us and that the patient is actually just a magnified edition of the only mildly neurotic, like you and me.

Obviously, at a conscious level, the average father in every society does not *wish* to kill his child, nor does he perceive it as a rival. However, as I mentioned earlier, among some monkeys and apes a new immigrant male who can vanquish the other males may proceed to kill off all the infants. The result is that the mothers, no longer nursing infants, rapidly resume their oestrus cycle and so become sexually available to the new male. It is dangerous to make many deductions about human behavior from primate behavior because every part of human behavior is subject to the influence of culture: apes and monkeys lacking speech cannot pass on ideas except through imitation and mime. However, it is tempting to see in customs like couvade an echo of a harsher past before we developed the cortical device, analogous to euphemism, by which we displace, substitute, and project our real feelings onto something else less threatening to our own self-image as being kindly and altruistic.

It would be an interesting exercise to study every society in which couvade occurs to attempt to see *why* men in those cases might unconsciously perceive a child as a rival. We might find in those societies cultural practices similar to those that seem to generate harsh initiation rites for boys at puberty.

Yet civilized Western people are not immune from the kinds of inner motivations that produce customs like couvade. The brutal conduct of some of the American troops in Vietnam—for example, at My Lai in 1968—should dispel such illusions. In the United States the thousands of cases of battered wives and children, the sexual abuse of small children, the incidence of rape and murder, and perhaps above all the enormous national industry of psychotherapy—all these indicate that we are still far from perfect.

A dozen years ago three social psychologists—John Whiting, Richard Kluckhohn, and Albert Anthony—studied male initiation rites by analyzing fifty-six societies which represented forty-five of sixty different culture areas of the world.[6] These included some "modern" industrial societies—France, Japan, and the United States.

Before examining the data, they assumed that "boys tend to be initiated at puberty in those societies in which they are particularly hostile toward their fathers and dependent upon their mothers." They suggested that "one feature of the rites is to prevent open and violent revolt against parental authority," particularly at a stage of physical maturity of the boys when it could be "dangerous and socially disruptive." The authors think that the conflict is over authority rather than sexual envy. One might observe that it is the possession and control of male coercive authority that has, in most societies, decided who should have legitimate sexual access to women.

A. R. Radcliffe-Brown also thought that authority is the major issue in intergenerational conflict, rather than sexual jealousy. Elsewhere he defined a political system as being concerned with three issues: order, territory, and the threat of force. In many ways, a family grouping (especially an extended family) is like a miniature political system. It is helpful to apply this concept to the family particularly where the son takes over from the father or the son's generation takes over from the father's generation as the person(s) in charge of land or herds or both. Some have asked, "What evidence is there for rebellious tendencies among adolescents in primitive societies?"[7] One could ask exactly the same question of any peaceable nation state, such as our own, which nevertheless feels it necessary to maintain a large army and police force. The extent to which the fathers' generation feel insecure and threatened by that of the sons has been dramatically revealed with the recent investigations of the activities of the CIA and the FBI when the latter was under the late J. Edgar Hoover. Recently a news item revealed that Hoover organized an investigation in the 1960s, into the dangerous nature of the British rock group the Beatles in destroying the morals of American youth (and turned down an offer by rock star Elvis Presley to be a secret agent in this campaign!). Thus, it seems unnecessary to me to search for active evidence of rebellion in the younger generation. The mere possibility seems enough for the more paranoid holders of authority.

Whiting, Kluckhohn, and Anthony set out in their study to test the following hypothesis:

Societies which have sleeping arrangements in which the mother and baby share the same bed for at least a year to the exclusion of the father, and societies which have a taboo restricting the mother's sexual behavior for at least a year after childbirth will be more likely to have a ceremony of transition from boyhood to manhood than those societies where these conditions do not occur (or occur for briefer periods).

What were the results of their survey? In 80 per cent of their cases, the data support their hypothesis: that is to say, in twenty societies which have a long post-partum taboo on sex—where the child sleeps with the mother and the father is not allowed into her bed—fourteen did have harsh rites. What then about the other six? In one case—Tepotzlán in Mexico—the data were inadequate to reach any firm conclusion. In four of the other cases, some kind of wrenching move of the boys from their parents' homes at about the time of puberty takes place; for instance, among the Nyakyusa of Tanzania, boys have to move out to form a new village as they reach about age eleven, and thereafter no boy is allowed to be alone with his mother and should only visit his home in a group with his comrades. In the last case—the Ganda of Uganda—a child is taken to his father's brother's at age three or so. Where descent goes in the male line, as it does with this group, a father's brother is often regarded as more authoritative and authoritarian than the father himself, whose actual direct blood tie might do something to ameliorate the otherwise harsh and punitive relations expected between the men of the father's generation and line and the son. Anyone who has ever gone to boarding school or something comparable will recall how painful and intimidating the experience can be and how easy it is to establish a pattern of subjection to authority.

In twenty-five cases studied by the team where there is a short post-partum taboo and no exclusive mother-child sleeping arrangements, only two of the societies had initiation rites: the Hopi in Arizona and the Timbira of Brazil. Evidently there is no innate human disposition to have initiation rites as such. Rather, some societies have set up arrangements themselves which seem to necessitate, as they see it, some dramatically painful method of establishing particular points. What about the Hopi and Timbira? Why then do they have rites and only a short post-partum taboo? The authors claim that the apparent predisposing factor in both cases is female descent, so that jural authority over the child is with the maternal uncle. Thus, they say, the child is more dependent on the mother (though I am not entirely convinced). It may be though that this emphasized yet another aspect of the rites in general: not only do they clarify who has authority over whom, but they also emphasize the sex to which the son belongs.

That this might be necessary was brought up by Freud long ago. In his *Three Essays on the Theory of Sexuality* he observed that "it is not until puberty that the sharp distinction is established between the masculine and feminine characters."[8] In a footnote to this, Freud noted—interestingly, in view of the prejudices he is alleged to be full of: "Observation shows that in human beings pure masculinity or femininity is not to be found in a psychological or a biological sense. Every individual on the contrary displays a mixture of the character traits belonging to his own and the opposite sex." Somewhat in the same vein he considered the question of homosexuality and made the observation that "the exclusive sexual interest felt by men for women is also a problem that needs elucidating . . . A person's final sexual attitude is not decided until after puberty and is the result of a number of factors . . ."

It is fashionable in most feminist circles today to denounce Freud as a male chauvinist misogynist, and certainly if one reads only his essay on anatomy as destiny, one might easily reach that conclusion. If, however, one reads his other works with their innumerable later footnotes amending and revising what he had assumed to be correct in earlier editions, one cannot escape the conclusion that he was, in his earlier years at least, extremely open-minded. Had he had at his disposal the ethnographic information we now have, he would probably have been in the forefront of the movement to reject the immutability of sex roles. One has to see people in their historical contexts. Freud was writing at a time and in a culture which emphasized extreme oppression for women, extreme authoritarianism, which, as we shall see, encourages masochism, and moreover, was dealing with the extremely neurotic. Had he been the total misogynist he is labeled by some at present (many of whom have probably never read a word he wrote), it is hardly likely that he would have trained his daughter Anna as a psychoanalyst.

Freud's ideas are relevant to the question of initiation rites. One purpose of the rites clearly is to determine for the initiand the sex to which he or she belongs and roles considered appropriate to that sex in that particular society.

Whiting and his colleagues make a fairly convincing explanation of the presence or absence of harsh and punitive initiation rites in terms of the predisposing factors involved: set up a childhood situation which will lead to an exacerbation of the Oedipal conflict and you will get one. In our society, indeed in almost every society (pace Malinowski), the son, as a child, becomes aware of the father as a rival in the affections of the mother. He may, and probably does, fear his father. Usually these feelings are fairly satisfactorily resolved in childhood, but reappear again in adolescence when the boy is beginning to challenge the authority of the father and that of his father's generation. Some people have suggested that the theory of Oedipal conflict was the product of Freud's bourgeois background and Western society. But ironically, the conflict is much more violent in non-Western societies, particularly where there is polygamy (more correctly, polygyny— multiple wives) and a long prohibition on sex between husband and wife after the birth of a child.

The Whiting team's article describes the society with whom Whiting himself worked, the Kwoma in New Guinea, as an example of the sort of conditions liable almost to guarantee the presence of harsh rites for boys.

While in our own society an infant sleeps in his own crib and the mother shares her bed with the father, the Kwoma infant sleeps cuddled in his mother's arms until he is old enough to be weaned, which is generally when he is two or three years old. The father, in the meantime, sleeps apart on his own bark slab bed. Furthermore, during this period, the Kwoma mother abstains from sexual intercourse with her husband in order to avoid having to care for two dependent children at the same time. Since the Kwoma are polygynous and discreet extramarital philandering is permitted, the taboo is not too hard on the husband. . . . the Kwoma mother . . . not only sleeps with her infant all night but holds it in her lap all day without apparent frustration.

The net effect of this is to establish an enormously strong emotional link between the child (of either sex) and the mother. At the end of the prescribed period of nursing, however, this sensuous, protective, warm, and loving period comes to an abrupt end, and the foundations are laid for the myths about a human couple being driven from Paradise, which doubtless have resonance in all humans because of some such experience at weaning. For the Kwoma child, as for many African children I have observed, weaning is traumatic. There is no gradual change from breast to bottle to spoon. Instead, being breast-fed on demand suddenly ceases completely. In many cases, red pepper or some bitter substance is put on the mother's nipples. The child is evicted from its mother's lap and bed, where it is replaced by the father. The Whiting team says the Kwoma child "varies between sadness and anger, weeping and violent temper tantrums." I have seen many African children in a state of acute misery at this time —deprived not only of the warmth and comfort of the breast, but in a very real sense deprived of nourishment and almost invariably suffering from dietary inadequacy; suddenly cut off from the day-and-night contact with the mother and apparently rejected by her in favor of the father. Small wonder that one might develop a hostility to the man who has apparently wrought this terrible change in one's condition. And what about one's feelings about mothers and perhaps women in general? A feeling of distrust would certainly be comprehensible. We shall consider this again later when we look at the images of women held by many peoples.

Male initiation rites in simple societies are very much concerned with authority, and especially with the authority of the fathers' generation over that of their sons. What kind of thing is involved in the rites themselves? There is tremendous variation from people to people. In some cultures the rites are of fairly short duration, but in others they may last for months. Very often they take place out in the bush or forest, the place of disorder, liminality, anomaly. There is frequently the following pattern of events: a total submission to the father's generation; an attack on the genitals or on the head as a phallic symbol; a belief in a ritual death in which the initiand is eaten by a monster or else descends to an underground place; a return to life in a new condition. The sequence has a powerful hold over human minds. Attending a performance of Bach's St. Matthew Passion a few years ago I suddenly nudged my wife and whispered to her that the whole story of the crucifixion follows exactly that path: total submission to the father; a crown of thorns; indeed the cross itself is thought by many to be a phallic symbol descended from the Egyptian ankh, or *crux ansata;* death and descent to the underworld; resurrection into a new form of life.

The male initiation rites, which Whiting et al. took as their example, were those of the Thonga of South Africa, described by Henri Junod in 1927, but the same kinds of ordeals could be found with probably a majority of African peoples.[9] Today many African boys may be sent to hospitals to be circumcised, but they are probably still a small proportion, and most boys still undergo the miseries and terrors of the initiation. The Whiting team's summary of the Thonga material describes it succinctly:

When a boy is somewhere between ten and 16 years of age, he is sent by his parents to a "circumcision school" which is held every four or five years. Here in company with his age-mates he undergoes severe hazing by the adult males of the society. The initiation begins when each boy runs the gauntlet between two rows of men who beat him with clubs. At the end of this experience he is stripped of his clothes and his hair is cut. He is next met by a man covered with lion manes and is seated upon a stone facing this "lion man." Someone then strikes him from behind and when he turns his head to see who has struck him, his foreskin is seized and in two movements cut off by the "lion man." Afterwards he is secluded for three months in the "yards of mysteries," where he can be seen only by the initiated. It is especially taboo for a woman to approach these boys during their seclusion, and if a woman should glance at the leaves with which the circumcised covers his wound and which form his only clothing, she must be killed.

During the course of his initiation, the boy undergoes six major trials: beatings, exposure to cold, thirst, eating of unsavory foods, punishment, and the threat of death. On the slightest pretext he may be severely beaten by one of the newly initiated men who is assigned to the task by the older men of the tribe. He sleeps without covering and suffers bitterly from the winter cold. He is forbidden to drink a drop of water during the whole three months. Meals are often made nauseating by the half-digested grass from the stomach of an antelope which is poured over his food. If he is caught breaking any important rule governing the ceremony, he is severely punished. For example, in one of these punishments, sticks are placed between the fingers of the offender, then a strong man closes his hand around that of the novice practically crushing his fingers. He is frightened into submission by being told that in former times boys who had tried to escape or who revealed the secrets to women or to the uninitiated were hanged and their bodies burnt to ashes.

A more dramatic literary description of initiation rites is given in one of the most beautiful of African novels: *The Dark Child* (*L'Enfant noir*) by Camara Laye.[10] In that novel, in Guinea, the rites are in two parts: an early terrorizing ceremony in which bull-roarers are used to simulate lions and a later circumcision.* The description of the first part bears repeating. The boys know for weeks that a creature called Konden Diara will summon them to the bush and that all the women will be confined to their houses:

> In a short while, when Konden Diara would start to roar, they [the women] would not be able to stop shaking with fright; they would all be shaking in their shoes, and making sure the doors were all properly barred. For them, as for us, though in a much less significant way, this night would be the night of Konden Diara.

The boys are taken by their elders out into the forest in the total darkness. Arriving at a huge bombax tree they find a great fire burning, near which they assemble:

> Our elders suddenly shouted, "Kneel!"
> We at once fall to our knees.
> "Heads down!"
> We lowered our heads.
> "Lower than that!"
> We bent our heads right to the ground, as if in prayer.
> "Now hide your eyes!"
> We don't have to be told twice; we shut our eyes tight and press our hands over them. For would we not die of fright and horror if we should see, or so much as catch a glimpse of Konden Diara? Our elders walk up and down behind us and in front of us, to make sure that we have all obeyed their orders to the letter. Woe to him who would have the audacity to disobey! He would be cruelly whipped.

The boys are now persuaded by the noise of bull-roarers that they are surrounded by lions—a truly terrifying experience. After a long period of this, the noise ceases.

---

* A bull-roarer is a piece of wood tied to the end of a string and swung round the head. In nineteenth-century Britain and the United States, children used bull-roarers as toys. Depending on the shaping of the wood, various noises are made.

A new command rang out, and we sat down in front of the fire. Now our elders begin our initiation; all night long they will teach us the songs of the uncircumcised.

One has to ask why all this terrorizing of boys and not of girls? We shall see that some African women are subjected to comparable misery, but not in anything like the same kind of brutally sadistic way that boys are, though in some cases, with quite terrible infliction of pain.

Part of the answer to the difference lies in our mode of bringing up children, and, as a corollary to that, our allocation of authority. Boys are expected to be, and usually are, much more aggressive and likely to challenge the holders of authority than girls. Most cultures would say that this is only natural; that women are naturally gentle and subservient, men naturally tough and strong. Indeed, experiments in our own society claim to show that boys begin to show these differences from girls within a few weeks. My own feeling about this is that parents have particular expectations about appropriate male and female behavior and give positive and negative reinforcement even to tiny babies. For instance, what is thought of as appropriate male or female behavior is rewarded by a smile, but inappropriate by a frown. An extraordinarily good survey of all the sources dealing with this topic was recently written by Ashton Barfield, a reproductive biologist, who describes all the differences claimed between male and female infants, but observes that "stereotyped sex-role attitudes are introduced very early."[11] And in describing the typical behavior of parents she notes that "while male infants are touched more, female infants are talked to and smiled at more." She also writes:

It should . . . be clear that neither biology nor socialization is the sole determinant of human behavior.

An economist, Ariana Stassinopoulos, who has strongly attacked the women's movement, makes much of the fact that girls exposed prenatally to androgens through medication develop what are thought of as male behavioral traits.[12] But Barfield points out that such traits "could be because their higher energy level causes them to associate more with boys," which would tend to reinforce their slightly male-biased behavior.

For most societies, boys are encouraged to break away fairly early from their mothers and to be independent; girls are encouraged to stay with them and be dependent. However, if one encourages boys to be tough, independent, brave, and fearless, there must inevitably be the incipient danger that they may wish to be independent also of their fathers when they become mature. To Western fathers this may be annoying and somewhat threatening. To peoples whose economic base is in the land or herds controlled by the fathers' generation, which will be taken over by the sons', the threat is much more alarming. This would be especially true where, as is almost always the case in such societies, there has been active encouragement of physical aggressiveness. If we add this threat to the situation brought about by the exacerbated Oedipal conflict I have described as brought about by the exclusive mother-child sleeping arrangements and denial of sex to the husband during this period, then we can see why some societies have apparently perceived the danger of rebellion by young males to be so great that its very possibility must be quashed by a brutal and painful act of intimidation.

Even where these preconditions do not exist, comparable acts of intimidation of young males take place in the name of "making boys into men." An anthropologist at a school of psychiatry, Howard F. Stein, in his critique of my 1977 article (see note 1, Chapter 2), noted:

In American society there is the slogan "The Marine Corps Builds Men"; so do Little League baseball, football, and warfare itself. As [anthropologists] Walsh and Scandalis suggest, warfare may be a means by which the father generation ritually jeopardizes and offers the lives of its beloved sons for the good of society.

An extraordinary act of intimidation of the younger by the older generation took place in the late 1970s in a small college town in New York State. The local police force claimed that with so many young men students around, they needed riot equipment. This request was denied by the town's budget committee so the police easily provoked an "incident" on a main street one evening. The police immediately appeared in force, assisted by their colleagues of the volunteer fire company. Witnesses of the incident to whom I spoke talked of their utter disbelief and bewilderment at seeing officers club every young man in range; and then the fire company turned hoses on the students, who, now sufficiently provoked, did indeed feel rebellious against those in authority.

Many of us have observed how fathers, while overtly sympathizing with their sons drafted into the Army, nevertheless revel in hearing about what a rough time the young men had in their initial training and proceed to recount their own boot-camp experiences. One scholar has suggested that far from fathers feeling hostile to sons, the evidence from Australia, where the Aborigines practiced not merely circumcision but subincision too—the slitting open of the penis to the urethra from the glans to the scrotum—indicates that fathers feel great sympathy for their sons. My answer was that if they were so sympathetic, why did they continue such a painful custom?

We can now begin to understand at least two of the three vignettes I presented at the beginning. We know why people think sex is dirty and why they find it so threatening. We also know why the Army insists on a haircut. The head is universally a phallic symbol. A ritual haircut is, then, a symbolic castration which, since hair grows rapidly, can be repeated at frequent intervals to remind those in a subservient position of the coercive authority of the power structure. Fortunately, for the recipients, the ritual is only a symbolic gesture which does not detract from the actual masculinity of the men! I was recently told by a teacher in upstate New York that fathers frequently use a rigorous haircut nowadays as a punishment for their sons. In Britain until recently it was customary to shave the heads of male convicts, as the most humiliating thing one could do to a man; released prisoners used to keep their hats on to avoid recognition. Presumably those in our own society who still persist in having crew cuts may perhaps feel that they are so wicked that they have to keep attacking themselves; alternatively, if they shave it off completely, they may feel that they thereby become—like Kojak and Yul Brynner—walking phallic symbols.

Needless to say, armies and fathers (or mothers) always produce a rationalizing explanation for short hair—it is sanitary, it is easier to treat head wounds, etc.—but the unconscious, underlying, symbolic significance is there.

10

Womb Envy

It is alleged that Freud once said that a cigar is, sometimes, only a cigar. However, when the proud American father of a new baby hands out cigars to his friends and colleagues, one can only assume that he is symbolically extolling his own phallic endowments. Perhaps there is an idea here that could be used by a chocolate manufacturer or baker for the benefit of nonsmokers.

Is there such a thing as penis envy? Freud and his followers thought so. Certainly males suffer great anxiety about possible castration, and symbolic castrations—circumcisions, haircuts, monks' tonsures, scalpings—have been, or are still, used as threats or reminders of the potential of enforced celibacy. Whether this means, though, that girls either feel that they have been castrated or envy boys remains dubious.

Many people today have considerable reservations about Freud's theory. There is the logical difficulty that must arise where children of one sex have never in fact seen the genitals of another. It is an *ex post facto* argument: it is not penises as such that women have envied, but rather the roles that men have universally arrogated to themselves through superior physical strength and for which they undoubtedly use phallic symbols as representations. What do we see again and again as symbols of authority but maces, swords, lances, guns, flagstaffs, towers, obelisks, steeples, minarets? And what do we see among the men who want to demonstrate their masculinity, since presumably they lack confidence in the adequacy of their natural endowments? If they do not have collections of swords, daggers, hand guns, and rifles, then they probably drive around in cars that are specifically designed to look like four-wheeled penises: Corvettes, Stingrays, Jaguars, and the like, or, as if the masculine noisy symbolism of a motorcycle or scooter were not enough, they put extension forks on a motorcycle to make that supreme mobile absurdity, a "chopper." Could it be fortuitous that so many of the phallic symbols are emblematic both of sex and death?

Bruno Bettelheim, a psychiatrist well known for his wide range of interests which have a general focus on children and their mental development, has written about kibbutz children in Israel and the value of fairy tales to children. Back in 1954, he wrote about the significance and functions of initiation rites; anthropologists have regarded this latter study, *Symbolic Wounds,* with mixed feelings.[1] Their criticisms are based on his equating the mentality of primitive peoples with that of the disturbed Chicago adolescents with whom he worked and the idea that rituals express more than social realities. Like many Freudians, Bettelheim is a firm believer in penis envy, but his great contribution to the theory lies in his insistence on the opposite as well: vagina envy, or as some have called it, perhaps more appropriately, womb envy, in males. We have, he suggests, "been far too engrossed in what seems to be destruction (damage to the genitals) and have overlooked the more hidden fascination with pregnancy and birth."

What led Bettelheim to this conclusion was his work with a group of disturbed adolescents who were housed together in his Chicago clinic. On the girls' side he found that they felt strongly that "something ought to be done to make the boys bleed." Like no doubt millions of women through the ages, they felt a sense of injustice and annoyance at having to cope with menstruation, what is often called "the curse." However, the appellation of "curse" to a perfectly natural function can also have the effect of conferring power (though cause and effect are hard to separate). Here we have another example of the power of words over the mind. In many cultures, menstruation is considered not only "dirty" but also polluting in a mystical way. What was curious in the Chicago case was that although in our culture we do not usually concern ourselves too much about ritual pollution (with the exceptions I noted in Chapter 2), the girls created a personal ritual out of the disposal of their sanitary napkins and, in some cases, wanted to save them for essentially magical purposes as a source of mystical power, believing that "the menstrual discharge is so powerful that it could poison the entire population of a city."

The boys were very ambivalent about the whole question of menstruation, being both repelled by what they perceived as its "dirtiness" and fascinated by the mysterious bleeding that in other circumstances would be clear evidence of an injury. Many of the boys explicitly stated that they wanted a vagina or both a penis and a vagina. One boy saw himself best personified as an androgynous clown. At a Halloween party there was strong evidence of wishes to be like the opposite sex: the girls wanted to dress as boys, often adding to their costumes with "guns, fishing-poles, swords, daggers and other masculine implements as penis-like tools." The boys, on the other hand, wished to dress as girls and stuffed their clothing to simulate breasts and pregnancy. Many people can think of examples of licensed revelry when they saw the same phenomenon with supposedly responsible adults— occasions like carnivals, when reversal of normal roles is permitted in controlled liminality.

Interestingly, the desire to circumcise the boys seemed to be generated by the girls. Some, in an angry reaction to their failure to produce a penis, declared that both penis and clitoris were ugly and that the latter should be removed. Some girls tried to stimulate the growth of a penis just before they reached puberty by pulling at their mons veneris. It is hard not to be struck by the similarity between these expressed desires and what is customary among many peoples in the world: clitoridectomy and the elongation of the labia minora by pulling on them regularly. The commonly expressed rationale for clitoridectomy is to reduce female libido, and the common assumption is therefore that it is a male-organized arrangement, as is well expressed in Harvey Graham's *The Story of Surgery:*

It seems reasonable to assume, particularly amongst the tribes who regard women as domestic chattels, that this crude excision was intended to remove a known organ of sexual sensitivity, the clitoris, in the belief that a woman so mutilated would be more likely to remain faithful.[2]

That clitoridectomy serves male purposes I have no doubt, but it has to be admitted that it is always carried out by women, and that in those societies where it occurs, its perpetuation is supported by women. That this sort of oppression of women can be strongly supported by women may seem astonishing unless we turn to our own country and observe how many American women oppose the Equal Rights Amendment (ERA) or who support the so-called Right to Life campaign.

Further notes from Graham on the practice in Arabia and elsewhere are as follows, which illustrate my point:

There is some evidence that excision of the external female genitalia was practised centuries before Mohammed, and that it was performed on all women irrespective of social rank when they were of age to receive their dowries, notably among certain Peruvian tribes, especially the Pano, the Campa, and the Tomagua. The mutilation or circumcision of girls by what is more properly called excision of the external genitals has almost as long a history as circumcision itself. It was certainly usual in Ancient Egypt, and to this day it persists in parts of Africa, Asia, and South America. In Arabia until quite recent times the profession of *resectricis nympharum,* or she-circumciser, provided steady and remunerative employment for elderly women, who would travel from village to village crying out their occupation rather like itinerant tinkers.

As I noted above, Bettelheim observed that it was the girls who wished to circumcise the boys to make them bleed. As Theodor Reik noted long ago,[3] one of the early accounts of circumcision in the Bible is that of Moses' son in an extremely enigmatic passage in Exodus 4:24–26:

And it came to pass by the way in the inn, that the Lord met him [Moses], and sought to kill him. Then Zipporah [Moses' Arab wife] took a sharp stone, and cut off the foreskin of her son, and cast it at his feet, and said, Surely a bloody husband art thou to me. So he let him go: then she said, A bloody husband thou art, because of the circumcision.

Apart from the fact that the passage seems totally unrelated to what precedes and follows it, the interesting point is that the cir-

cumcision of a boy is carried out by a woman. Of course, once in-
stitutionalize the idea that either men or women or both must be
circumcised, then either sex will reject any member of the society
who is not operated on as being immature and dirty. As Robert
Seidenberg points out, however, such conditions have never de-
terred either sex from having relations with an uncircumcised person of another group.

Observation of the Chicago adolescents led Bettelheim to the
conclusion that initiation rituals at puberty "appear as attempts to
promote personal integration in a difficult, transitional period of
life." He thus rejects the Freudian (and Whiting-ian) position
that a major purpose of initiation rites is to express the hostility
of the older to the younger generation. Instead, he says, they
should "be understood as efforts of the young, or of society, to resolve the antithesis between child and adult, between male and
female . . ."—nothing that a social anthropologist could object to.
True, but what about Bettelheim's contention that the rites are an
expression of male-female and female-male envy of each other's
sexual capacities? Moreover, I would, as usual, contend that one
explanation does not have to invalidate others—that the rites
could be about both intersex envy and about intergeneration
conflict, about resolving sexual identity, and about transferring a
child from the asexual to the sexual world.

The ideas and wishes of the Chicago adolescents may be extreme in Western society, but not wildly so. The idea of dressing
in clothes of the opposite sex during adolescence is very common
and strikes a responsive chord in many Western adults—witness
the British pantomime, costume parties, carnivals, and the like.
That really men are far more envious of women than women are
of men can be seen by the fact that transvestites are almost always
men. A Kinsey Institute study reports:

In a questionnaire distributed by Virginia Prince to 390 transvestites
only 13 percent reported any fetishistic feelings. Two-thirds of the
males said that they felt they had a feminine component which was
seeking expression through transvestism. The remaining 11 per cent
were transsexuals who felt they were women trapped in male bodies.[4]

It is difficult to document, but there are suggestions that many
men would in fact like to wear female clothing but are restrained

by fears of ridicule. One might argue that the widespread adoption of pantsuits and jeans by women over the past twenty years suggests the reverse phenomenon. I would not agree. In many cases, the intention has been to de-emphasize the sexual aspect of the clothing. In the second, transvestism in males usually involves an obsession with delicate lingerie, but I have yet to hear of women wishing to wear male underwear.

If we turn to the ideas of peoples in the non-Western, nonindustrialized world, it is possible to produce some rather startling examples of male envy of femaleness. Perhaps one of the most dramatic is that of the Wogeo people of New Guinea described in Ian Hogbin's book *The Island of Menstruating Men*.[5] The Wogeo are a people who trace descent in the female line, i.e., matrilineally; thus a man's heir is his sister's son and not his own son. (We must never confuse female descent with matriarchy. While the latter only exists in mythology, matrilineal descent is fairly common. Men still hold all the authority roles and are usually the property holders.) Whereas in many matrilineal societies the husband moves in with his wife's people, at least for a time, the Wogeo have patrilocal marriage: a wife moves in with her husband's people. The whole Wogeo society is divided into two moietes (halves)—Hawks and Bats—and one always has to marry someone in the other moiety. Usually, each moiety performs the services for the other of initiating boys and carrying out burials.

Wogeo myths could provide fertile ground for analysis, containing as they do elements of cannibalism, fratricide over competition for a woman, confusion of sex roles, and the transposition of sex organs, and so on. But it is their ideas about sexual pollution and menstruation on which I wish to concentrate.

Sexual activity is approved of but considered highly polluting— even hand contact with one's own or one's partner's genitals is dangerous. Thus, women urinate standing and men squatting (the latter custom common today in many areas of the world, to prevent urine touching clothing). Normal blood is not thought polluting, but menstrual blood is regarded as so dangerous that it can be lethal to anyone else if touched or, for instance, to a man if introduced into his food. Indeed, Hogbin reports that Wogeo women are able to stop their menfolk from beating them by threatening to do just that. Sexual intercourse the Wogeo believe to be highly polluting, but for the women this poses no lasting problem because, Hogbin says, they "are regularly freed from contamination by the normal physiological process of menstruation." What about Wogeo men?

If the premise of a society is that sex is polluting but that women can rid themselves of this pollution by their flow of menstrual blood, then logic demands that men, too, must somehow eliminate contaminated blood from their systems. A menstruating Wogeo woman has to be sequestered from the rest of her family and society in a special hut. Her menstrual blood is believed lethal to anyone but herself. This is, one would think, enough to provoke enormous anxiety about sex among both men and women, but the situation for men is much worse.

Wogeo boys approaching puberty have their tongues scarified until they bleed profusely, which gets rid of some of the bad blood. However, when they reach manhood, much more drastic measures are thought to be necessary. When a man decides that the time has come for him to "menstruate," he eats nothing (one could equate sex and food or argue that fasting makes it dramatic; both are true) on the chosen day. In the late afternoon he goes alone to a quiet beach and wades out until he is knee-deep in water. He stimulates his penis until it is fully erect and then slashes the glans with a crab or crayfish claw. Since the penis is engorged with blood, it will no doubt bleed violently and profusely. The sheer physical pain the man suffers when doing this is dismaying to contemplate, but the mental anguish and terror of pollution must surpass it. The woman's blood, we have seen, is believed to be lethal to others but harmless to herself. Not so the man's. His blood is believed to be lethal to others and fatal to himself should it fall or drip onto his hands or legs.

The snake is generally recognized as a universal phallic symbol (an indication perhaps of the male authorship of Genesis since Eve was unable to resist the serpent). In the case of Wogeo men the symbol must achieve a hideous realism for the man as he handles what must seem analogous to a poisonous snake. It is impossible to believe that sometimes his blood would not splash on his fingers and thighs; and one can picture his terror-stricken washing off, his realization that frantic rinsing of one place has allowed some more blood to spatter somewhere else, his incredible relief

when death does not follow, his gnawing anxiety for the next day
or so, exacerbated by intense physical pain.

After this operation the man waits until the blood clots, then
wraps his penis in leaves and retires to the men's clubhouse for a
few days to recuperate in safety. It hardly needs to be said that
Wogeo men do not "menstruate" every month as women do or
they would never have any sex at all. Only before occasions of
moment, or if, when ill, they are diagnosed as having had contact
with some female impurity, do they consider such an agonizing
course necessary.

As noted above, Wogeo women keep their contamination by
men in check by menstruation, but when a woman gives birth, the
blood she loses is believed to be supremely polluting in that it
contains nine whole months of male contamination that has not
been removed by monthly flows. In consequence, some women
elect to give birth alone so as not to burden anyone else with such
a load of pollution. If an old woman should act as midwife, she
has to undergo a special rite of purification. (In a reciprocation of
the female acquisition of male impurity through sexual congress,
it is believed that the men's close contact with the embryo through
sex will cause him to suffer morning sickness—and no doubt in
consequence he does.)

What is at the root of these bizarre beliefs, one might ask?
There are two main ways one could interpret the information, sociologically and psychologically. First, the sociological. Mary
Douglas points out, as Hogbin notes, that the dogma of ritual contamination by females will be found "where males find that their
authority can be challenged." I agree. And in the Wogeo case the
evidence of this is unusually strong. The self-inflicted bleeding of
the males has the effect of "proving" the superiority of males to
females, since females naturally get rid of their impurities from
males by their monthly flow while males, voluntarily and with
great pain, rid their bodies of the accumulated bad blood. The
friend who observed to me that she wished she got a week off
housework every month took a comparable view of the Wogeo situation and remarked that in her view Wogeo men were symbolically shown to be inferior to the women in that they did not naturally get rid of their bad blood and had more dangerous blood
than women's. One *could* look at it this way, but I doubt that the

Wogeo do. Their beliefs are analogous to the chivalric ideal of
self-sacrifice making one more noble than the common run of
men.

Among the Wogeo the whole of men's lives is a kind of obstacle
course to be overcome. As babies their ears are pierced; later they
are admitted with ceremony to the men's clubhouse and are
shown the sacred flutes, symbol of male authority; prior to puberty their tongues are slashed; at puberty they are taught to slash
their penises. It is interesting that in accord with Whiting's hypothesis, we find that a boy is taken from his mother by the elders
as an infant, who demand that the child should sleep in the men's
clubhouse. Girls merely have a rite of celebration rather than
achievement when they reach menarche. This is something often
found: that boys *achieve* manhood whereas girls just *arrive* at
womanhood—a cultural declaration of the relative evaluation of
the sexes.

The beliefs and practices of the Wogeo illustrate vividly the
locus of authority: older men over younger men, all men over
women. Beliefs about sex and the sexes, about pollution and
purification, about the relationship between the world of humans
and the world of spirits not only emphasize the world view but
also provide drama and excitement in a humdrum progression
from birth to death. Religious leaders in Western societies constantly deplore the erosion of attendance at religious services.
Apart from an increase in education bringing a slight increase in
rationality, one of the major reasons for the decline in attendance
at churches and synagogues may lie in the availability of other
forms of dramatic entertainment: the theater, ballet, opera,
movies, radio, and, of course, television.

Psychologically, following up on this point, one could say that
the drama of rituals in life serve to "gift-wrap" the unpalatable
truth of the inevitability of death. If we follow Bettelheim's argument, however, we can see a very vivid example of males wishing
to make themselves like women, while at the same time emphasizing their claimed superiority over women.

Before I turn to other examples of primitive societies, I should
like to consider whether the curious notions of the Wogeo do not,
perhaps, have some parallels in the West. First, a fairly recent
study in South Wales showed that working-class women had feel-

ings very similar to those of the Wogeo about menstruation and menstrual blood, which they regarded as dirty.[6] The flow they thought of as a means of cleansing their bodies of impurities, and women spoke of feeling full of "badness" before their period, of having an "excess" of blood of feeling "huge, bloated and poisoned," and of feeling a need to get this out of their systems. There were very great concerns about menopause: some women were delighted at being finished with all that—it being assumed that menopause heralded a cessation of sex as well as of menstruation; others were very worried about the build-up of poisons in their systems which would not be cleared out monthly. An interesting research project for a student would be for him or her to study the use of aperients by women like this. I would predict that the use would rise after menopause.

The similarity between the Wogeo beliefs and these is interesting enough, but recent discussions with a student about the subject produced a much more startling perception. When I told her that the idea of getting rid of dirty blood from the body was widespread, she suddenly remarked: "I suppose that's what leeches were for!" I regard this idea as brilliant in its simplicity. Could it really be that all the centuries of bleeding (phlebotomy) and the application of leeches was a form of artificial menstruation to imitate the women's natural flow, believed to remove poisons from the system? Perhaps so.

The Encyclopaedia Britannica, 1963 edition, says: "Beneficently, the practice of bleeding with leeches has *almost* ceased . . . [my emphasis]." As recently as the 1938 edition, however, we have a long essay on the subject of leeches and blood letting by one William M. Marston, A.B., LL.B., Ph.D., Lecturer in Psychology at Columbia and New York Universities, who wrote:

In the past blood-letting was used to such excess, as a cure for almost every known disease, that public opinion became opposed to it. Latterly, this prejudice has disappeared to a great extent. In certain pathological conditions it brings relief and saves life when no other means would act with sufficient promptness to bring relief.

Plainly Dr. Marston approved of the practice, for the following conditions: "stagnation of the blood on the right side of the heart"; acute pneumonia or bronchitis, to lower arterial tension;

cerebral hemorrhage; various "convulsive attacks" as in one type of uremia and in eclampsia. He advocated the use of leeches as being desirable in what he called "small numbers"—ten to twelve —applied at a time! Remember, this is only forty years ago.

If we go back to the 1882 edition, we are really into leech-mania. Noting approvingly the use of leeches since Galen and in ancient China, it then goes on to recount that in 1846 it was calculated that

there were from twenty to thirty millions used in France; and [Rudolf] Leuckart mentions in 1863 that in London seven million and in the Parisian hospitals five to six millions, were annually employed. At the great American leech-farms the average sale is one thousand per day.

One wonders what happened to these great leech farms!

Let us go further back yet. In a wonderful, delightful, yet utterly appalling book, edited by Warren Dawson, entitled *A Leechbook: A Collection of Medical Recipes of the Fifteenth Century* on the subject of blood letting we are told that:

. . . blood-letting in measure, it cleareth thy thought and closeth thy bladder and tempereth thy brain. It mendeth thine hearing, it restraineth tears, it closeth thy maw, it defieth [digests] thy meat, it cleareth thy voice, it sharpeth the wit, it easeth thy womb [abdomen] it gathereth thy sleep, it draweth away anguish, it nourisheth good blood, wicked blood it destroyeth, and lengtheneth thy life.[7]

In the same work there are a variety of strange remedies for bodily ailments: four separate ones recommend the use of a woman's milk who has borne a son; one for the "aching of the eyes" requires the milk of a mother *and* her daughter; perhaps my favorite is the cure for the bite of a spider: "Take flies and rub the place." This is all rather comic, but not for the poor people who had to suffer under such primitive medical practice. Why it was so primitive can be laid squarely at the door of the Church. In Graham's *The Story of Surgery* the part religion played not only in hindering medical research but in casting away what humans had achieved centuries before is made abundantly clear.[8] As in the Middle Ages, so in earlier times. Graham praises the skill of the ancient surgeons of India but says,

As in Egypt, religion destroyed far more than it could ever create. A debased and bastard craft was bequeathed by priests abhorring surgery to the lowest castes . . .

Returning to the more specific point of blood letting and what it was for, Graham suggests that leeching was probably introduced to the West by Alexander the Great. Of very widespread provenance in many parts too was (and in some countries, still is) the practice of "cupping," whereby a vacuum is formed under a glass or similar vessel on some part of the body and blood exudes from the skin. The makers of "hickeys" have a long ancestry!

The most elaborate work directed to the practice is Simon Harward's *Harward's Phlebotomy* published in 1601.[9] The entire book is devoted to "one of the greatest remedies of corporall griefes" so that "other humours are . . . by Phlebotomy evacuated out of the whole body . . ." After going through a list of ailments for which bleeding is appropriate, an enormous number of which Harward called, significantly, "putrefied agues," "putrefied vapours," and "putrefied humours," he quotes the second-century Greek physician Galen approvingly as saying:

Phlebotomies do avoyd the good bloud, but as for the ill bloud which is gathered together in the first vaynes, especially that which is about the liver and mid bowels, they disperse and spread it throughout all the body.

The relevance to my hypothesis—that all this bleeding was to imitate the natural process of menstruation, itself seen as a mode of eliminating poisons from the system—appears when he discusses why one should bleed a person. It is, Harward says, "either to ease nature, being overburdened, or to expell some dangerous causes of putred matter . . ."

Plainly, most of the bleeding was done to men, but for women he claimed that the "fittest age to let blood in" was "about the fortieth yeare"—that is to say, what in those days was called "about the beginning of old age" but more to the point, when menopause was reached and "the courses suppressed." Further to my point, in another discussion about women, Harward says there was great debate whether pregnant women should be bled. If women are "having their courses," he quotes an earlier scholar as laying down that "if they have them immoderately, then they may open the vayne basilica for diversion.[10] But if moderately and naturally *then is Phlebotomy not requisite* [my emphasis]."

The whole of medical practice, stifled by religious intolerance, was based for centuries on the theories of Galen, who derived his ideas from the Hippocratic theory of the so-called four humors: blood, phlegm, black bile, and yellow bile and hence the four temperaments: sanguine, phlegmatic, melancholic, and choleric— a notion that to this day captures the popular imagination. The humors had to be diagnosed, treated, moved, and so on. But since any real knowledge of how the body functioned was lacking because the religious authorities would not allow dissection, medical men for centuries worked with the basic idea that the body absorbed or built up impurities which were the causes of sickness. Thus, the major forms of treatment were emetics, purges, and bleedings—all designed to remove poisons. Precisely the same treatments still occur among peoples who have not yet grasped the germ theory of disease, frequently accompanied by a notion of spiritual causality: the malevolence of a witch or the wrath of a slighted spirit.

Since menstruating women did not need bleeding and menopausal women did, the intent of all those centuries and all those millions of gallons of blood unnecessarily, if not harmfully, removed from men was to simulate menstruation. So let us not think of the Wogeo as being irrational if our Western medical profession was advocating rather the same idea up until about forty years ago.

Another excellent example of the use of rites designed to make men bleed and at the same time demonstrate their superiority to women comes from the Gisu people in Uganda, as described by Jean La Fontaine.[11] This society prescribes a public display of the achievement of manhood, if manhood is defined by the ability to withstand agonizing pain without flinching. Boys are circumcised before the assembled people and standing in the full view of all. Any sign of pain, any grimace, any sound will be remembered for life. The operation, which takes place in some areas in two stages, with a pause between them, is so supremely painful that the boys she spoke to afterwards stated that they did not know how they managed to bear it. Although they had witnessed it many times, they said that they had not the slightest idea of the degree of intense physical anguish involved. Indeed, two boys died after the operation.

In Gisu society, La Fontaine tells us, "men and women compare childbirth explicitly with circumcision: in the comparison both sexes emphasise the pain that must be endured and the fact that it makes full adults of the immature."[12] Men explain, too, that circumcision is superior to childbirth in that it involves *voluntary* submission to pain and bleeding as contrasted to the natural and involuntary pain and bleeding of childbirth. As with the Wogeo people of New Guinea, the message is plain: men are superior to women because they voluntarily undergo pain and bleeding from the genitals.

The Luguru of Eastern Africa, among whom I worked for some years, are a matrilineal people where women have three advantages over their sisters in similar patrilineal societies: they keep the children in the event of a divorce; unusually, they have inherited rights in land similar to those held by men; they choose and theoretically can depose the head (male) of the subclan, the autonomous religious, political, and landholding group.[13] Women hold no positions of authority, however. If potential male rebellion against the rule of the elders is quashed by harsh puberty rites for boys, the possibility of a female takeover is effectively snuffed out among the Luguru.

At her first menstruation a Luguru girl is confined to a dark hut where she lies curled up on a tiny bed on which it is impossible to stretch out. She only wears a loincloth, which, like her body, is never washed. She is never allowed out except after dark and only in the company of a small prepubescent girl, from whom all knowledge of menstruation must be strictly concealed. She may only speak in a whisper. She is fed as much as she can eat. She is given a doll that incorporates male and female physical features and has to care for it in prescribed ways. Today some Luguru girls are only incarcerated for a few weeks, but in the 1930s it could be for six years. Many women I interviewed had spent two to three years inside. During the incarceration, the girl receives instruction from older women—not her mother—about appropriate sexual conduct. The end of the ordeal arrives, as I described in Chapter 1, when a girl goes to join her husband (there is no wedding ceremony), but this is at the conclusion of an elaborate coming-out ceremony. At the end of a day of drinking and dancing, the maiden is brought out riding on the shoulders of a brother of her husband-to-be. She is almost naked, covered in oil, and spattered with seeds. She has her eyes tightly shut and holds a fly switch in her right hand. She shakes and shimmies to the drum music, twitching the fly switch, and after being carried round and round the crowd, she is set down on a mat between her grandmother's knees. Obviously the entire rite is a symbolic rebirth—the fetal position in the dark hut, her pale and helpless physical condition, her closed eyes and her shaking to free herself, her twitching of the switch/cord—but it is a rebirth from a man. Women may have babies, but only men give birth to adults.

One can view the whole affair in structural-functional terms and be quite correct. The emphasis is undoubtedly on authority—of older women over younger; of maternal uncles and fathers over their nephews, nieces, and children; of all males over females. The complementarity of the mother's clan and father's clan and the pre-eminence of the former similarly are emphasized. But out of thousands of possible ways of doing all these things, why choose a mode of expression which relies on the symbolism of gestation and birth—organized, controlled, and, in the final rites, performed by men? Bettelheim would say because of male envy of female procreativity.

Female initiation rites do have the educational function of teaching the girl all about what the society believes to be the truth about menstruation, conception, gestation, parturition, and lactation. All these are customarily shrouded in mystery and secrecy. Even to the sophisticated and scientifically educated person these are matters of some secrecy not freely talked about before children. How much more dramatic and mysterious must they be to people whose ideas of anatomy and physiology are very vague? Women then are the possessors of a mystery which confers on them a potential superiority. In consequence, men have often developed initiation rites for themselves which are shrouded in dreadful mystery. Dark secrets are disclosed to the initiands, it is believed, which would be revealed to women at the peril of supernaturally caused death. And what is the tremendous secret revealed to the men then? The secrt is that there *is* no secret.

The most extreme example of this kind of thing occurs with some of the peoples around Mount Kilimanjaro, in Tanzania. The boys are told that women believe that not only are boys circumcised—which they are—but that their anuses are plugged so that thenceforth they never defecate. Of course, the boys are told that this is not really so, but this is what the women believe, and it gives men great superiority over the women. Therefore, they are told, they must never allow their wives or other women to know that they still defecate. Should they have an attack of diarrhea, a male age mate will fix up a lodge in the woods. The supreme irony of this is that in the secrecy of the girls' initiation, the girls are told that the men believe that they believe that their anuses are plugged and that to preserve the male egos they must never let on that they know this is not so. The belief was quite a hindrance during a government health campaign to encourage the construction and use of pit latrines in the 1950s. On the other hand, I found that among some people in northern Uganda, it was the women who refused to use pit latrines, as squatting over a hole was believed to make them sterile.

Returning to the Luguru case for a moment, the long incarceration of young girls did have one other important effect, though it was probably unintentional: it removed potentially fertile women from childbearing for several years and also ensured that the women would not be exposed to the dangers of childbirth before their bodies were relatively mature. Even in the poor dietetic circumstances of the Luguru, some girls reach puberty by age eleven or twelve, long before their bodies are fully grown. (Even with the seclusion, a proportion of Luguru women die in childbirth.) The removal of potentially fertile women from childbearing for some years, combined with a long post-partum taboo and a 50 per cent child mortality before age five, woud have the effect of maintaining a relatively stable population size.

The physical and psychological effects of the ritual seclusion on adolescent Luguru girls are difficult to assess. A German nurse, Anna von Waldow, who worked in the 1930s with a neighboring people who have the same custom, reported on forty cases which she observed. After their debut, five were, she said, "mentally deranged" and "two of these later become quite mad"; six died shortly after their coming out; all the rest were "very unfit and sickly."[14]

One pauses to try and be culturally relativistic and avoid ethnocentrism. Try as I may, I find it impossible not to be appalled by the idea of condemning adolescent girls to several years of solitary confinement in the dark. As though this were not terrible enough, Von Waldow reported that if a young woman failed to conceive within a short time after joining her husband, or if she produced a stillborn child (very common where there is a high incidence of syphilis), the local doctor (male) would diagnose the problem as being due to a failure on the young wife's part to give proper attention to the male/female dolls kept in seclusion with her, and she would be returned to the prison for from two to nine more months. As I noted earlier, Luguru women have unusually liberal rights for women in Africa. With this degree of intimidation, it is hardly surprising that they do not try to usurp more.

The Iatmul of New Guinea provide another example of what I was discussing earlier: intimidation of the young and male envy of female procreativity. The Anglo-American anthropologist Gregory Bateson describes how during the boys' initiation "the spirit in which the ceremonies are carried out is . . . of irresponsible bullying and swagger."[15] The boys have their backs and chests scarified with bamboo knives in what is plainly an extremely painful manner. If the boys scream with the pain, the initiators beat on gongs to drown the noise. Bateson tells us explicitly that when pain is inflicted, it "is done by men who enjoy doing it and who carry out their business in a cynical, practical-joking spirit." He also tells us that during the "early period of initiation when the novices are being mercilessly bullied and hazed, they are spoken of as the 'wives' of the initiators whose penes they are made to handle." After the first week of bullying, the initiators are known as the "mothers" of the novices.

Throughout peoples' lives in this society, events of cultural significance are celebrated by a rite which gives Bateson the name of his book—*naven*. On these occasions, he tells us, "The outstanding feature of the ceremonies is the dressing of men in women's clothes and of women in the clothes of men." He describes a *naven* carried out for a little girl who had caught her first fish on a line. Four of her classificatory maternal uncles were dressed as "mothers" but with their genitals exposed. One of the uncles was tied to a stretcher and the little girl placed on his belly.

His wife meanwhile danced with her skirts up to expose her genitals and held a digging stick. Bateson comments: "The whole of this ritual pantomime . . . appears to me to be a representation of the birth of the little girl from the belly of her mother's brother . . ."

The structural-functional explanation all this seems to focus on the emphasis on authority, on appropriate sex roles, and on reversal of roles. The latter may be to emphasize what the normal should be; reversal often takes place, as I mentioned earlier, in an attempt to generate mystical power. The simulated birth from a male of the mother's clan could be said to emphasize: (1) the importance of this clan in providing a wife and mother, and, (2) the fact that males hold authority and are the ritual representatives of the clan. True, but the symbolism chosen does seem to underline Bettelheim's notion, that men envy women's procreativity.

A final example of womb envy is from a fascinating article by Alan Dundes called "A Psychoanalytic Study of the Bullroarer."[16] To the astonishment of some of the early anthropologists, the bull-roarer was found to be very widely used in male initiation rites and for sacred purposes among native Americans, Africans, and Australians and was reported to have been similarly used in ancient Greece. Its use as a toy in Europe and the United States was therefore regarded as a "survival." Dundes goes through an extensive literature on the subject, noting that it was often linked to thunder and wind; that in some cases the use of the bull-roarer in initiation went along with the covering of the initiands in filth such as goat dung or clay; that many observers considered it a phallic symbol; that there are often myths that it was first owned by women. Dundes, following the Dutch anthropologist J. van Baal, describes how some Australians have an initiation ceremony for males in which two bull-roarers are tied together, which Van Baal calls a phallus, a term Dundes finds inept since "the native language term for the [bull-roarer] is *ambilia ekura,* amnion, womb!" I find it most odd that Dundes regards "phallus" as inept, particularly in the light of his subsequent ideas. He tells us, for example, of two myths. In one, a man kills his wife; vegetables sprout from her body; he swallows them and they pass into his penis; he marries a new wife with whom he has sex and when withdrawing from her he scatters vegetables. In the second myth, a man hears a noise from a woman's belly; he sends a bird which extracts a bull-roarer from her vagina. This, Dundes observes, "represents the male equivalent of female procreativity, but the question remains of why does it function in symbolic form—through the making of noise, wind, thunder, etc.?"

Dundes only briefly mentions Bettelheim, but they reach the same conclusion—that men envy women their ability to bear children. He shows that the relevance of the bull-roarer to this idea comes from the widespread dream equivalence made between thunder and paternal flatus. This is probably the explanation of why it is that men concerned to demonstrate their masculinity remove the baffles from the mufflers on their motorcycles, scooters, "hot rods," and sports cars. He notes also the widespread idea that a wind can be a fertilizing agent, of which the best-known example is the Holy Ghost. He draws attention to the semantic links between "spirit" and "breath." Also, in semantic linking, he shows an Australian linking between "shadow," "soul," "hidden secret," "ancestors," "excrement," and "bull-roarer." Finally, he shows that the initiation rites link feces and creativity to bull-roarers and suggests that a boy "becomes a man by passing through a faecal ritual. It is as if to say that a man is moulded from faeces."

It seems to me that in Dundes' article we find the Bettelheimian notion that male rites are partially about male envy of female procreativity, an equation being made between anus (male) and vagina (female) between male rectum and female uterus. We also see that there is a linking between sex and feces, but in addition, an association made between male authority, male fertilizing power; between the noise made by fathers breaking wind and authority and indeed male divinity.

11

Authority, Violence, and Sex Roles

Mutilatory rites at puberty in simple societies originate partially from sexual envy, particularly the envy that males have always felt for women's "mysterious" qualities. This leads to the notion that man can menstruate, men can give birth, that men have a great and mysterious secret analogous to that of women. In the West, millennia of misplaced medical practice in the custom of phlebotomy, leeching, and cupping was almost certainly based on the wholly mistaken idea that the physical reason for menstruation was to rid the body of impurities.

These beliefs have always served the purpose of upholding the male-female status quo. In every society the major political and authority roles have been the prerogatives of men. When one considers that everywhere women do a greater proportion of child rearing and socialization than men, and that it takes place at the most impressionable age, this denial of authority roles to women is astounding.[1] If the right to hold authority were based solely on intelligence and mental capacity, authority roles would be evenly divided between men and women. Nowhere is this so. What then is the basis for the acquisition and retention of authority by the male?

Earlier I mentioned Radcliffe-Brown's definition of a political system which suggested that any system is concerned with the establishment and maintenance of social order within a particular territorial area by the threat of the use of force. I return now to this point as it seems to me to have great relevance to what I am discussing.

Among the English poet Hillaire Belloc's satiric verses is one about Britain's colonial empire in which he says:

> Whatever happens we have got
> The Maxim gun and they have not.

A parallel to this, and a revelation of the true basis of what governs sex roles, was brought home to me a couple of years ago. My neighbor in a small American city, a construction worker, lost his job. His reaction to this was, first, to get drunk so that his social inhibitions became relaxed; second, to come home and beat up his wife. Since the man in question was known to possess more firearms than are allowed for the entire population of an English city and, moreover, was a part-time police deputy, no one interfered. Indeed, his wife did not complain and capitalized on his subsequent guilt. She was not powerless in a psychological sense and took pride in manipulating her husband in a variety of ways. There is a fluctuating ratio between power and authority: where women hold the least authority they are most likely to manipulate power.[2] Where authority is shared, there is less manipulation of power. Put otherwise, if women are denied all access to authority and responsibility in a particular society, one can almost guarantee that the beliefs of the society will ascribe to all women the qualities of scheming, malice, damaging gossip, deviousness, and spite. At the same time they will be seen as coquettish, flirtatious, and seductive.

My neighbor's action was like that of a ruler, colonial or domestic, who periodically "shows the flag," rolls out the tanks and rockets, or parades the troops, National Guard, and police. Such a parade of coercive power apparently takes place frequently in American society. The publication in 1978 of Terry Davidson's *Conjugal Crime* has revealed how widespread it is:

One of the nation's most affluent communities, Montgomery County, Maryland, reported having seven hundred incidents of assaults against wives by husbands each year . . . Findings showed that incomes of reported wifebeaters ranged up to $40,000 a year, educational levels up to the doctoral degree.[3]

One of the other disturbing points chronicled by Davidson is this:

In middle-class conservative Suffolk County, New York, an agency dealing with victims of spouse abuse and sexual assault logged more than 4,500 hotline calls, and had 468 clients in the Counseling Center during the first year after opening June 1976; 96 per cent were victims of spouse abuse.

She also notes:

A recent Gallup poll showed that for over half the Americans surveyed, their religious beliefs were "very important." And "nearly all people" questioned said that they belonged to some church.

In fact, Davidson reveals that she herself was a child of a mother who was constantly beaten up before her children by their father, who was a Christian minister. It will be recalled that most incest offenders are very devout. The doctrine of repentance covers a multitude of sins.

Countries that have tried to insure equality between the sexes, such as the U.S.S.R., China, and Cuba, may have achieved a great deal, but somehow one has yet to hear of many major female political figures today in any of those countries. It reminds one of the situation in Zaire when it was the Belgian Congo. Africans were trained for and held all the low-level jobs—truck and locomotive drivers, office clerks, and so on—but all the top jobs were reserved for Belgians.

Authority is always thought of as legitimate and is always conferred on the holder by some external agency, if not human, then divine. Authority is never *sui generis* except in the case of deities. One might argue that since deities are only created by human imagination, the same really still applies. The legitimacy of authority is upheld by a consensus of the people ruled. It is supported by a conceptual and symbolic system which is subscribed to by the members of the society. The support may take the form of beliefs about the right to hold authority; it may also depend on beliefs about the nature of those who do not hold authority. And always behind authority, if it is to have any real meaning, is the threat of the use of force. Usually the force is physical; sometimes the physical force may be supported or reinforced by some supernatural force—ancestral spirits, the wrath of God, the fear of hell.

Colonial rulers could only maintain their regimes provided that the population being ruled believed that the authority to rule was somehow legitimate and that it was backed by the threat of the use of force, which was physically demonstrated from time to time. It may even be that in extremely authoritarian cultures, the possession of overwhelming force by the rulers may confer legitimacy on the regime in the people's eyes. When the population at large will no longer accept the legitimacy of the rulers, even the rulers' application of overwhelming physical force is insufficient and the regime collapses. The cases of Portugal's overseas colonies of Mozambique, Angola, and Guinea demonstrate this well.

My wife-beating neighbor, referred to at the beginning of this chapter, was, as it were, showing the flag. Such "colonialist" parades are not infrequent. Further, the feminist writer Susan Brownmiller, in her remarkable study of rape, *Against Our Will: Men, Women and Rape,* suggests that the rapist in our society "performs a myrmidon function for all men by keeping all women in a thrall of anxiety and fear."[4]

In her view, "rape became not only a male prerogative, but man's basic weapon of force against women, the principal agent of his will and her fear." She also speculates that "[man's] discovery that his genitalia could serve as a weapon to generate fear must rank as one of the most important discoveries of prehistoric times, along with the use of fire and first stone axe."

Throughout history, rape and the fear of rape have been a threat to women which, because of the nature of male and female genitals, female receptivity at any time, and superior male physical strength, could only be countered by enlisting the aid of a male as a husband who would thus protect a woman against all the other males. But, as Brownmiller writes, "the price of woman's protection *by some men* against an abuse *by others* was steep." Because of the inability of women to assist one another in the face of male physical superiority, she believes that they tend to mistrust one another. This mistrust of women for women has, she considers, allowed men to reduce them to chattel status. This is good polemic stuff and her case is very persuasive, but the snag in these kinds of speculations is that they assume some act of creation that suddenly put men and women together, whereas previously they somehow lived as two separate species. In reality, they must always have lived together in social groups of which they were an integral part. The division of labor between gathering and hunting necessitated relatively equal numbers of males and females in any one band.

Let us draw another parallel to the colonial situation. The policy of apartheid in South Africa is rightly seen as evil. Its evil lies not merely in the policy of segregation and discrimination, but in the fact that the policy has legal sanction in the laws of that country. Precisely the same used to be true of many states in the United States. Today, discrimination on racial grounds still takes place in the United States, but it does not have legal backing. As for sexual discrimination, in courtrooms around the country, abused women face judges reluctant to act in what they see as domestic disputes. Nevertheless, wife beating is not sanctioned by law. This is not true in all countries. I recorded dozens of court cases in Tanganyika in the early 1960s. I vividly recall two about wife beating. In both cases the wife sued her husband for assault. In the first case it was established that he just beat her because he was drunk. He received a jail sentence. In the second it was established that the husband came home late and told his wife to prepare food at once. She told him to ask his other wife. He beat her up. The case was dismissed as it was seen as justifiable provocation to the husband.

What about Brownmiller's point that men reduce women's status to that of chattel? Long ago the French anthropologist Claude Lévi-Strauss suggested that the earliest item of exchange among humans was women. Yet the primatologist Jane Lancaster's observations of primate band society indicate that exchange in early human society of either males or females could have been practiced, depending entirely on the numbers of male or female children born in a particular band. If the adoption of a taboo on incest among humans goes hand in hand with the linguistic capability of naming and classifying kinsfolk, then some form of marrying out—exogamy—must have been inevitable. But Brownmiller uses the concept of exogamy to illustrate her point that rape was the basic way of obtaining a mate (like the thousands of cartoon drawings of a caveman clubbing a woman and dragging her off by the hair). She quotes a statement from the Gusii people of Kenya who say, "Those whom we marry are those whom we fight." Superficially, this sounds persuasive, but in reality it shows a profound misunderstanding of both the statement and of exogamy. Anthropologists have recorded innumerable times statements to the effect, "We marry our enemies." The point is not that one group seized women from an enemy group by raping them, but rather that by marrying women from an enemy group (and they would reciprocate by marrying the other group's women) one group converts enemies into relatives. To me, my wife's brothers, sisters, and parents are "in-laws," or affines. To my children, they are uncles, aunts, and grandparents—"blood relatives." The same is true in reverse for my wife. One may dislike relatives and quarrel with them, but one does not usually fight them. One of my fantasies of being world dictator for a brief period would be to force every Israeli to marry an Arab, every Russian a Chinese or American, every Indian a Pakistani, every Ethiopian a Somali. And, of course, the reverse. In the past, kings often married off their daughters to the sons of other kings in the hope that it would promote peace and prevent war between the two peoples. It never worked for long. It did not work because only two patrons were involved; but if, for example, every English person had had to marry a French person and vice versa in the late eighteenth and early nineteenth centuries, the Napoleonic wars between England and France probably would never have taken place.

This defense of exogamy should not, however, obscure the very real point that women were exchanged. Logically, one could exchange women or men, and band society—the aboriginal human form—does allow for this. There are some matrilineal societies where marriage is matrilocal—where the husband moves to his wife's people rather than the other way round (patrilocal)—but they are a small minority of the world's societies. And even where this is the case, men are commonly the holders of authority and property. They also frequently get permission from their wives' relatives to remove their wives to some other location after a child has been born and weaned—that is to say, after the continuity of the wife's brother's line is assured.

The British anthropologist A. R. Radcliffe-Brown suggested that in law the marriage of a man to a woman potentially brings three sets of rights over a woman to her husband and indeed to his kinsmen. These are given Latin names and are (1) rights *in personam*, (2) rights *in rem*, and (3) rights *in genetricem*. Rights *in genetricem* imply rights over the offspring from the union. In a patrilineal (male descent) society, these rights belong to the husband and the group to which he belongs. I recall hearing about a distressing case in Kenya in the past few years. A schoolteacher absconded with all the tuition money brought in by the pupils, abandoned his wife and children, and was not seen again. This was disaster enough to the poor wife (and the school). However, education had to go on, so she was asked to leave her house immediately so that a new teacher could take it. While she was worrying about this, her husband's brothers arrived from the country and removed her children. Since the husband and wife were effectively separated, the children then belonged to his descent group, and she had no hope of recourse in law.

In patrilineal societies the children always stay with the father. In a matrilineal society the woman takes the children after a divorce because the rights in the offspring belong not so much to her as to her group, and more particularly to her brother, whose potential heirs they are. It is very important to realize, though, that in neither case do the rights *belong* to the woman. She is merely the means by which the children are produced. It is this attitude which logically leads to the belief that it is wrong for a woman to practice contraception or, even more importantly, to have an abortion because it is believed that the fetus belongs to the father.

Recently, in England, a husband who was divorced from his wife found that at the time of the divorce she was pregnant by him. The wife was about to have an abortion, but the husband sued to restrain her, as he claimed the fetus was his child. The judge, in what was considered a landmark decision, ruled for the woman. It is doubtful if she would have been so successful in other countries or with other judges.

In Islam, when a divorce takes place—very easy for a man, very hard for a woman—the wife is kept in seclusion for forty days to make absolutely certain that she is not pregnant by her former husband, in which case he would claim the child.

The other two rights acquired by a husband and his group in

most societies indicate more blatantly the status of women. Rights *in personam* imply exclusive sexual and domestic rights of a husband over his wife. In other words, no one has legitimate sexual access to her but her husband (and his brothers in the event of the husband's death, under the provisions of the levirate, the widespread practice whereby when a husband dies, his wife is inherited by his brother; see Deuteronomy 25:5). The "domestic" right means that the husband has the right to expect that she will perform those domestic and farm tasks that the particular society considers it appropriate for women to perform. Her failure to cook, sweep, pound corn, do farm work, fetch firewood, and so on would give her husband grounds for divorce. Along with a husband's exclusive rights over a woman's sexuality is the presumption that if she does not produce children, she is not fit to be his wife and can be divorced. With the usual double standard that prevails in most societies, sterility is usually laid at the woman's door, unless she can prove that her husband is impotent. The idea that a man's sperm might be infertile while he can physically produce semen is a notion which relies for its proof on the availability of microscopes. Moreover, even in Western society some men feel that it would be such a blow to their male egos to discover that they could not impregnate a woman that they refuse to be tested. To most women in simple societies where there is a tremendous value placed on fecundity, both to provide a labor force and bear children to carry on a line of descent, not to be able to have children—I hesitate to use the pejorative term "to be barren"—is a terrible affliction. The disgrace, the humiliation, the sending back to one's family involved in societies where there are no wage-paying jobs—what could be more corrosive to one's self-esteem?

Rights *in rem* are very similar to those *in personam* but with a subtle legalistic twist. The meaning, literally, is "in the thing." What this means is that the husband not only has the exclusive sexual and domestic rights already discussed; he also possesses the woman as a "thing," a piece of property. Suppose you have a new car and someone bumps into it in a parking lot and damages it, you will, presumably, demand compensation. Similarly, a husband who has rights *in rem* over his wife can sue for damages against anyone who damages his property or uses it without his permission. Thus, it is very common in Africa for husbands to sue their wives' lovers for compensation payments. If we are tempted to be smug and think of ourselves as being superior to this kind of thing, we should consider whether the old grounds for divorce in most states—adultery—was not merely an extension of the same idea. According to the 1875 edition of the Encyclopaedia Britannica, in Scotland "the husband may claim damages from one who has committed adultery with his wife in a petition for dissolution of the marriage or for judicial separation." It also notes that "damages may be recovered against an adulterer in an ordinary act of damages in a civil court." As a further discouragement to extramarital affairs, "A person divorced for adultery is, by the law of Scotland, prohibited from intermarrying with the paramour."

Of course, once it is possible for a wife to claim a divorce on the grounds of the husband's adultery, the situation is rather different and based, at least theoretically, on a mutual contract of exclusiveness in sexuality. The notion of "possession" by a man of a woman's sexuality dies very hard, however. One still finds the use of phrases like "he possessed her" for performing an act of sexual congress. Similarly, the submissive "she yielded to him" implies a degree of passivity which reminds me that in Swahili a man "marries"; a woman "gets married"—the passive form of the verb.

Most anthropologists go to great lengths to claim that the institution of bride wealth or bride price does not imply a purchase of the bride. What is involved is a payment by the groom's family to the bride's family. One can make a very good case for the theory that it performs all kinds of useful social functions: it places a value on marriage, it shows that marriage is not to be undertaken lightly, it legitimizes the marriage, it legitimizes the children, it involves people in systems of gift exchanges, and it helps form alliances between groups. All this is true, and the abolition of bride wealth by missionaries in, for instance, South Africa, led to a great decline in morality since people no longer placed a value on marriage; all the same, when people protest that it is not a sale, a niggling strand of doubt unravels in my mind. Young men in Africa certainly perceive it that way and one finds letters in papers asking "For how much longer are our sisters to be sold as slaves?" With the human capacity for rationalization, the same young men will take a totally different attitude when they have marriageable daughters; then they will start pontificating about placing a value, etc., etc. Along with all the important and valuable aspects of bride wealth goes the acquisition of rights *in rem*. It may not be a purchase, but it's very like one. Where one finds the institution of dowry, which involves a payment from the bride's family to the groom, one might expect that the acquisition of rights would be reversed. On the contrary, the husband, not his family, gets the payment and he also acquires all the other rights too.

Brownmiller notes that since women have universally been regarded as a form of property, it has always been considered the prerogative of conquering armies to rape the women of those conquered. This accomplishes three purposes: it satisfies the conquerors; it acts to demonstrate their political power in the most dramatic manner; and it humiliates the men of the group conquered, who may well subsequently reject their poor wives afterward, as occurred recently in Bangladesh. Perhaps, at an unconscious level, much of the resistance to the ERA and to having women in the armed forces may arise from the fear that David (or preferably Davida) armed with a sling can easily become a match for massive Goliath.

Rape is a crime of violence, hatred, and contempt rather than merely a satisfying of a sexual need. Its political aspect is illustrated by this passage from Brownmiller's book referred to above:

Torture of female political prisoners traditionally includes rape or variation of genital abuse. Whether sadistic torture leads by its own logic to the infliction of sexual pain, or whether the motive of eliciting political information is merely a pretext for the commission of hostile sexual acts, the end results for a woman is almost inevitable. As German soldiers in 1944 tortured and raped Maquis supporters, and as French paratroopers tortured and raped Algerian resistance leaders a decade later, so in the year 1972 beyond the horrors of the interrogation centers in South Vietnam one heard of electric shocks and rape applied to political prisoners in Argentina and severe beating and electric shocks administered to the sexual organs of male and female prisoners in Brazil, including the doubly vengeful act, "a woman raped in front of her husband by one of his torturers." Six months later the pattern was repeated by the Portuguese in the colonies of Angola and Mozambique, and a year after that by the government of Chile.

Both men and women are reared within the same cultures and thus tend to subscribe to the same values. The resistance by many women to the ERA is good evidence of this, as is the support of women for the continuance of clitoridectomy in those cultures where it is found. Brownmiller describes in grim detail the actions of the Russian second-line troops (not the front-line troops, she carefully notes), who, in raping German women, were acting in political retaliation for what the Germans had done to Russian women. As one who was in Germany at the end of the war and for a year afterward, I should like to bring up a point that, I think, illustrates both the political aspect of the sexual possession of women and their acquiescence in that value.

While no doubt some men would prefer to rape, most, one hopes, would not. When World War II ended the air was filled with the revealed horrors of the concentration camps and then the rapine of the Russians. Thousands of Germans fled from the Russians into the areas occupied by the American, British, and French troops. Many German women then voluntarily placed themselves at the disposal of the Allied troops. The popular legend in the newspapers at the time was that they were doing it for food or stockings. Perhaps a few were, but a majority were not. This temporary submission by the German women was probably a cultural result of an authoritarian indoctrination that saw women as property to be used by whoever has seized political power, a value shared by the women.

Against Our Will should be compulsory reading for all of us. I do not entirely accept Brownmiller's thesis that it is rape or the threat of rape alone that is responsible for the relative status of the sexes. My view is that the basis is physical strength and coercive physical force; that rape is a most important aspect of that threat can hardly be denied.

One aspect of this problem which has not, I think, been sufficiently taken into account by feminist writers speculating on the facts of male dominance and female subservience, is the question of the relative ages of spouses at the time of marriage. Where there is no formal education in a Western sense, it was and is customary to find that girls marry as soon as they reach puberty. Their husbands may be ten or more years older. To understand how this comes about, we have to return first to the concept of incest. We have seen that once the taboo on incest is established and marriage instituted, the whole idea of kinship and affinity stems from them. At the same time, all these ideas are utterly dependent on language and speech. If we are not to commit incest, then we must be able to know and to identify who our parents and siblings are. As we have seen already, the idea that incest can occur unwittingly is the point of the Oedipus myth. The divine retribution that inevitably followed Oedipus' sin is also part of the theme. In the book of Leviticus we are commanded not "to lie" with a number of close kin nor to uncover their nakedness. Those who do so have "wrought confusion" and should be put to death. Killing the participants of an incestuous act has two important results. First, the moral code has been rigorously upheld and the proper forms of conduct between particular categories of person ruthlessly re-emphasized. Second, the dangerous possibility of an unintended outcome—the birth of a child—has been averted.

Most societies believe that acts of incest are followed by awful retribution: natural disasters like crop failures or a cessation of rain, earthquakes, a drying up of cows' milk, or, at a more personal level, the affliction of those involved with leprosy. Even in our society today there is a widespread popular belief that all childred born of incestuous unions will be, if not monsters as some societies have it, at least mentally deficient. With the human belief that reversing the natural order of things generates mystical power, it is often believed that the performance of an act of incest with conscious evil intent will thereby confer the quality of being a witch on the doer. The effect of all these beliefs is strongly to deter people from breaking the prohibition.

The possibility of incest occurring as a result of uncontrolled sexuality, leading to what Leviticus calls "confusion," that is, a confusion of appropriate roles, is a very frightening one to humans. Incest is a very real possibility given the enormously strong nature of the sexual drive in humans and the reduction of moral principles that can easily occur under the influence of intoxicants or purely through sexual arousal. After all, men can be aroused very quickly and women are sexually receptive 365 days of the year from the time of their physical maturity until they die. These facts together with the fragility of our construct of society which is based on rigid control of them, explain our obsession with virginity in women at the time of marriage.

That virginity continues to fascinate as an ideal, both to males and females, everywhere in the world, is evident from the sales of Barbara Cartland's romances. She now can claim 150 published novels and says herself:

In the past two years the sales of my novels have leapt into astronomical figures and have now reached seventy million. Twenty-six novels will appear in Britain this year. I am a bestseller in Europe, North America, and also in Turkey, Singapore, India, the Philippines and Sri Lanka. Why? Because all my heroines are virgins.[5]

As Francine du Plessix Gray explains:

This writer's staggering oeuvre includes the following titles: *Again This Rapture, An Arrow of Love, The Call of the Heart, Desire of the Heart, The Heart Triumphant;* and all of them champion that virginity particular to chaste pulp fiction which is constantly trembling on the verge of ravishment.[6]

Gray also very pertinently observes:

One can't forget that the worship of the Virgin Mary—and the contiguous cult of woman as inhumanly good and pure—has thrived in those Latin countries which are infested with the most brutal sexist machismo.

This kind of ideal of saccharine purity is linked to the idea of woman as property. Property and authority have been and largely continue to be male prerogatives in most countries. It is, therefore, logical that men should be in control of women, if authority is based on physical strength. I said nothing about justice.

Human obsession with female virginity lies partly in the concept of women as property and partly in the very real fear that incest might take place and pregnancy ensue. Because men do not have babies, virginity is rarely considered important for them. It has been said, with ironic aptitude that if men were able to become pregnant, then abortion would probably be a sacrament. The vociferous denunciation of contraception and abortion by some men has never for one moment prevented the same persons from taking sexual advantage of any woman who happened to be available. If men could become pregnant, then virginity in men would be as closely guarded as it is for women in most societies. Men have two advantages: they cannot get pregnant and have no hymen. While many women have little difficulty and no bleeding involved in the perforation of the hymen, popular belief certainly holds otherwise. Consider the conversation of Gogyrvan Gawr, the father of Guenevere, with Jurgen:

". . . a woman's honor is concerned with one thing only, and it is a thing with which the honor of a man is not concerned at all."

"But now you talk in riddles, King, and I wonder what it is you would have me do."

Gogyrvan grinned. "Obviously, I advise you to give thanks you were born a man, because that sturdier sex has so much less need to bother over breakage."[7]

If a man has sex, it has no lasting physical effect on him; if a woman has sex, she can easily become pregnant. If the father of the child is not a person in the permitted categories with whom one may mate, then confusion will result in our system of ordering society. Let me give a practical example. In a village where I lived as a teen-ager was a girl of my age who seemed like anyone else, but an aura of mystery and oddness hung over her. I finally discovered that her father was also her grandfather. Consider how confusing that is to people who categorize everything semantically. She was, of course, the result of incest between a man and his daughter. Anthropologists tell of the man who, when asked if he could marry his sister, replied vehemently, "No!" When pressed to say why, he thought for a little and then answered, "Well, if I did, who would my mother-in-law be?" If the kind of thing that resulted in the girl in my village took place with any degree of frequency, then we should just not be able to have the kind of kinship systems that we do. As it is, the very occurrence of the odd incestuous birth is so dramatic in its impact that it serves to point to the rule: in the same way, carnivals and other rituals of norm reversals make clear what the norms are.

This danger of women becoming pregnant from puberty on is probably the real cause of the obsession with virginity. Since women are as likely to want to have sexual experiences as men, societies arrange for the pubescent girl to be guarded and chaperoned every moment until she has been handed over still intact to her husband or arrange for her to be married at or before puberty to make absolutely sure that incest will not occur. Thus, women customarily were (and are) married in many societies at anywhere from eleven to fifteen years of age, or even younger, whereas men frequently do not marry until their late twenties. Because of this large age difference and consequent disparity in mental and physical maturity, it is extremely easy for men to establish a pattern of psychological and physical dominance over their wives, who enter marriage as little more than children. To take a famous example, the Prophet Mohammed's favorite wife, Aisha, was only six when she married him; the marriage was consummated when she was nine. Hollywood's "moppet" stars, whether of legitimate or pornographic movies, remind us of an earlier custom. Could their popularity be an unconscious response to the growing strength of the women's movement—a wish on the part of some men to have a relationship with a woman where the man's dominance is assured?

Let us go back to initiation rites. Our anxieties about sex may be the basis of the mutilations often practiced in the rites. But the effect of the rites is often to intimidate the younger generation through physical and psychological anguish and to educate in a dramatic and never-to-be-forgotten manner who has authority over whom. In the case of boys, the rites are carried out by men in the prime of life and physical strength, usually on boys who have not yet reached that point. The rites are not usually carried out by the grandfathers' generation, with whom the boys (and girls) have a relaxed easygoing relationship. The grandfathers can afford to be relaxed because they have no authority over the boys; their authority is over their own sons, the boys' fathers.

Plainly, at this stage of life the grandfathers could not vanquish the fathers physically. Even in our relatively informal kin system, most people go on being restrained and respectful to their parents even when the latter are old. How much more would sons be respectful if they had still the memory of the agonizing pain inflicted by the parents' generation on them when they were in adolescence? Of course, the respect accorded to parents in their old age often has a moral and religious basis as exemplified in the Ten Commandments or in the belief of the power of ancestors. Without these, would humans go on respecting their parents when they are no longer economically productive? If culture is to survive in nonliterate societies, it is essential to have old people around as repositories of knowledge—walking libraries. Thus those societies which preserved the old beyond their practical usefulness would have had a better chance of survival. But how does one persuade the young that they should preserve the old? By fear, seems to be the rather unpleasant answer. By fear of God's wrath, the vengeance of the ancestors, by a memory of ability to inflict agonizing pain or psychological humiliation, the remembrance of which remains active.

Consider for a moment the case of the Nubians of southern Egypt, described by the anthropologist John G. Kennedy.[8] Both boys and girls undergo genital operations long before puberty. Kennedy argues that this shows that initiation rites and puberty are unrelated. While it is true that in many cases the anxiety surrounding sexuality reaches its peak at adolescence and that therefore the rites take one from an asexual to a sexual world, nevertheless, if we find some cases occurring long before (and in a few cases after) puberty, it is still illustrative of the anxiety felt by humans about sex. The effect of the rites is also to intimidate and ensure respect for and fear of those in authority. In the Nubian case, the relative value placed on the sexes is well demonstrated.

Boys are circumcised by the local barber and the operation is simple—one swift cut—though the celebrations are great. With girls the operation is appalling and complex but has little attendant celebration. Kennedy describes how the midwife takes a razor or knife and cuts off the clitoris, the labia minora, and part of the labia majora. Women chant and shout with joy which, according to some, "serves partially to drown the screams of the child." Raw egg and henna are applied to the wound and then the child's legs are tied together, sometimes for "only" seven to fifteen days, sometimes for forty days. According to Kennedy, "This healing process generally provides the scar tissue for the complete closure of the vulva, except for a small urination orifice which is kept open by a match or reed tube." When a girl is married her virginity is certainly assured since penetration is only possible after cutting the vulva open again. Kennedy reports that "old women vividly remembered this period of misery even fifty or sixty years later." He also tells us that most girls get married between age ten and fourteen.

Does emphasis on pain and the genitalia serve to focus one's attention on those who hold authority? Or is the pain and threat of further pain the basis for the authority and what prevents it being challenged? To answer this question, we must revert to my point that it is anxiety lest incest should occur that leads to so many social rules. Over 90 per cent of the time that humans have spent on earth was in the Paleolithic period—the Old Stone Age. At that time (and indeed in many parts of the world even today) societies were so small that the possibility of incest was ever present. This was particularly true of those societies which practiced unilineal descent—matrilineal or patrilineal. In these systems relatives were classified in broad categories so that dozens of people with whom one came in contact were classified as brothers and sisters, mothers, and fathers. Remember the case of the young chief in Africa who told me that all the young women in his village were forbidden to him because they were his "sisters." And Maxine Hong Kingston's account of a Chinese village where everyone was related.

Virgins have often been used for ritual purposes. The most celebrated examples are the Greek goddess Artemis, her Roman successor, Diana, and her heir in Christian mythology, the Virgin Mary. There are contradictions in each incarnation in that while each is a virgin, she is also believed to help mothers. In her form as the Virgin Mary we have the even more profound contradiction that she is said to be both virgin and to have been a mother through the mechanism of the Virgin Birth. In many cases it is believed that a planned act of incest may confer mystical power and in the case of royalty, as in ancient Egypt through brother-sister marriage, may define its sacred quality. The same idea is at work in the doctrine of the Virgin Birth as we can see by looking at the doctrine of the Trinity. If the Father, Son, and Holy Ghost are indeed one and the same, then Mary was in some sense impregnated by her son, so that Jesus is, at one and the same time father, husband, and son. This in itself is mystery enough, but if we add the additional factor of her perpetual virginity, the mystical power is enormously enhanced. Mary Douglas' interpretation of the mystical nature of virginity is an interesting one. She believes that it arose in the Christian case as an extension of the Pauline aim of establishing a sense in which there would be neither Jew nor Greek, male nor female. Moreover, she considers all concerns about bodily orifices to be a manifestation of anxieties of a small persecuted minority, whose concerns "lend themselves to beliefs which symbolise the body as an imperfect container which will only be made perfect if it can be made impermeable." Since it is the female body rather than the male which is in danger of being invaded by seed from some other group, this interpretation fits well with some of what I have suggested. Douglas' idea about the extension of St. Paul's notion, however, strikes me as a rationalization of a long-held belief about the sacred nature of virginity. Its sacredness is more connected to the concept of celibacy. If I am correct and we make an unconscious equation between sex and death, then avoidance of sex equals a conquest of death— precisely what is claimed as the reward for nuns and priests. As St. Paul puts it (Romans 8:6), "For to be carnally minded is death; but to be spiritually minded is life and peace."

One symbol can stand for many things, and virginity, for example, may be generally seen as a symbol of purity and innocence— that is to say, the opposite of sexuality. The attraction of Barbara Cartland's novels is, perhaps, the mental vision of purity flirting with its loss, which means sex, which, through the unconscious equation, implies death and filth. But it is always a heroine who has to preserve that magical quality. The physical nature of women and men guarantee this. A man may lose his innocence but it is of little consequence compared to that of the loss of virginity. Thus virginity is more than a symbol of purity-life-cleanliness; it has come to be a symbol for property, in that husbands have claimed the right to be the first to penetrate their lawful wives over whom they gain property rights through marriage. The concept of property and authority and their relation to virginity and rights over women has been best illustrated by the feudal *droit du seigneur,* also known as the *jus primae noctis.* This was the right of the lord of the manor to spend the wedding night with the new bride of any of his vassals, so that he could exercise his authority over his inferior and take what would have normally been thought of as the husband's own privilege. There is some doubt whether this practice in fact ever took place or actually served as a source of the overlord's revenue, the husband paying his lord for giving up his right. That it did or did not take place is not really relevant. What matters is the idea that it could take place as a supreme gesture of authority.

One would think that the availability of adequate contraceptive methods should have got rid of the mythology surrounding virginity, since sex and pregnancy are not inevitably linked. This has not so far taken place except for a very few people. That women are the willing victims of the system is frequently only too painfully obvious.

12

"The Fear of the Lord Is the Beginning of Wisdom": Authority, Authoritarianism, and Submission

I ended the last chapter with the observation that women are often the willing victims of systems that impose on them such examples of the double standard as premarital chastity and virginity. Yet Freud is attacked for having suggested that women are naturally masochistic. Am I then saying the same thing? My answer is given by Freud's pupil and associate Theodor Reik: "If masochism is the expression of feminity, as Freud believes, it certainly is a distorted and caricatured one."[1]

In Freud's defense, we must remind ourselves of the values held by the Germanic culture in which he was working and of which he was a product. By today's standards, most liberal-minded, educated people would regard the child-rearing practices common in Freud's culture at that time as harsh and authoritarian in the extreme; more particularly was this the case for girls. A rigidly authoritarian upbringing makes anyone somewhat, if not markedly, masochistic. Thus, the neurotics who came in desperation to Freud for help probably exhibited an exaggerated form of what was at that time and in that culture a type of masochistic personality commonly found among women. With this kind of exposure, it seems hardly surprising that Freud reached conclusions that we, the children or grandchildren of his generation, regard as absurd. The idea that men *or* women are naturally of any particular type of personality should have been exploded long ago by the work of Margaret Mead, among many others, but the notion persists because it is useful to some people that it should; and it continues to provide a self-fulfilling prophecy.

How does masochism come to be part of a personality? Reik wrote:

Under the effects of anxiety and fright, of fear and horror, children are sometimes stimulated sexually and begin to masturbate. Such effects as anxiety certainly are unpleasant in themselves and yet they initiate sexual excitement.[2]

He found that this statement continued to be true for many adults, if there was some reinforcing experience that made the unpleasant experience in some way pleasurable. For instance, a young woman who only had sexual satisfaction after being slapped around, finally recalled that as a child she was told that rosy cheeks were pretty and so slapped her own face so that she might be (and was) praised for her prettiness. She also heard and took to heart the saying that "Vanity must suffer."

He recounts a number of case histories of patients who could only achieve sexual satisfaction by fantasizing highly masochistic situations. One young woman had to imagine that she would go to the butcher and ask to be slaughtered. She would undress and lie on a block with calves, also due to be killed. She would fantasize that the butcher would check the calves and then come to her to examine her. The instant he laid his hand on her vagina she would have an orgasm. A man, similarly, would fantasize that he was a sacrificial victim to the god Moloch. The priest would check on the other potential victims and castrate those who were unsatisfactory. When this took place the man would identify with a castrated victim and at once reach orgasm.

Bizarre and odd as these examples might appear to most of us, perhaps they and the preceding information about the sexually exciting effect of fear on children, do explain the attractions of horror movies and the apparently endless stream of films about sharks, exorcists, and buildings collapsing through earthquake, fire, or flood. One might even suggest a publicity campaign based on a slogan like "Is your love life dull? See *Quivering Catastrophe* and really make it!" The attraction of the dozens of violent films and television shows of recent years probably arises from an attraction to sex which the avid viewers are reluctant to face in themselves.

The starting point of masochistic fantasies, Reik claims, is "infantile sadism." As a child matures, gets teeth and muscles, and gains control over its bladder and bowels, it also develops the desire to overpower and hurt those more powerful than itself. Since this is plainly beyond its physical powers, it seeks satisfaction in imagining such a possibility. However, this satisfaction is thwarted by the fear that the person the child is attacking in fantasy will retaliate by punishment for its rebellion. "The sadistic need, eager for gratification, is replaced by anxiety on account of this gratification which is felt to be forbidden," says Reik. "The idea of one's own aggression and the punishment slowly blend." He sees the total development of masochism as taking place in three stages:

1. As you do to me, so I do to you—*sadistic phase.*
2. As I do to you, so I do to me—*intermediate phase.*
3. As I do to me, so you do to me—*true masochism.*

To Reik, these phases take place while the child is under the control of the mother. As he puts it: "The sequence of yielding and defiance, punishment and instinctual satisfaction then would be the echo of long-forgotten difficulties of the education by the mother." It is these memories, he claims—and I entirely agree—that have led to the development of beliefs about terrible and terrifying mother goddesses such as the Hindu Kali, a creature of awful malignity portrayed as having protruding eyes, a huge extended tongue, wearing a necklace of skulls, eating a baby, and trampling on the corpse of a man. I shall return to her when we consider male hatred of women.

The same kind of sequence of events that Reik saw as leading to masochism was considered by the psychoanalyst Melanie Klein, who saw a progression and development through childhood of (1) a rivalry with the parents, (2) a wish to grow out of one's perceived deficiencies, (3) a wish to overcome one's destructiveness and inner badness, and (4) a progression to all kinds of achievements.[3] The child, angered by its helplessness, Klein saw as wishing to grow tall, strong, rich, and powerful while its parents grow weak and powerless. As in all these kinds of cases, the line is thin between the neurotic and the normal for the culture. These kinds of wishes must be common to all children, to a lesser or greater extent. Some children may develop into murderers, rapists, or torturers. Some, because of guilt at their feelings, says Klein, "are obliged to remain unsuccessful, because success always implies to them the humiliation or even the damage of someone else, in the first place the triumph over parents, brothers and sisters." Some remain normal within the confines of the culture but have a potential for cruelty and violence that may come out in the circumstances of a war. Perhaps, as Hannah Arendt so vividly brought to our attention, one of the most appalling aspects of so many of the Nazis like Adolf Eichmann was their ordinariness, their respectability, their banality: their quality of being like reputable businessmen.

This concealed propensity for brutality does not imply a natural human aptitude for aggression. Humans are not naturally aggressive. But the malleability of the human character makes frighteningly possible the development of sadistic pleasure in cruelty, the other face of which is masochistic pleasure in pain to oneself. Writing of Malaysia, the novelist and travel writer Paul Theroux speaks of the apparently kindly and gentle nature of the people. But, he says,

. . . the Malay smile is misleading: it was shortly after I decided that it was one of the quietest countries in the world that Malays came howling out of mosques with white rags tied around their heads. When they were through, 2000 Chinese lay dead and hundreds of shops had been burned to the ground.[4]

Let us consider what I regard as a tremendously important work which shows in further detail how humans produce the sort of horror described by Theroux. Five years after the end of World War II, four authors—Theodor Adorno, Else Frenkel-Brunswik, Daniel Levinson, and Nevitt Sanford—carried out a major study which they called *The Authoritarian Personality*.[5] The authors were inspired by the ghastly revelations of what Nazism had meant in practice and a desire to try to understand how the German people were persuaded against their own self-interests to be antidemocratic. How could a nation thought to be civilized have countenanced such fantastically atrocious acts as those committed in the extermination camps? And did or does the same frightful potential exist in our own society? Plainly there is no simple answer. The reason may lie in economic conditions, in mythology, in political circumstances. But none of these alone could account for Auschwitz and Buchenwald. How then did people become that way, and do we have the same potential?

What comes out in this study with complete clarity is that there is strong relation between discipline and punishment on the one hand and the development of prejudice and hatred on the other. The authors describe a major dichotomy in child-rearing practices in American society, which has, I believe, a universal human application and which explains a whole range of human conduct that might otherwise appear as "natural" and innate.

The dichotomy the four authors describe is based on two radically different modes of imposing discipline. There are people who see no need for disciplining children, and their own children may be very unhappy and frustrated because no boundaries are ever imposed. If, however, one does accept that boundaries on the behavior of the child must be imposed—to prevent it from being obnoxious to the world at large and a burden to its parents and itself—then there is the question of how they should be imposed. It is this question that is addressed by Adorno et al.

They believe that the two ways of imposing discipline on children are by "rules" and by "principles." Rules are moralistic rather than moral. Discipline is thus "handled as a *vis major,* as a force outside of the child, to which at the same time he must submit." The child is constantly forced to obey, not because it understands why but because the external coercive force of the "rules" demand that it does. The following slogan, often carved over the doorways of English schools, admirably sums up this attitude: THE FEAR OF THE LORD IS THE BEGINNING OF WISDOM. It is the difference between the obedience to morality of the religious person because of fear of divine punishment, and the adherence to a moral code of the rational agnostic, whose adherence rests upon an understanding and acknowledgment of the necessity for the code to preserve order in society.

The other way of imposing discipline is through what the authors define as "principles." Under this method, the application of discipline "invites the cooperation and understanding of the child and makes it possible for him to assimilate it." Thus, the authors observe, the difference between the two methods of imposing discipline "is the differentiation between a *threatening,* traumatic, overwhelming discipline, and an *assimilable,* and thus non-ego-destructive discipline." The first method—discipline imposed arbitrarily by moralistic rules—"forces the child into submission and surrender of the ego." Of course, a deeply religious person might raise a child by the second method, particularly if the religion involved were something like Quakerism, where the basic assumption is of the potential goodness of humans rather than of the unavoidable and inescapable evil, which is implied by self-hating doctrines like "original sin."

In the Adorno study it was found that the high-scoring subjects on the question of prejudice toward other racial, ethnic, national, or religious groups almost all had histories of undergoing arbitrary, cruel, or at least harsh punishment for infringement of the code of rules set up by their parents. Those who had little prejudice toward others and were tolerant of human differences were almost all products of a principle-oriented childhood, where parents explained the reasons for refusing or allowing particular actions.

There is a reasonable way of dealing with everything. I recall a young man who was a volunteer in a Peace Corps training program some years ago who achieved very low peer ratings, though he was good with small children and older people. It was revealed that his parents, both clinical psychologists, had gone to such lengths always to be logical and rational, that their son had never once seen them lose their tempers and hence saw them as hardly human. In consequence, he found it difficult to deal with more ordinary people of his own age. It is all right to be angry with a willfully disobedient child and even to deliver a sharp smack on occasion, provided that afterward, when tempers are cooled, one discusses it with the child and gets it to admit the reasonableness of the anger. What is truly awful is a parent's storing up of anger to be vented on the child in cold blood later on.

According to Adorno et al., the subjects who scored highly for prejudice—the potential Nazis, communists, terrorists, Klansmen, believers in simplistic solutions—had a background of moralistic, pietistic, rigid adherence to rules which were treated as immutable and almost divinely inspired. As the authors note: "This finding is highly important since it seems to uncover a source of the basic fear so frequently exhibited by high-scoring men—and so often compensated for by sadistic toughness."

This plainly has relevance to a lot of human behavior. First, consider the mode of training military personnel like that found in the Marine Corps in the United States or the Guards regiments in Britain. The whole intention is to produce a man who is totally rule-oriented, who will obey without question, who will be prepared to undergo great hardship and suffering in the name of a condensed symbol like honor or patriotism or regimental pride and who will, of course, be a highly efficient killer of other men whom the rules identify by another condensed symbol as the enemy. To achieve this end, the recruit is treated like a child of peculiarly brutal and sadistic parents who punish every act which is seen as disobedience, no matter how trivial, and reward slavish obedience with grudging kindness. Arbitrary changes of plan; fanatically rigorous inspections of uniform, equipment, living space, lockers; constant physical demands; petty regulations about every aspect of life—in short, insistence that one carry out instantly and without reasoning any orders, no matter how objectively senseless they may appear to a "reasonable" person. The ever-recurring theme of the drill sergeant to the man who has the temerity to say when questioned about something he is alleged to have done wrongly, "I thought that . . . ," is to shout at him, "Shut up. You aren't paid to think! You're paid to do!" Some men, like some children, do manage to come through this by shutting off parts of their minds in a determination not to be corrupted. Most do not. For much of my life one of the great puzzles about humans was cruelty. It was a matter of bewilderment to me that humans could take pleasure in watching the pain and suffering of others and even take part in inflicting it. There is plainly a link between this pleasure and a harsh rule-dominated childhood. Cruelty to a child frequently tends to result in the child's cruelty to its own child, as studies of battered children make clear. Rigidity, sternness, strict moralistic rules, putting "the fear of God" into a child—these are what produce the Buchenwalds and the My Lais. Presumably, this was well understood by the Spartans. If you wish to produce ruthless efficient soldiers, then treat children with ruthless discipline and top that off with more of the same in military training.

Cruel, brutal people are usually extremely sentimental. Cruel people not only enjoy ordering others about, but usually acquiesce in if not actively enjoy being ordered around by someone more powerful than themselves. This is relevant to harsh and punitive initiation rites. We recall that one cause of the rites may lie in intersex envy. Bettelheim suggested that circumcision and similar painful rites may be "not necessarily only or mainly imposed on the adult by the young . . . but . . . to a large degree . . . may gratify the desires of youth."

Let us look at this matter from the point of view of language. Language is important to humans in classifying, categorizing, and defining the world in which they live; by changing the way in which they categorize they can change not merely the world view but the actions that people take in particular circumstances. This would be very obvious, for instance, if one were to examine the dictates of the Communist party to its followers in all its extraordinary changes of direction.

In 1964 Basil Bernstein, an English sociolinguist, wrote a most interesting article entitled "Elaborated and Restricted Codes: Their Origin and Some Consequences."[6] In this article he showed that a complex heterogeneous society like our own does not have a uniform mode of speech. He divided the types of speech into two major categories: elaborated and restricted codes. The former is characteristic of the relatively well-educated and articulate person who can converse intelligently and descriptively about a wide range of topics. Restricted codes he broke into a number of subtypes. For instance, there are the codes characteristic of a variety of in-group societies such as army, navy, or air force units; clubs and associations; hospitals; special trades or professions; jail populations; and so on. The members of each group share common assumptions and experiences, and often use words or phrases, which might be meaningless to the outsider, as kind of condensed symbols. The average user of an elaborated code can usually comprehend this type of restricted code and use it after a while. Then there is the restricted code found among members of the lowest socioeconomic group in any complex society. While such a code does not hinder communication about immediate needs and is often supplemented by a whole range of nonverbal devices—gestures, facial expressions, body postures—it does severely hamper the articulation of complex abstract ideas and is much more geared toward the concrete, the simple, and the immediate.

Mary Douglas was attracted by this notion and applied Bernstein's schema to religions in a fascinating way in her book *Natural Symbols*.[7] She explored some of the ideas that Bernstein developed, and showed how a restricted code tends to emphasize authority roles without rational explanations—the very same kinds of ideas that Adorno and his colleagues wrote of in their study of authoritarianism. As an example of the kind of behavior to which she directs our attention, consider a conversation like this:

"Don't do that!"

"Why not?"

"Because not!"

"Yes, but why not?"

"Because I said not!"

"Why?"

"Because I'm your mother!" (or "Because your Dad said so!") The effect is not to emphasize why a particular act is bad or foolish or ill-advised or what its results might be. Rather, the effect on the child is to emphasize its own helplessness, dependency, and subordination to the older person.

Douglas analyzes the effect of an exchange between parent and child like the one I used above. In what Bernstein calls the "positional" family (as opposed to the "personal" family), she writes:

The child . . . is controlled by the continual building-up of a sense of social pattern: of ascribed role categories. If he asks "why must I do this?" the answer is in terms of relative position. Because you're a boy (sex role). Because children always do (age status). Because you're the oldest (seniority).

Bernstein himself notes that in situations like these, "the relationship can quickly change to reveal naked power and may become punitive." What is also interesting is that these kinds of codings, emphasizing conduct appropriate to age, seniority, and status, are typical of both the working class and the aristocracy. It is notable that inventiveness, innovation, and scientific curiosity in a Western educated sense have rarely manifested themselves in either of these groupings. It is commonly in the middle classes where these have appeared and, one might confidently predict, where one finds Bernstein's personal family—or, put in other terms, the Adorno team's rearing by principles rather than rules. Of course, there are still plenty of rule-oriented, positional families within the middle classes who can easily be identified by their conservative right-wing views. Their rebellious offspring may well adopt radical left-wing views. Critics of Bernstein have also pointed out that there are elaborated code users in the working class, just as there are restricted code users and positional families in the middle classes. His point about codes is important all the same.

Where I think it has further relevance is in the case of tribal societies. Bernstein noted in passing that tribal languages are likely to be restricted codes because the culture is likely to be fairly if not very homogeneous. Status and roles are more likely to be ascribed than achieved—that is, who and what you are is more likely to depend on your birth than on your ability. In a small-scale, simple society which has agriculture or herding (or both) as its economic base, there is very little differentiation of people by occupation or achievement, since everyone does virtually the same thing. True, there may be a few specialists—smiths, potters, weavers—but these are often subsidiary jobs, and the specialists still depend on farming or herding or fishing for their subsistence.

Think of Western society for a moment. You arrive late at a large cocktail party. Your host or hostess comes over, briefly introduces you to some strange person and leaves you. After a minute's exchange about the weather, the number of people, the noise level, and so on, you probably will not be able to go much further until both of you have exchanged certain information. What does the other person do? But how utterly pointless this question would seem in a society where everyone does exactly the same thing.

Again, imagine my class of students. I bring in a series of strangers to address the class on different occasions, whom I announce variously as Senator Jones; Dr. Jones, professor of psychiatry; Bishop Jones; Mr. Jones who runs a garage. Each was called Jones, but by applying a tag referring to the person's occupational status, our expectations and feelings about him are immediately adjusted. Categorization is at work on our emotions.

In a simple society obviously the occupational label is no use. In these circumstances, one of the commonest ways of identifying and relating to people is by the use of kin terms. Indeed, when you as an anthropologist start work in such a society, you can often not be accepted until classified as a brother, sister, son, or daughter of some relatively well-thought-of person. The moment this is achieved, everyone knows how to behave toward you: the kinship terminology gives a kind of mental blueprint for the rights, duties, obligations, and expectations entailed by the particular status to which you have been assigned. On one occasion in Tanzania, my adoptive elder brother took me to a very remote hamlet to visit "our" eldest brother. While I was there, a small boy came out of a house and saw me, his first white person. He gave a scream of dismay and ran off, but my "brother" called after him, "Hey, come back! This is your grandfather!" Grandfathers are supposed to be kind, loving, and indulgent. They have no legal or domestic authority over grandchildren and so can afford to be. The boy stopped, turned round, came over, and presently climbed onto my lap. The tag of "grandfather" made one safe, whatever strange color I might be. If you think for a moment, you will realize that we often do the same with "aunt" and "uncle," for whom first names alone seem too familiar, but for whom "Mrs." or "Mr." seem too formal.

That is about as far as we go except for using occasional parental or sibling terms such as "father" and "sister" for priests and nuns. The system often used in a simple society of classifying whole blocks of people under one term certainly simplifies the problem of appropriate behavior in any circumstance of interaction between persons. It is also an enormously more rigid system than the one we in the West are accustomed to. In a simple society one's father is often called by a term which is applied to everyone whom one's father calls "brother," which may mean every man at his generational level in an entire clan—dozens, scores, or even hundreds of people. But fathers are rarely treated with love by their children after their infancy; instead, the relationship tends to be stern, distant, harsh, and forbidding. Fathers punish. A father's authority is often backed mystically by the supernatural force of the ancestral spirits. Boys usually have to be respectful to elder brothers, and girls have to be respectful to all brothers. As we can see from Bernstein, Douglas, and Adorno et al., this kind of categorization and rigidly applied role behavior is the perfect breeding ground for authoritarianism.

The psychiatrist Robert Seidenberg suggested that the origin and basis of social, ethnic, racial, or religious prejudice lay in a rigid inculcation of the incest taboo, which tends to make people categorize ourselves and others into "we" and "they." "We" are the people with whom one is supposed to mate by the rules of society, but often this mating is surrounded by anxiety because of too close a resemblance of our people to the forbidden categories of parents or siblings. "They" are the people we despise as too different from ourselves to marry, yet with whom we may have real or fantasy sex to achieve the fulfillment denied to us by the fears aroused with those of our own group.

I have mentioned several times that people in small societies, particularly those which use classificatory kinship terminologies, suffer great anxiety and often severe sexual frustration because of worries about incest. In such a society one may have dozens of persons with whom one interrelates and whom one calls "brother," "sister," "mother," or "father," all of whom are forbidden sexual partners, but because one may not have been raised with them in the close proximity that might have inhibited one's sexual feelings toward them, one might easily worry about one's impulses. One should remember too that the act of incest is often ascribed to the enemy within the society: the witch who is responsible for death, disease, and misfortune. Thus, if one felt sexual attraction toward someone included in the enormous number of prohibited persons, one could easily feel twinges of guilt and wonder whether one was not perhaps a witch responsible for the disasters which might have befallen the community.

If we now put together some of these strands and twist them into a larger rope—restricted codes leading to emphasis on authority rather than reason; discipline based on rules rather than principles; fears of incest leading to great anxiety about sex, nakedness, defecation, and urination—we begin to see, perhaps, what it is about some societies that encourages unquestioning submission to authority, submission to pain if administered or sanctioned by those in authority, pleasure in giving pain, torturing, bullying, and hazing, and, probably, great anxiety about bodily emissions and ritual pollution generally.

In these circumstances, it seems to me hardly surprising that some societies have developed painful and mutilatory initiation rites. The rites express a whole range of ideas: anxieties about sex and incest; a way of hurting others legitimately as one was oneself hurt; a way of emphasizing the location of authority; the fact that authority is backed ultimately by the capability to administer pain; a way of undergoing a supremely masochistic experience legitimately and so satisfying a psychological need to submit totally to those whom one acknowledges as having authority (and probably at the same time having a feeling that one's soul has been wiped free of all guilt). One is also defined in one's own eyes and to the society as an adult who is capable of withstanding pain, engaging in sex, different from the other sex, and different from and superior to members of other groups. Mircea Eliade and Jean La Fontaine would also emphasize, that, as the former puts it:

. . . it is through initiation that men achieve the status of human beings; before initiation they do not yet share fully in the human condition precisely because they do not have access to the religious life.[8]

And Jean La Fontaine comments:

Initiation emphasises the distinction between ignorance and secret knowledge, which confers power on initiates.[9]

As Whiting, Kluckhohn, and Anthony showed, painful initiation rites are most likely to be found in those societies that impose a long post-partum taboo on sex and where the child sleeps with its mother to the exclusion of the father until it is weaned.[10] The weaning is usually harsh. The combination of these factors together with the other ones given above is almost certain to produce extremely authoritarian personalities.

Do the other conditions for the development of authoritarianism, sadism, and masochism exist in belief systems more familiar to ourselves? Let us look at a system for which we have a written record extending back thousands of years, that of the Jews. Throughout the Old Testament there is a constant stress on obedience and submission to God, who is conceptualized as a fatherlike, patriarchal figure. His covenant with Abraham demands total submission. First, this is expressed in acceptance of a symbolic castration—circumcision—of himself and of all males. This is commanded to continue in perpetuity. The initial covenant demanded the circumcision of all males regardless of age; in successive generations the covenant is to be ratified by circumcision of each male child eight days old.

Doubtless some would argue that the circumcision of an eight-day-old child is a very different matter from the taming of a rebellious adolescent. There are a number of answers to this argument which seem to me to be appropriate. One is that infant circumcision bears a similarity to ideas surrounding couvade: an expression of the ambivalent feelings, perhaps hostility, felt by the father for the potential rival his son. One could argue that if a child can be affected by things that happen to the mother during her pregnancy and that if the birth trauma experienced by a child is a reality, as I believe it is, then an eight-day-old child can certainly be aware of pain unnecessarily inflicted on it by those in whom it should presumably repose trust. The physical evidence of what took place is there for life to reactivate the memory. Finally, the perception of circumcision being a harsh manifestation of coercive authority is not a figment of psychoanalytic imagination, but was recognized as such by the ancient Jews, for Deuteronomy 10:16 says in an injunction to obedience to God: "Circumcise therefore the foreskin of your heart, and be no more stiffnecked."

As Proverbs 23:13–14 puts it:

Withhold not correction from the child: for if thou beatest him with the rod, he shall not die. Thou shalt beat him with the rod, and shalt deliver his soul from hell.

Returning to Abraham, we have the terrible story in Genesis 22 of how God commands Abraham to sacrifice his son Isaac to prove his total submission to his will. It may well be that fathers at some level of their minds perceive their newborn sons as rivals. It may be that at adolescence, particularly where the son will take over the father's authority and property, the father will resent the son. But in early childhood and after the son is weaned, then it seems to me that fathers are highly emotionally involved with their sons in a manner that would make a sacrifice of this nature so agonizingly painful that it would be almost impossible to contemplate. It is thus a sure measure of Abraham's utter submission to God's will that he goes forward with all the preparations for the rite: building an altar, placing the firewood on it, binding his acquiescent son on it, drawing his knife to cut his throat. Providentially, a ram is trapped in a thorn bush, and in accordance with the new orders of "an angel of the Lord," Abraham looses his son and slays the ram instead. Imagine the public outcry that would occur today if it were revealed that a father did this to his son! The point being made by the story for the listener, though, is to emphasize the absolute condition of obedience to rules rather than principles.

Always we find a tremendous premium placed by the Old Testament on unquestioning obedience. Consider the case of Saul and David (1 Samuel 15:3, 7–9, 22–23, 33). Why did God, according to the prophet Samuel anyway, transfer his affection and support from Saul to David? Because Saul did not carry out to the letter the orders of God transmitted through Samuel. What then were these orders?

Now go and smite Amalek, and utterly destroy all that they have, and spare them not; but slay both man and woman, infant and suckling, ox and sheep, camel and ass.

And what did Saul do about this ruthless command, which today would fill us with dismay?

And Saul smote the Amalekites from Havilah until thou comest to Shur, that is over against Egypt. And he took Agag the king of the Amalekites alive, and utterly destroyed the people with the edge of the sword.

But Saul and the people spared Agag, and the best of the sheep, and of the oxen, and of the fatlings, and the lambs, and all that was good, and would not utterly destroy them: but everything that was vile and refuse, that they destroyed utterly.

This was not enough. It did not comply totally with God's order to destroy Amalek utterly. When Saul tried to excuse himself to Samuel by saying that he and his people had brought the best of

188 THE LAST TABOO

the livestock back to sacrifice to God, he received the dusty answer:

. . . Hath the Lord as great delight in burnt offerings and sacrifices, as in obeying the voice of the Lord? Behold, to obey is better than sacrifice, and to hearken than the fat of rams. For rebellion is as the sin of witchcraft, and stubbornness is as iniquity and idolatry. Because thou hast rejected the word of the Lord, he hath also rejected thee from being king.

Saul begged for forgiveness in an access of humility, but Samuel scorned him and, moreover, "hewed Agag in pieces before the Lord in Gilgal."

If we follow the career of Saul's successor David, there is the heartbreaking story of Absalom, his loved son. Plainly, the tale goes, David spared the rod and spoiled the child by being kind and merciful to him. Absalom's gratitude was to try to usurp his father's throne. Ultimately, he met a humiliating death for his rebellion against paternal authority.

Some of us think of the message of Christianity as being one of kindness, tolerance, and gentleness, though the anthropologist Marvin Harris challenges this rather persuasively in his book *Cows, Pigs, Wars and Witches.* The Sermon on the Mount, Jesus' reaction to the woman taken in adultery—these seem to typify more the difference between the ruthless savagery depicted in stories like that of Saul and the Amalekites and the idea that God is love. Yet the final tragic drama of the crucifixion represents the ultimate in filial submission. As Jesus says in his agonized prayer at Gethsemane (Luke 22:42):

. . . Father, if thou be willing, remove this cup from me: nevertheless not my will, but thine, be done.

Certainly, the interpretation of Christianity through the last two thousand years has stressed much more the harsh, punitive, intolerant attitudes of the Old Testament. The person most responsible for the interpretation and propagation of Christianity, St. Paul, was evidently a man obsessed with a fear and disgust toward sex, particularly to any deviance from what was permitted in the injunctions of Deuteronomy and Leviticus. Contrast Jesus' tolerant and forgiving attitude to the adulterous woman with that of Paul toward homosexuals, male and female, whom he described, in Romans 1:29–32, thus:

Being filled with all unrighteousness, fornication, wickedness, covetousness, maliciousness; full of envy, murder, debate, deceit, malignity, whisperers, Backbiters, haters of God, despiteful, proud, boasters, inventors of evil things, disobedient to parents, Without understanding, convenant-breakers, without natural affection, implacable, unmerciful: Who, knowing the judgment of God, that they which commit such things are worthy of death, not only do the same, but have pleasure in them that do them.

Reading this impassioned denunciation and recalling Paul's constant denunciations of women, one is reminded of Lear:

> Thou rascal beadle, hold thy bloody hand!
> Why dost thou lash that whore? Strip
>   thine own back;
> Thou hotly lust'st to use her in that kind
> For which thou whippest her. . . .

The stress on rules rather than principles permeates Christian teaching until recent times. The bloody wars, crusades, persecutions, burnings, pogroms, and oppressions carried out in the name of Christ make somewhat hollow the Christian claims of love, kindliness, and tolerance. Whatever the message of the founder may have been, many of His interpreters have seen to it that Christianity has often provided a vehicle for the perpetuation of authoritarianism.

If we turn to Islam, we find no question of whether or not the message is of gentleness and tolerance: quite plainly it is not, though many Muslims (like Jews and Christians) have been merciful and gentle. God is seen as being forgiving and merciful, it is true, but only if one is unquestioningly obedient to His will. The very word "Islam" means a surrender—to the will of God. It was often said that British administrators in the former colonial territories, themselves the product of that pillar of authoritarianism, their "public" school system, found themselves more in sympathy with their Muslim subjects than anyone else they ruled, since, like Sir Richard Burton and T. E. Lawrence, they could easily identify with their similar system of beliefs.

One religious system after another conveys the message that unquestioning obedience to those who hold authority is the greatest good. But it is during an earlier period of human life—weaning—when some children undergo an experience that tends to produce the kind of authoritarianism that revels in cruelty. In Western society today many women do not breast-feed their children—in many cases an acknowledgment of fear and disgust with sex—though in the recent swing toward a less repressed attitude to sex, many women are returning to this practice. Even among those women who do nurse their children, however, one rarely finds a child unweaned by the time it is anywhere between six to nine months old. Dana Raphael, of the Human Lactation Center, writes that after four to six months, a child cannot be maintained by breast milk alone.[11] In Western society, however, weaning is always a gradual process ameliorated by a change to a bottle, which allows a child to go on sucking to obtain comfort and nourishment for a long time before it finally is fed only by spoon and cup. (That far too many children are weaned too early seems to be indicated by the number of people who feel a need for a cigarette, a pipe, or gum.) It is rare for sexual relations between the parents not to be resumed within a few weeks after a child is born, and there are not many people who relate the resumption of sex to nursing or not nursing, as is the case in many non-Western cultures, though occasionally one finds folk beliefs that pregnancy is unlikely to ensue while breast-feeding continues. In any case, weaning is not usually a traumatic affair either physiologically or psychologically for the child.

In many non-Western societies we find a very different picture. In many cases we find weaning and the resumption of marital sex concurrent; and both take place after anything from one to three years after the child is born. In one case, sex was not resumed for ten years! Frequently it is believed that if the parents have sex while nursing is still going on, it will harm the child by curdling or poisoning the milk or cutting off its supply. The last belief has some justification, in that if a woman gets pregnant too soon after one child is born, either her milk supply *will* cease or, at the very least, not be available for two children, so that one probably will die.

Freud and Durkheim assumed that since the Australian Aborigines were the people with the most primitive culture in the world,

their culture must be the same as that of all our stone age ancestors. The snag to this assumption is that all humans have all been
on earth for the same length of time, whether Europeans, Africans, Eskimos, or Australians and there is no way of knowing
whether today's Australians have the same ideas and beliefs as our
early ancestors. However, they do still have much the same sort of
material culture, and presumably have consumed much the same
foods for thousands of years. All humans doubtless lived in the
same manner—gathering and hunting—for at least half a million
years (if we reckon *Homo erectus* as human), perhaps more than
three times as long as that. While holding to the caveat about
changes in ideas over time, we might look at another people
who have lived in the same area in much the same way for the
past 11,000 years: the Bushmen of the Kalahari Desert in southern Africa.

The environmental constraints of this area made it impossible
for the people to have lived in a very different way from what they
do now. Particularly crucial are the types of food available. Although the foods are perfectly healthy and nutritious for adults
(and doubtless the average adult of this area is far more healthy
than the average sedentary Westerner), few of them are suitable
for consumption by a small baby. The British anthropologist
James Woodburn, who lived with a similar people, the Hadza, in
a very dry and arid area of East Africa, says that the problem
with food is not availability but unpalatability: most of the roots,
nuts, and berries consumed are hard and fibrous and frequently
leave an inedible residue in the mouth that has to be spat out.[12] In
these circumstances, it is necessary for the mother to continue
breast-feeding a child for as long as possible, at the very least, in
order to supplement the hard and fibrous foods it is weaned on.
The foods available to the mother similarly cut down her bodily
capabilities so that the old Western folk belief about not getting
pregnant while nursing is here somewhat validated. One study
among women in the area of the Kalahari shows that the age of
menarche among the nomadic !Kung is about 15.5 years and that
the people have a very low fertility rate.[13] A reporter for *Science*,
G. B. Kolata,[14] relates these findings to those in a study R. E.
Frisch and J. W. McArthur made in the United States showing a
direct relation between the ratio of body fat to size and the onset

of puberty and resumption or cessation of menstruation after parturition.[15] She suggests that the late puberty and low fertility of the !Kung are probably due to the diet. In this society children are nursed for a least three years and sometimes longer.

When one gets a very long nursing period there is often a very abrupt cessation of it at the end. Plainly a child of three or four cannot be adequately sustained on breast milk alone and must consume other foods for some time, so that the dietary change is not a major problem when the breast feeding stops. The psychic deprivation must, however, be acute. Suddenly the child is denied its greatest source of comfort, which for years has been available on demand. In some cases red pepper or some similar substance is put on the nipples; in others the child is physically removed from the mother's care and placed in the care of another relative. The general misery of recently weaned children in such circumstances is painful to see. The child's place in the mother's arms and bed is taken by the father.

Among the !Kung Bushmen, Kolata reports, "the average length of time between giving birth for a nomadic !Kung woman is four years." G. B. Silverbauer, an anthropologist, who carried out research among the G/wi (the various symbols of ! and / indicate clicks in the speech), reports that a G/wi child is nursed for four years, the wife must not conceive during that time, and it is obligatory for the husband to abstain from sex with his wife for the entire period.[16] These statements would seem to imply an exclusive mother-child relationship which, according to Whiting's theory, should produce father-son and son-father antagonism, and hence one should expect harsh initiation rites. The Anglo-South African anthropologist Isaac Schapera writes of the boys' rites among these people that they are "roughly handled and half-starved" and terrorized by a variety of mythical (and female) monsters and finally have incisions made between their eyebrows.[17] Even more interestingly, he notes that several early and reliable observers claimed that it was once customary to cut out one of a boy's testicles. Some people may be skeptical of the idea that circumcision represents a symbolic castration of the sons by their fathers. In this case, not only was there mutilation of the head, but an actual semicastration. Surely this must be the nearest that any group has actually come to castration of the sons by the fathers.

Where there is a three-to-four-year period of total warmth and security for the child which suddenly ends, here is the stuff from which myths of a golden age are made. We should realize that this must have been the situation in the gathering-hunting phase of all humans—here is our paradise, from which we are driven by a stern father figure. And if the child feels hostile and angry toward the person who has supplanted it and toward the mother for this act of rejection (the bitterness of which will surface at every emotional rejection throughout life), how does the father feel toward this creature who supplants *him* for the first few years? It would be difficult for him not to have (at least unconsciously) ambivalent feelings toward it, since he can no longer sleep with his wife nor have any sex. In these cultures it is easy to believe that, for a man at least, the marital bed is a reminder of the glorious period of infancy and that pregnancy and birth is a reminder of the feeling of rejection generated by his own weaning when a child.

Is hostility between parents and children inevitable? For humans in cultures where there are no adequate weaning foods, the answer may be yes. However, in cultures where contraception is available, where there is a knowledge of nutrition and weaning foods can be obtained, there is no reason at all for antagonism to exist between fathers and children. Particularly should this be so if we understand and prevent the potentially detrimental effects on the child of harsh toilet training, of inculcating the idea that sex is dirty, and of imposing arbitrary, stern, and inflexible rules rather than guiding and disciplining through rational principles.

It should be possible to deduce from much of what has gone before in this work that some of what have seemed to be the most intractable problems in the human condition—cruelty, brutality, prejudice, intolerance—do not have to be part of the condition at all. Over the past centuries there has been an accelerating movement, particularly in the West, to esteem gentleness, tolerance, generosity, and concern for others above the more aggressive qualities. That this movement as yet represents only a minority view is evidenced by the continuing strength of the military; organizations like the Ku Klux Klan, the American Nazi Party, the John Birch Society, the National Front in Britain, and other products of a rule-dominated childhood; and the other traits found in that constellation.

The women's movement has been responsible for a shift in the direction of greater male involvement in the care of children and domestic tasks generally. Nothing could be more important for our future.

It is worth reflecting on the fact that we often laugh at what causes us most anxiety. To most people, some of the funniest jokes are about sex, death, and bodily functions. But the one sure way to make almost everyone laugh is to show authority overturned, oppression subverted, pride and pomposity punctured: the very targets that Charlie Chaplin so unerringly hit. One can show an old silent movie of Chaplin in the most remote village in Africa and people will roar with delight. And what are the most frequent targets of the Monty Python television show? The military, the police, bureaucrats, the clergy, the politicians. There is a lesson for us here.

13

Ritual Pollution and Sex Roles

Theodor Reik recounts how his strictly religious Jewish grandfather, wishing to discuss important matters concerning religion with him, said to his grandmother, "Mach den Tisch rein!"—make the table clean. She should remove herself so that the men, ritually pure, should be able to discuss theological matters which would be nullified or profaned by the ritually impure presence of a woman.

Women are often thought of as inferior. Painful initiation rites reinforce this subjection both to the authority of older women and to all men. The basis for male authority lies in the possession of overwhelming physical force. Yet humans have developed another way of emphasizing the differences between the sexes—ritual pollution.

"Pollution" is often used to define internal and external boundaries. Mary Douglas thinks the fact that in various societies people put different emphases on bodily parts, orifices, and emissions proves that there is no universal human psychological concern with these matters. Yet the fact that most orifices and emissions are matters for concern in varying degrees to all societies may be proof of the reverse. If a handful of societies is *not* bothered about bodily emissions, then we should seek the psychological reasons why this is so.

Mary Douglas argues: "Spittle, blood, milk, urine, faeces or tears by simply issuing forth have traversed the boundary of the body. So also have bodily parings, skin, nail, hair-clippings and sweat."[1] Her concept of the body as a vessel is a good one, so that emissions from it have traversed its boundary and are liminal and therefore polluting. But there is one exception which does not fit: tears. A student of mine made what I think is the correct observation on this subject. The best that Mary Douglas can offer to explain the nonpolluting quality of tears is to say that they are connected neither to food nor sex and they are cleansing in nature. The correct solution lies, I think, in two characteristics of tears not found with all the others. They do not putrefy and only humans shed them. One could object that hair and nails do not putrefy either. But there is also a sacred and dangerous aspect to these two which gives them a special quality: they go on growing after death. Every type of emission but tears reminds us of death by its associations with decay. It is this quality, coupled with liminality, which confers the polluting aspect on all the others and also accounts for their widespread use in destructive magic. Tears, because of their unique and human, nonanimal quality, emphasize our nonanimal side. Bodily emissions emphasize nature; tears then symbolize culture.

Douglas suggests that "when rituals express anxiety about the body's orifices the sociological counterpart of this anxiety is a care to protect the political and cultural unity of a minority group."[2] Let us examine this idea.

Let us look first at Hinduism. A German scholar, Johann Jakob Meyer, examined all the Hindu beliefs pertaining to sex, using the two major bodies of tradition, the Mahabharata and Ramayana and the Code of Manu, as well as many other sources.[3] Much of his work is in the form of direct quotations translated from these sources, and it is these that are used to illustrate my points. Among the Hindus each caste can be regarded as a "minority group," and certainly pollution rules are what define the boundaries between castes. For instance, it was said that "[the] Brahman who lies with a slave woman goes to hell [and] if he goes to a Pariah woman he becomes a Pariah himself." But these are universal rules which apply to all castes, regardless of their position in the hierarchy. And one could hardly call the Hindus a minority group, except where they live in another country such as England or the states of East Africa. Here pollution rules tend to get eroded rather than enhanced, which they should do if Douglas is right. Probably the rules *would* be emphasized if the minority were oppressed. It is probably oppression and discrimination against the Jews over the centuries which kept their religion alive.

Among strict Hindus, sexual activity may only take place with a woman during her *ritu,* i.e., four days after her menstrual flow has ended and she has taken a ritual wash and until her next flow begins. For, "At this time the woman is not only well fitted and with the right and duty to procreate, but also she is clean." Note that this cleanliness is not really concerned with hygiene, even if one were mistakenly to suppose that intercourse during the period is unhygienic. Rather, it is because "uncleanness dwells in her, and every kind of magical harm, and in the peculiarly mysterious menstrual blood are concentrated all these dread powers." There are endless and quite frightening injunctions against having sex during menstruation. It is strictly forbidden. To visit a menstruating woman "is one of the seven things whereby a man forfeits his happiness or long life." A Brahman who does this must "as a penance, for six months wear a wet garment and sleep on ashes." A woman in her period "must not be in the neighborhood of the ancestral offering." If she even looks at food, it cannot be sacrificed to the gods—"Food thus spoiled is the very portion of the demons." Finally, it is recorded that "to have connection with a woman during the monthly flow is reckoned among the dreadful crimes set forth in Arjuna's formula of self-cursing."

Since we fear sex, we attribute righteousness to voluntary abstention from sex by priests and nuns. They emulate St. Paul, who said (Romans 8:6, 13): "to be carnally minded is death; but to be spiritually minded is life and peace" and "if ye live after the flesh, ye shall die . . ." If we equate sex with death, then celibacy means life (though not, perhaps, living). The same idea is expressed in Hinduism—but only applied to men. Although St. Paul considered women weak, he was at least able to allow them the same chance of holiness as men through celibacy (1 Corinthians 7:8–9): "I say therefore to the unmarried and widows, It is good for them if they abide even as I. But if they cannot contain, let them marry: for it is better to marry than to burn." In Hinduism a woman is believed to be unable to control her lubricity, but for man "an irresistible power dwells in perfect asceticism" at which the gods tremble, so that Indra (a warrior god) would send temptresses to ascetics, who, poor things, "at the mere sight of a lovely woman are thrown into an orgasm." For men, "seed and the shedding of seed is . . . magically dangerous."

Thus Hindu women are seen as a snare, a hindrance to the achievement of spirituality. Just as in the Genesis story in which Eve brings the knowledge of sex and death to Adam and so ends mankind's golden age, so in Hinduism we find that "in the golden age there was no sexual union whatever [and] there was no fear of death." Significantly, the passage continues: "In our own evil or Kali age it is now needful; but it is regulated." Kali is the mother goddess. As in the Bible, there are strict injunctions against male and female homosexuality, bestialism, and oral sex, any of which was grounds for expulsion from one's caste. Interestingly, coitus in the daytime is "among the most dreadful sins." But it is the menstruating woman who carries an overwhelming load of evil: "[Her] very glance makes unclean . . . even speaking to her sullies . . . food she has touched must not be eaten" and if "she willfully touches a twice-born man, she shall be flogged with a whip."

Modern Hindus still hold many of the same ideas, and the doctrine of celibacy for men is very important. Men's life force is believed to be concentrated in their semen, so that any depletion of the supply implies a concomitant diminution of the life force. Women are believed to be not merely weak and potentially polluting; they are a perpetual trap to weaken a man and diminish his virility and shorten his life. It can do little for marital happiness if, on the one hand, the old scriptures prescribe that it is a husband's duty to satisfy his wife in her nonpolluting times, while, on the other, there is a strong belief that every seminal emission depletes one's vigor irreplaceably. Some might argue that the Tantric tradition in Hinduism (which can involve worship through an act of intercourse), extols sexuality. If it does, it is in a very strange way, and one which merely uses the woman.

In Islam, at least, this fear is not one which nags at the conscience of the sensual male. However, the cultural view of woman is very similar both to that of classic Hinduism and ancient Judaism. The Muslim writer Fatima Mernissi finds ironic the contrast between the Freudian view of female passivity and the Islamic view of female aggressiveness in sexuality.[4] Examination of the views of Muslin scholars, she observes, shows what they believe: "The Muslim woman is endowed with a fatal attraction which erodes the male's will to resist her and reduces him to a passive acquiescent role." There are numerous comparisons made between a woman and Satan. Meeting a woman and feeling desire for her can only be countered by rushing to one's wife and having sex, so the Prophet enjoined. Under this kind of visual assault on the ever-susceptible male, logically the only salvation for him is to keep women out of sight—either indoors or behind a veil. The opinions of women on this subject have not been solicited.

The Koran says (XXIV:31):

And tell the believing women to lower their gaze and be modest, and to display of their adornment only that which is apparent, and to draw their veils over their bosoms. . . .[5]

For women who have reached menopause, these restrictions are relaxed. For them "it is no sin if they discard their outer clothing in such a way as to show adornment." However, the end of the above passage (XXIV:60) says: "But to refrain is better for them. Allah is hearer, knower."

The Islamic views on women are not quite so negative as that of Hinduism, but are hardly in accord with feminist thinking. This view provides a major modern ethical problem, as its equivalent does for the orthodox Jew, Christian, or Hindu in the modern world, since the Koran, like the scriptures of other religions, is regarded as the word of God revealed to man (and I use the word "man" intentionally; scriptural revelation never seems to occur to women, though visions and messages may). Any challenge to the doctrines laid down in any holy book believed to be of divine inspiration can only be viewed as heresy and blasphemy. A terrible impasse.

If the scriptures are indeed the word of God, there can be no change in the relative position of the sexes. If they are viewed as the works of men, then it becomes possible to believe that the scriptures are historically interesting and inspirational, but do not necessarily provide an unchangeable blueprint for human conduct.

After death, according to the Koran, men who have been good Muslims are destined for Paradise. Women are not mentioned. In Paradise, however, there *are* women—not the earthly wives but "those of modest gaze, whom neither man nor jinni will have touched before them" (LV:56), who are described as "fair ones, close-guarded in pavilions" (LV:72). In a later passage, the condition of Paradise is described as consisting of gardens of delight, where beautiful youths bring bowls of heavenly liquor (which gives no hangover) to the men, who lie on soft couches eating fruit and "the flesh of fowls" and have at their disposal "fair ones with wide lovely eyes" (LVI:22), who, by a special act of creation, are perpetual virgins. In a work of James Branch Cabell, once very popular, his hero, Jurgen, shown a variety of men's dream worlds by Anaïtis, the Lady of the Lake, remarks that he feels a sense of shame because apparently the ideal of felicity held by most men is rather like a glorified brothel. The Islamic notion of Paradise seems comparable. Hinduism, Buddhism, and Christianity all commend celibacy as a means of conquering death and ensuring eternal bliss. Islam does not and foretells a sexual Paradise.

Earthly women may not aspire to Paradise, but they must be kept in their place. According to the Koran (IV:34):

Men are in charge of women, because Allah hath made the one of them to excell the other, and because they spend of their property (for the support of women). So good women are the obedient, guarding in secret that which Allah hath guarded.

There is little difficulty, one would think, in upholding the status quo and preventing a female *coup d'état,* but to ensure this, the same passage tells men:

As for those from whom ye fear rebellion, admonish them and banish them to beds apart, and scourge them. Then if they obey you seek not a way against them. Lo! Allah is ever High, Exalted, Great.

Plainly the nature of women is thought to be weak though sexually voracious. An East African Islamic theologian, Al-Amin bin Aly, writing in 1955, put it this way:

Almighty God created us female and male, and in his mercy He has arranged that women are weak in strength and weak in intelligence. And in His mercy He has arranged that men are the strongest and have great intelligence and fine thoughts, and for this reason He has arranged that it is men who supervise women in their affairs . . .[6]

Women then are physically and mentally deficient, incapable of ordering their affairs, and sexually a constant threat to the integrity of men. However, through veiling, segregation, and harsh discipline, one would think there was no great problem in keeping them down. Just to be absolutely sure, however, there is the added weapon of pollution ready to hand.

A man may not go to prayer if he is drunk, has come from the latrine, or has touched a woman until he has purified himself by washing with water or clean sand.

The things Islam laid down as being ritually polluting are blood, pus, vomit, dirty phlegm, milk from an unclean animal (ritually unclean, that is), urine, feces, alcoholic drinks, a dead body (except human, fish, or locust), meat cut from an animal still alive (an old Ethiopian custom), everything connected with a dog—its saliva, hair, claws, etc.—everything connected with a pig. Pollution can usually be removed by washing. Very strict rules are laid down for latrines and using them: they must be far from the house, completely private, out of sight and hearing. A person should enter left foot first and come out right first. A man must always urinate squatting, the main reason being, according to Al-Amin bin Aly, to avoid the possibility of any drop of urine falling on the clothing, which would, he tells us, completely invalidate the carrying out of any of the required five prayers daily.

In addition to the list of polluting things above, for men, contact with a woman is classified as being comparable to visiting a latrine (sex and feces). Until one has washed, one is in a state which precludes religious activity. Contact with a menstruating woman in any manner is considered bad; sexual contact would be too awful to contemplate. The cessation of blood, followed by washing, is, however, sufficient to allow a married woman to engage in normal sex life, whether after her period or after childbirth. There is no required four-day hiatus as prescribed by the Hindus.

Many defenders of Islamic culture, aware of the critical attitude of the West to the position of women in Islam, take a variety of defensive stances. At one extreme are writers in the monthly magazine put out by Aramco (Arabian-American Oil Company) at immense cost and distributed free to schools and universities in the United States. If one took this publication seriously, one would gain the impression that most Arab women are disporting themselves in bikinis on water skis or becoming airplane pilots and other high-status persons.

Some claim that far from imposing an inferior position on
women, the Koran marked the first step in the emancipation of
women from their prior chattel status.[7] The injunctions of the
Koran may lay down regulations about treatment of women and
their rights to property which put them in a more favorable position than had earlier been the case, but what this viewpoint entirely neglects is that if the Koran is the word of God, as orthodox
Muslims believe, and if there can be no prophet after Mohammed
until the Day of Judgment, then it is quite irrelevant that the
Koran marked the "first step" in women's emancipation: there
can never be a second step.

Since men may not approach menstruating women, the women
must be ritually inferior to men. Yet there are those who hold
that:

. . . God enjoins men not to approach their women [during menstru-
ation] except in normal ways. Is there not then in this the suggestion that men used to approach women in "abnormal" ways and,
therefore, that they are perverted and inferior ritually?[8]

In the Torah, the first five books of the Old Testament, believed
by Orthodox Jews to be the word of God revealed to humans
through Moses, we find the same kinds of ideas once more. In
Leviticus 15:16 we are told that all kinds of bodily emissions are
unclean, particularly semen:

And if any man's seed of copulation go out from him, then he shall
wash all his flesh in water, and be unclean until the even.

Successive verses declare that clothing polluted by semen is
unclean. A menstruating woman is far more polluting, however.
She has to remain apart for seven days and any person who
touches her is "unclean until even." There are two statements
about having sex with a woman at this time (Leviticus 15:24):

And if any man lie with her at all, and her flowers be upon him, he
shall be unclean seven days; and all the bed whereon he lieth shall be
unclean.

This is serious enough—in effect, the man by contact with menstrual blood has been reduced to the status of woman, with seven
days of exclusion from any ritual activity. In Leviticus 20:18
however, we find a more serious view taken of this sin.

And if a man lie with a woman having her sickness, and shall uncover her nakedness; he hath discovered her fountain, and she has uncovered the fountain of her blood: and both of them shall be cut off from among their people.

A natural bodily function is labeled as "sickness" and is comparable to the attitude of some Western hospitals toward childbirth. Male superiority is also symbolically stressed at childbirth. For a boy child, a woman is unclean for seven days; on the eighth day the boy is circumcised and then she is unclean for a further thirty-three days; but for a girl child, the mother is unclean for sixty-six days (Leviticus 12:1–6).

Mary Douglas notes that St. Paul tried to reduce the importance attached to exterior bodily conditions by Judaism and emphasized instead the inner condition, to the extent that he thought "bodily states are irrelevant to ritual."[9] This viewpoint met much opposition, and in the seventh century A.D., Archbishop Theodore of Canterbury enjoined the avoidance of all blood, including that of menstruation. We shall look at our modern society presently to see how we stand today. Douglas makes one very interesting observation about menstruation which fits her liminal-danger category. This is that the Maoris regard menstrual blood with horror as "a sort of human being *manqué*." Yet pollution rules, and particularly ones which pertain to menstruation, have incalculable social *and* psychological effects.

The Luguru of Tanzania, as I have noted, incarcerate girls in the dark at puberty, a practice which has a devastating effect on the potential position of women in that society, effectively quashing any possibility of rebellion. Just to make doubly sure, however, women's dangerously polluting nature is explained to a Luguru boy in his puberty rites, rites which are themselves well adapted to ensure respect for the authority of fathers, maternal uncles and elder brothers. At the final rite the boy is told this by a grandfather:

You are big. Your pubic and axillary hair must always be shaved off. This hair must always be removed or you will stink. You are big, you will want women. You will lie with women and find it good. Later you will lie with your wife and make her pregnant, and she will have a child. A child will come from the vagina of your wife. But if a woman has her period, don't lie with her or your penis will die. If it dies, you will never have sex again. Women won't want you because you are useless. The penis dies with menstrual blood.

Although Western industrial society is not what Douglas calls "pollution-prone" in the same way as other cultures, at the same time we are not entirely free from these notions. First, all committed Catholics differentiate a state of grace from a state of sin, sin often being defined as some kind of sexual offense, sometimes as a rejection of parental or religious authority. In spite of the insistence of Christianity on love, mercy, and forgiveness, the Catholic view of life is a highly authoritarian one. The potential results of authoritarianism in terms of prejudice, cruelty, and sexual difficulties we have already seen. Much the same attitudes are to be found among Orthodox Jews, whose attachment to the idea of ritual pollution is still strong. It is no coincidence that both these groups in American society are strongly opposed to equality between the sexes.

But what about those who are not religious, in the sense of being attached to a formal faith? How would they respond if asked to handle cloth soiled by semen, menstrual blood, feces, urine, and so on? One could probably set up a mental revulsion scale (1 meaning the lowest score) which might run something like this:

	1	2	3	4	5	6	7	8	9	10
Saliva	▓									
Sweat	▓	▓								
Nails & hair trimmings	▓	▓								
Blood	▓	▓	▓							
Nose mucus	▓	▓	▓	▓						
Pus	▓	▓	▓	▓						
Vomit	▓	▓	▓	▓	▓					
Urine	▓	▓	▓	▓	▓	▓				
Feces	▓	▓	▓	▓	▓	▓	▓			
Semen	▓	▓	▓	▓	▓	▓	▓	▓	▓	
Menstrual blood	▓	▓	▓	▓	▓	▓	▓	▓	▓	▓

Of course, different members of our culture might assign slightly different scores. Probably the scores would be radically different if the material was totally dried out. There would also be a major modification contingent on kin or marital relationship. Nevertheless, for most not formally religious people the highest scores would probably be for feces, semen, and menstrual blood. This takes me right back to the beginning where I suggested that our fear of sexuality stems from our knowledge of death. Because of our unique human need for anal cleaning after defecation, we not only absorb the idea that sex is dirty, but also subconsciously link sex, incest, feces, and death. Just a small test for ourselves: Do you detect any difference in your reaction to finding hair or nail trimmings in a bath as compared with finding pubic hair? Most people react with greater disgust to the latter. Some people claim that on the emissions scale, they would find vomit most disgusting of all. It is no coincidence that many peoples (including ourselves) often equate food and sex. It also smells strongly and thus becomes like feces.

So far so good, but all this illustrates is that in spite of our rationalism all of us are still subjectively affected by what is objectively harmless and by what causes no apprehension whatever to other animals. Remember, animals do not know about death and their conceptual systems are not based on verbal symbolism. What we should examine closely is whether our "rational" and secular symbolic system is used in any way as a weapon in discrimination between the sexes (there is no doubt that it is often used between ethnic groups).

In Meyer's book on India he includes a fascinating footnote in which he gives an example of how prejudice against menstruation exists throughout the world. At one boarding school for girls in England it is reported that "the cook had her courses, and therefore did not dare to touch the meat, as it would thus be spoiled."[10] Many Welsh women today are obsessed with a wish to reach menopause or have a hysterectomy so that they can, in their view, be finished with sex; conversely, others wish to be purged of their "bad blood." If they did not have a good flow, they "would feel unclean." The essence of this belief is that the "sexual processes produce poison which is eliminated from the woman's body through menstruation."[11] This concept, that menstrual blood is poisonous, is clearly objectively wrong, but continues in folk belief. Centuries of bleeding and leeching have been linked to this

idea. The basis for having male chefs and probably also one of
the major reasons why churches continue to refuse to ordain
women priests is the notion that a menstruating woman is unclean,
impure, poisonous, dangerous, and ritually polluting. I recently
received dramatic confirmation that this idea has some substance.
Someone was arguing in favor of women priests in the Catholic
Church. Her mother gave what to her was the final judgment:
"How would you like to receive Holy Communion from some
woman who had her period!" It would be interesting to follow up
this statement with inquiries among large numbers of comparable
persons.

The writer Nora Ephron, with her usual marvelous ability to
see beyond the rhetorical wrappings to the real inner meaning of
anything, has, in her book *Crazy Salad,* gathered together a number of essays which relate to feminist subjects.[12] In her essay
"Vaginal Politics," concerning the book of the same name by
Ellen Frankfort, she attacks some of the more radical members of
the women's movement for emphasizing bodily functions to the
exclusion of more important issues as though it were not enough
that:

For some time, various scientists have been attacking women's libera-
tion by insisting that because of menstruation, women are unfit for just
about everything several days a month.

The "self-help women" from Los Angeles who were advocating
the use of the "period extractor" (what she describes as "a
syringe-and-tube contraption that allows a woman to remove her
menstrual flow, all by herself, in five minutes") were, she suggests, saying of menstruation, "Yes, it *is* awful, it is truly a curse
and here is a way to be done with it in five minutes." Trying to
eliminate the fact of menstruation, she remarks, "springs from a
self-hate that is precisely parallel to the male fear of blood that
underlies so many primitive taboos toward women."

Another of Ephron's sharp and witty essays is called "Dealing
with the, uh, Problem." In it, she describes how a particular pharmaceutical manufacturer went from a small scale to $182-million-
a-year sales of which $40 million comes from what is called the
"feminine hygiene spray," which has been attacked since 1966
"by women's liberationists, who think it is demeaning to women;

by consumerists, who think it is dangerous." In spite of this, she says, there are now twenty different companies manufacturing some forty different brands, which, it is claimed, are being used by 20 million American women. Who are these people so hung-up about everything connected with sex and elimination that they can be persuaded into buying what must rank as one of the most supremely unnecessary products in a world obsessed with consuming unnecessary products? The answer of a drug store was "stewardesses and secretaries." As Ephron says:

It figures. Scratch any trend no one you know is into and you will always find secretaries and stewardesses. They are also behind Dr. David Reuben, contemporary cards, *Jonathan Livingston Seagull,* water beds, Cold Duck, Rod McKuen, and Minute Rice.

Nora Ephron's polemic on deodorants coincides with reflections on the same subject by an anthropologist, Shirley Ardener.[13] She writes that women in Cameroon use sexual insults to men to express female militancy: "Cameroon women particularly abhor the imputation that vaginas smell, an accusation that does not seem to have been common in England and America until recent years." She quotes from Mary Douglas: "[When] male dominance is accepted as a central principle of social organization . . . beliefs in sex pollution are not likely to be highly developed . . ." and Ardener suggests that it "is tempting to follow this by arguing that it was the weakening of the authority of the American male which led to the sudden discovery of the need for vaginal deodorants."

Is Douglas right? Will one only find beliefs in sex pollution where male dominance is *not* the central principle of social organization? Surely almost every society is organized around that very principle. Certainly Islam, Hinduism, Judaism all emphasize it and also believe in sex pollution. Perhaps more important is the idea that where men, for whatever reason, feel threatened by women, then beliefs about the sexually polluting qualities of women will emerge. The examples of Islam, Judaism, and Hinduism illustrate that the more women are deprived of authority, the more they will manipulate power. Who has not heard tales of the intimidating Muslim, Jewish, or Hindu mother?

If women have no authority but much power, then there is a perceived need to keep them down. Therefore, fears of sexual pollution crop up. These fears of sexual pollution make men more paranoid about women. They then deny them authority on the grounds of their polluting nature. This forces women to be more manipulative to obtain power illicitly since they are denied authority which will make them appear threatening to men. It goes on and on. The answer is to allow women to hold authority positions—but try and tell that to an orthodox religious believer of whatever persuasion and see how far you get. The only way women can improve their position is by fulfilling two conditions: they must have an economic base beyond mere subsistence, and they must be organized in groups.[14]

Let us look again at the suggestion that the rise of the feminist movement created a threat to the male establishment and that this led to the promotion of vaginal deodorants which stress the "inferior" nature of women. The fashion and pharmaceutical industries are not interested in women de-emphasizing their sexual difference from men; on the contrary, they want to draw attention to and if possible exaggerate those attributes of women which differentiate them from men. Men do not develop breasts, so women's clothing is designed to draw attention to the bosom; women have smaller waists in proportion to their hips than men do, so clothing stresses this; sexually mature women have proportionately longer legs than men, so stockings and high heels accentuate this. What women *are* encouraged to de-emphasize are what are thought of as their more "animal" attributes in physical terms. (Unlike men, they are *not* encouraged to repress their natural emotions.) Body hair in women is often regarded as repellently animal-like and so women are encouraged to remove it from their legs and armpits. In many cultures they remove all their pubic hair too. To return to the question of deodorants, unwashed vaginas do smell. But this fact is not something that has suddenly burst on an astonished world. African, Arab, and Indian women invariably wash their genitals before as well as immediately after sex, specifically to remove any trace of vaginal odor.

Yet the situation for men is rendered different so that it can be used to demonstrate male superiority. First, male genitals smell just as much as female ones if the male is not circumcised and if he does not wash behind the foreskin daily. This may be the real reason for male circumcision (and perhaps some forms of female

circumcision had the same imitative aim). Peoples who circumcise their male children (and that includes a majority of modern
Americans) tend to regard peoples who do not as dirty. But, of
course, the secretions from both males and females, in which bacteria thrive and produce the characteristic odor, are actually perfectly natural and relatively harmless. What makes them offensive
and disgusting is, I suggest, that as emissions they are marginal
and threatening and that the smell once more reminds us of death
and decay and also of our animal—i.e., natural, as opposed to
cultural—human origins. Animals, unaware of death, are not in
the least put off by body odors or emissions of any kind; on the
contrary, they probably associate them only with sex and so find
them attractive and pleasurable. Americans are encouraged to us
underarm deodorants and to wash their feet—both bodily are
which potentially smell the same for both sexes. With genit
however, it is much easier for the male, especially if circumc
to keep himself odor-free and use this fact as an indication
superiority to the more natural and animal-like woman. Ve
quently societies ascribe more of nature to women and of
to men, mainly because of childbirth and lactation.[15] Iror
is largely women who are responsible for enculturating b
and females.

Women are also thought of as being emotionally le
and more prone to weep or scream. Men are often c
ditioned (usually by women) to restrain their em
weep, not to cry out in pain. There is great cultu
the level of pain that either sex believes one is
East Africa, for example, African nurses are cor
dian women who scream constantly in childbir
relative stoicism of English women. Studies ir
have shown great variation between ethnic
amount of pain each thinks its members sh
Whether we are dealing with how much
with the question of bodily emphases, bot
the net result is a self-fulfilling prophecy:
to be superior to women. No doubt the
of New Guinea who, by "menstruating"
manner, were able to use this els
"prove" their superiority to women.

One last example of how sexual pollution is used to draw boundaries and make equivalences. Humans place much symbolic emphasis on gateways, portals, thresholds—e.g., opening a building or bridge, carrying a bride into a house, and so on.[16] In some places neither a corpse nor a menstruating woman can leave or enter a house by a main door but has to use a back or side door. Notice the association of death and sex.

When I worked in East Africa I came to realize that people were very careful always to use their right hands to give or receive anything.[17] When they ate from a common dish as a group, only their right hands were ever used. Why? I asked. I was told that the left hand was used to clean the anus after defecation. Most people have had the same thing told them in those regions where this is the rule—throughout Africa, India, the Middle and Far East—and leave it at that. But that is to confuse the cart with the horse. It is not that the left hand is "bad" because it is used for this purpose, but rather that the hand is "bad" because it is left and so is selected for it. When an unconscious equivalence is made between sex-feces-incest-death, then this too adds to the discomfort already attached to what in Latin was called the *sinister* (left) hand. (Incidentally, that the practice of cleaning oneself with the left hand used to be common in England may be shown by the English vernacular term "cack-handed" (left-handed), perhaps from *cack,* which Webster's Third New International Dictionary gives as Middle English *cakken,* "from Latin *cacare;* akin to Greek *kakkan* to void excrement . . . and perhaps to Greek *kakos* bad.)

Some of my Western colleagues thought I was overly sensitive to local feelings about the use of the left hand in Africa. To prove my point, I carried out a survey with school children from all over Tanzania; the results were the same. To give or receive with the left hand was an insult. According to one African teacher, a child had to know the difference between the two hands by the time "he old enough to walk across a room and hand something to a est"—in other words, about the age of two. The left hand is , evil, dirty, unlucky, connected to witchcraft. Many older ple in the United States can remember having their left hands to their bodies to prevent their using them. Why this apparent

insistence on differentiating between two virtually identical parts of the body?

Once more the answer lies in the area of our old friends categorization and symbolism. Most humans are right-handed.

The institutionalization of behavior is a human universal which had a great adaptive value in evolution, i.e., if norms of conduct can be established for a particular society, it becomes much easier for that society to exercise controls over its members ("We do it this way because we have always done it this way"). Thus, if most humans are right-handed, then the left-handed minority must be coerced into being like everyone else. How better to do this than through verbal symbolic categories? Six centuries before the Christian era, the Greek philosopher and mathematician Pythagoras set this out clearly in a set of dualities or oppositions in a manner similar to those explicitly or implicitly accepted by most cultures even today:

Dark	Light
Night	Day
Evil	Good
West	East
Death	Life
Left	Right
Women	Men

In some languages, e.g., Hadza and Swahili, the very words for "right" and "left" mean "male" and "female." But did you ever hear of a "right-hand woman"? And check every restaurant you go in—you will find that if the men's and women's bathrooms are situated side by side, the men's is nearly always the right-hand door.

Beliefs about witchcraft, as I shall discuss further in the next chapter, always ascribe to witches the reverse of everything considered "right," correct, normal, proper, decent. Witches are believed to engage in acts that would be most likely to disrupt human society. These acts are also those that we most fear might be manifested in ourselves in our darkest imaginings: incest, sexual perversions, killing those closest to us, cannibalism. Many regard the communion service of the Christian churches as a form of ritual cannibalism, which indeed it is; but if we recall that something which is reversed in a controlled manner for ritual purposes is believed, because of the human obsession with categorization, to generate great mystical power, then the point of the communion service becomes clear. Outside the ritual setting, it would be considered witchcraft; within, it is mystically overwhelmingly powerful to the believer.

If right is good and left bad, then men are pre-eminently categorized as everything good and desirable, and women are categorized as just the opposite—of everything evil and undesirable. Witches are everything the opposite of good: they even dance "widdershins" (counterclockwise); they are connected with darkness and death. And if you stopped a child in the street and asked it to describe a witch, what would the answer be? Probably "an old woman."

14

Witches and Mothers

The belief in witchcraft is a very ancient one which goes back, I believe, to the time when humans adopted farming as a way of life.[1] Belief in witchcraft accounts for what otherwise would appear meaningless and arbitrary. In most Third World countries (and in the West until Pasteur), the average expectation of life was about forty years or less. About half of all children born died before they were five, and many more before they were adult. Today we recognize that there is a feedback between mind and body: that although bacteria and viruses certainly exist, they sometime only seem to attack those who are psychologically vulnerable too. If unconsciously you feel sorry for yourself, in need of sympathy, hate your work, don't want someone to go away—a multitude of reasons—you may be afflicted by a cold or flu. This is what gives the witchcraft explanation some validity. Witchcraft is about hatred, envy, covetousness, spite, malice. If you feel that someone is directing any of these at you—and, of course, you may well really be projecting *your* feelings onto the person you suspect—then you may easily get sick. If you really believe, as many people in the world do, that death only occurs because of someone's malevolence, then you may die if you believe someone is bewitching you.

A young African woman assistant of mine, a graduate of an

American university, unwittingly expressed the reality to me once. When I asked her if she believed in witchcraft, since she came from an area reputedly rife with it, she replied, "Oh yes! But you know, it's funny: my father doesn't believe in it so it can't hurt him!" Here once more we have the extraordinary power of the mind to affect the body through symbolic categorization. Say and believe, "I am bewitched! I'm going to die!" and sure enough you will die. People do every day in some countries. An autopsy would reveal nothing organically wrong, but someone has died all the same.

What people usually believe about witchcraft is that it exists as a psychic quality of which some people are possessed and some are not, somewhat as some people have blue eyes and some brown. A better analogy would be the ability to dowse for water, which some seem to be able to do and some not. It is often thought to be inherited: most often from mother to daughter. Alternatively, it is sometimes believed that one can *become* a witch. In the Christian tradition, the way for one to achieve this was by making a pact with the devil—that is, by reversing what is believed to be what one should do. Elsewhere, one may become a witch by performing one of the acts ascribed to witches. These are all the things most calculated to shatter the structure of the family: incest, wanton killing, and cannibalism.

Evans-Pritchard found that the Zande, in the Sudan, like most peoples, differentiate witchcraft from sorcery.[2] Witchcraft is believed to be a property of the person's physical-mental makeup. Sorcery is learned (remember Mickey Mouse as the "Sorcerer's Apprentice"?). Witches may be men, but most often they are thought to be women. Sorcerers may be women, but most often they are believed to be men. Thus, although both sorcerers and witches are evil, sorcerers who *learn* their wicked trade and master the use of spells and potions and hence achieve their status are intellectually more active than witches who are just naturally bad.

Like the men who "menstruated" voluntarily or the men who are believed to plug their anuses or the men who through circumcision are less smelly than women, we find that somehow men are made to appear qualitatively superior to women.

Beliefs about witchcraft never seem to bother people in gathering and hunting societies. These kinds of societies one can always leave if irritation and tension build up in one with another person. It is easy to go to another band or perhaps to go off in a smaller unit for a time. We can do the same. If you cannot bear your boss, your colleagues, your mother-in-law, it is possible to move to another company, another state, or even another country. For everyone between our condition and that of the gatherers and hunters, moving away is, if not impossible, at least extremely difficult because you are tied to the land on which you depend for your living. Therefore, you have to go on living with people you detest.

The norms for a society usually prescribe that brothers and sisters love and respect one another and their parents; the reality is that jealousy, envy, hatred, and spite are often present to a marked degree. If one constantly has to mask one's feelings and stifle one's anger, the almost inevitable psychological result will be depression. Other results may be headaches, ulcers, colitis—a whole range of complaints. These results produce the extraordinary irony that beliefs in witchcraft become self-fulfilling. One must always be restrained and well-mannered in case one should be suspected of being a witch. Conversely, one is always polite to other people in case they are witches. Therefore, one suffers from psychosomatic complaints brought about by always masking one's anger or frustration. But these complaints are often the classic symptoms of being bewitched! Thus, by the simple expedient of believing in witches and behaving accordingly, one has guaranteed the effects of their postulated existence.

When I first worked in rural Tanganyika I was greatly impressed with how polite and good-mannered everyone was. Most foreigners have the same impression. I was also impressed by the great solicitude for a sick person in the family or neighborhood: everyone would come to visit daily. It was only when I became an anthropologist and learned to ask different questions that I became disillusioned. I found that unless one visits a sick person every day, it will be assumed that one is the evil witch or sorcerer responsible for the sickness; unless one is polite, "normal," restrained, deferential at all times, the same is true.

One human universal is a proclivity to blame others for our misfortunes rather than ourselves. Whatever occurs is someone else's fault. If we add this to the restraint imposed partly by custom, partly by fears of being thought different, odd, nonconformist, and the very formal and authoritarian nature of many small-scale societies, then the reason for beliefs about witchcraft begins to be clear.

If we can grasp the stifling social atmosphere in which beliefs about witchcraft thrive like fungus in dark dank woods, how then are witches conceptualized? The British anthropologist Lucy Mair suggests there are two sorts of witches: "everyday" witches and "nightmare" witches.[3] The everyday witch is mean, petty, spiteful, inhospitable, stingy, unhelpful, greedy, doesn't share food and beer, lives a solitary life, either doesn't respond to or give greetings immediately or is over effusive. If someone is any of these, then in the dark moments of the night, it is easy to imagine the person might easily, secretly, be a nightmare witch. It would be interesting to plot a graph of how beliefs in witches decline with the presence of electric light and rise with the use of candles and poor, flickering lamps.

I asked a man with whom I was working once in Africa to tell me how he conceptualized witches. He thought for a moment, and then gave me the very same description recorded by another anthropologist, Roy Willis, for another people many hundreds of miles away. "Imagine a road at night," he said. "Two people are dancing on it naked: a man and a woman. But the man is hanging upside down on the woman's front, with his legs clasped behind her neck." After some of the musicals and ballets of the past fifteen years, this vision may not seem very shocking to us, but to the people in this culture it represents everything that is the reverse of what they see as the proper and normal order of things: people are out at night when one should be at home in bed with the door tightly shut (and no windows); they are naked, which one should never be except in the dark of one's own room with one's spouse; they are naked in the most public place possible. Finally, in what to them is the most awful reversal, the man is dependent on the woman.

Kings in some societies marry their sisters to prove their difference and mystical superiority to their subjects. Mary is mystically impregnated by the Holy Ghost, who is also her son. In the Roman Catholic Church, Jesus' body and blood is believed to be consumed in a rite which, if performed by ordinary persons, would be thought of as cannibalism. Killing may be a sin and a crime. Categorize the victim as an enemy, and the act may become ennobling. Think back to the English pantomime or the carnival: reverse the norm in a controlled way and it is not merely acceptable, but often mystically powerful. Reverse the norm in a way *un*controlled by society and once more the mystical power is believed to be unleashed, but in an illicit, dangerous, evil manner: for the benefit of the individual rather than that of society.

In many societies there is a strong belief that ancestral spirits discipline the living and mystically uphold the authority of the elders. The power that is used by the spirits is the very same power used by witches and sorcerers; but elders-ancestors are using it licitly; witches illicitly. To make an analogy: the "power" is available in the world to make humans sick or die. Elders tap into it via the ancestors, who are concerned to uphold the elders' authority and the norms of the society. Their tapping of the power is quite licit and approved, and it serves to keep younger men and all women firmly in line. Witches and sorcerers use the very same power, but it is as though they went out at night and put clips on the power lines illegally to channel the current to their evil ends.[4]

There is a branch of the feminist movement which, like many men of the J. Edgar Hoover type, see plots and conspiracies all around them. It may be comforting to explain one's subservient position in terms of a wicked plot that cheated one of one's rightful inheritance, but it is totally unnecessary: coercive force, rape, pollution rules, religious injunctions—what more is needed?

Yet people persist in clinging to myths about "matriarchy" even though every feminist anthropologist regards the idea as long ago exploded, and have even built up another strange mythology based on the idea that witches were early feminists. Some women actually believe that they *are* witches, belong to what they call "covens," practice what they call *wicca*, and see themselves as votaries of the Roman goddess Diana. It may be harmless gameplaying, but let us look briefly at this idea.

It all stems from the work of an English woman Egyptologist called Margaret Murray who wrote a book called *The Witch-cult in Western Europe* in 1921, which received a lot of popular acclaim. It would be instructive to analyze why it was so uncritically received at the time—perhaps because, in the aftermath of the slaughter of World War I, people were seeking for romantic ideas; perhaps because so many people had been sickened by the insistence of the clergy on both the Allied and German sides that God was on their side. The book was reissued by Oxford University Press in the late 1960s at a time when many young people, revolted by the bloody and corrupting involvement of the United States in Vietnam, were seeking answers in a range of mystical experiences. Yet no serious scholar now regards the Murray work as more than fantasy. These seekers after spirituality do not perceive that science is not the villain, but the misapplications of science sanctioned by the very religious systems that they are avidly pursuing.

It was Murray's hypothesis that the medieval witch trials in Europe were really an effort to suppress the worship of the old pre-Christian deities. While many old religious beliefs probably lingered on long after the forcible imposition of Christianity, it is unlikely that they survive the hundreds of years that passed before the witch trials, except in odd customs sanctioned by the Church, such as the Maypole rituals and the mummers and morris dancers who still are with us. One story brings out rather vividly the irrationality of ideas about the "Dianic cult." Again and again people in sixteenth-century England accused of witchcraft, many of whom were women, were tortured terribly and commanded to reveal the names of the deities they worshiped. All most could come up with were the names of Satan and the demons of Christian mythology. One poor old woman, pressed beyond endurance to reveal her spells in recently Protestant England, finally said "Three 'aves' and a creed."

The medieval witch trials in Europe were an example of the mass hysteria that seizes humans brought up in a rule-dominated way, who think that human problems must have some simple solution. Other examples of the same phenomenon have been the pogroms in Czarist Russia, the Stalinist purges in the Soviet Union of the 1930s, the McCarthy era of the 1950s in America, the "cultural revolution" of the 1960s in Communist China. Always there is some disaster for which an explanation must be provided—the Black Death of the fourteenth century and subsequent outbreaks of plague every ten years, the beginnings of the breakdown of feudalism, the disgust with the oppression and corruption of the Church—these were doubtless some of the reasons for the medieval witch trials. Perhaps in some cases, the cause of the disaster could be blamed on climatic changes and disastrous harvests.

Some of the feminists who support the Murray position, such as Barbara Ehrenreich, see the medieval trials as a device for controlling the power of women midwives and equate witches with herbalists, folk-medicine experts, and so on. No doubt some of these women *were* identified as witches. When one thinks of the number of women and babies who die at the time of childbirth or soon after (for instance, among eighty families with whom I worked in rural Tanzania in 1965–66 at least 4.6 per cent of all children born died as infants) often as a result of the administrations of traditional midwives in Third World countries, it is no surprise that midwives were often identified as witches by grief-stricken survivors. If it is supposed that the male medical establishment of the Middle Ages was trying to monopolize the obstetrics field, as it indeed has done today in America, this plainly is fantasy. In 1522 a Dr. Wertt of Hamburg, long after the witchcraft trials had reached their peak, was so desirous of seeing the birth of a child, from which all men had been rigorously excluded, that he dressed as a woman to accompany a midwife. He was detected and burnt at the stake. The first recorded book on midwifery was published by a man, Eucharius Roesslin, nine years before this, but it is believed that it was constructed from hearsay and that he never saw a birth.[5]

No, the reasons for the medieval witch trials must be sought in economic, climatic, and political areas. Consider the Black Death. It began in the Orient and moved inexorably west. In China 13 million people died, "India was almost depopulated [and] the population of the earth was reduced by a quarter in the space of a few years. Sixty millions of people died."[6] Every decade or so from 1347 onward, when it first reached Europe, there was another outbreak. It was centuries later before greater care in personal hygiene and garbage disposal brought a cessation to the scourge of plague. Fleas and rats were the carriers. Death on that scale had to be explained somehow. What better scapegoat than a new heresy—witchcraft—allegedly a worship of Satan involving all the sexual fantasies of the celibate priests of the admittedly misogynist Roman Catholic Church?

If bubonic plague were not enough, syphilis became epidemic in Europe in the sixteenth century and spread like wildfire. Whether it was, as some allege, brought back from the Americas by Columbus' crewmen or whether it was a new mutant form of an old European disease is still debatable. The point I wish to make, though, is that life in Europe was extremely insecure in terms of health, quite apart from the thousand and one minor ailments that caused pain, misery, and death to people still unaware of how the human body functioned for a very major reason—an ignorance fostered by the religious leaders, both Catholic and Protestant, who were busily seeking witches.

That midwives, herbalists, and folk-medical practitioners were among the thousands accused of witchcraft is probably true, but it was what they were believed to do rather than what they did that is important. Human minds love oppositions—dark-light, female-male, evil-good—as Pythagoras chronicled so long ago (see above, Chapter 13). If one has a God who is all-good, rather than the kinds of deities held responsible for both good and evil elsewhere, then, logically, there has to be a devil to explain the evil in the world. By the process of ritual reversal, we have the devil worshiped instead of God and a belief in rituals like the Black Mass. In this, it was alleged, the Lord's Prayer is said backwards, black candles are used, and everything done in reverse. Of course, what is important to grasp is that there were no witches, are no witches, nor ever will be any witches. They only exist in imagination, though imagination can bring very concrete results. Admittedly, there are people around who call themselves "Satanists," who self-consciously do all these things for some kind of thrill. Rather like the young men who burnt the American flag during the Vietnam war, showing clearly that they recognized its symbolism, the Satanists plainly believe in God.

But why have women so often been identified as witches?

The answer is, I think, complex. One reason is the omnipresent male envy of females of which I have spoken. Envy often wraps itself in some rationalization.

The second and perhaps most important reason of all lies in child rearing. It cannot be separated from the facts of childbirth and human evolution. Many of our psychological difficulties in life stem from the very rapid evolution of humans. Only a million and a half years ago our hominid ancestors had heads of not much more than half our present cranial capacity, that is, about 900 cc compared to the present *Homo sapiens* average of 1,400 cc (and 900 cc seems to have been unusually large: most of the *Homo erectus* skulls were much smaller).[7] The present *Homo sapiens* brains range in size, from 1,000 cc (absolute minimum) up to 1,600 cc, imposes certain requirements. To get a baby's head whose brain is going to grow that large to pass through a female pelvis, one of two things have to happen: either the pelvis must be so wide that birth can take place easily with a fairly mature infant, as it does with most cows in a short space of time; or the child must be born physically very immature and with a still-soft skull. As we know, the latter alternative is the one which evolution produced. This has a number of results, all of which need to be considered at once like the objects kept in the air by a juggler. Since this is manifestly impossible, we shall have to take them one at a time, but ideally they should be taken all together.

If you have ever seen the birth of a calf or a foal you will notice a great difference between its condition and that of the newborn human child. Within minutes it is up on its feet and walking around—clumsily and awkwardly, but nevertheless walking. In a few weeks it is running around. Within two years it is physically and sexually mature. Contrast this with a human infant. It is usually about a year before it reaches the ability to stand on its feet that is reached by a calf in its first five minutes after birth and several more years before it has the mobility that a calf develops within a few weeks.

Among the nomadic, pastoral Masai of East Africa, an extremely tough, hardy and independent people, seven-year-old boys are sent out to help with the herding and seven-year-old girls help their mothers with fetching water and firewood. The Masai have no time for pampering their children, but even so, they see seven years as being the earliest possible age at which one could expect a child to be mature enough to carry out tasks of this kind. Returning to our hypothetical calf, by this age a female would probably have already given birth to several calves or long ago would have fulfilled its destiny in steaks and hamburgers if it were male.

Most Westerners in farming areas would consider seven as

being a very tender age for a boy to be out herding sheep and
goats, but it can be done. Even so, a seven-year-old child could
hardly be expected to cope with all the problems of life. If Westerners in general are looking for sexual maturity, they would
have to wait a further seven years. By this time our cow may be a
great-grandmother. Full physical strength is not attained with humans for yet another seven years, by which time our elderly cow
has probably become ground beef.

With humans, a child *has* to be totally dependent on adults for
at least seven years and would find it difficult to survive by itself
for about seven more years. It is inevitable that a child will be
subjected to the authority of some adults, probably its parents, for
many years. We have seen the effects of a stern, rule-oriented upbringing in producing potentially cruel and sadistic people, but we
need to go back further in time.

Because of the human infant's utter helplessness, it can initially,
like all mammals, only receive food by suckling. It is also quite
incapable of controlling the evacuation of its bowels and bladder, and, in fact, even when it has achieved the muscular control
needed, it still has to be taught to exercise it to achieve the quality
of humanness commonly taken for granted. Severely retarded
children may never achieve this control. Those animals most
closely associated with humans for thousands of years—dogs and
cats—can be, as we put it, "housebroken," (though horses have
no sense of social occasion).

The human animal, then, not only has to master control over
bladder and bowels; it also has to learn where and when it is considered appropriate to empty them; it has to learn the positions
considered appropriate—sitting, squatting, standing—by its particular culture. Most important of all, I believe, it has to learn to
clean itself after defecation. The incalculably important results of
this necessity form part of my hypothesis as to why humans universally regard sex as dirty and threatening. Dirty, because
mothers have in the main found it hard to conceal their disgust toward urine and feces, particularly the latter. This attitude is inevitably extended to the genitals and sex in general. Threatening, because of our knowledge of death acquired through language, and
the association made between the stench of feces and the horror
we feel for a putrefying corpse. The small infant, as yet happily

unaware of death, decay, or the facts of sex, has no horror of feces: on the contrary, small children (and some mentally deranged adults) play with their feces.

As the child matures and begins to be aware of its bodily functions, its mind too is becoming active. It feels aggressive, and, as we saw, Gregory Rochlin suggests that because of the child's early awareness of the mortality of itself or its guardians, any threat to the self arouses an aggressive response. But helpless as the child is because of its undeveloped limbs and muscles, it is frustrated by its total inability to do anything to defend itself. This situation parallels that of people in agricultural societies contrasted with hunter-gatherers. In the latter case, one can always move away if relations with kin and neighbors become insupportable, irritating, or filled with animosity. Not so for the farming peoples: whatever their feelings about their siblings, parents, in-laws, spouse, neighbors. There is very little they can do about it because they are so dependent on the co-operation and assistance of others in the production of their food.

Just so for the child. However angry it may get, it can do almost nothing about it because of its dependency on the adults for food and protection. It is this total dependency that no doubt produces the fantasies of witches and demons. Think how many tales for children deal with giants, ogres, monstrous persons— who are always defeated in the end. I am sure many of us recall the common terror dream of childhood when a monstrous towering figure looms threateningly, growing ever taller until it fills the sky. Here is the stuff not merely of giants and ogres, but of gods and demons, always something like humans, usually enormously large and awe-inspiring. Many of us, even as adults, recall being in hospital completely helpless and supine and how very tall the nurses appeared. And our astonishment at finding them normal size, or even short, when we recovered and stood up straight again? Is it then surprising that adults, who are indeed five or six time the size of a baby, appear to be absolutely monstrous to the child lying in its crib? Turning to the question of toilet training, the psychoanalyst Geza Roheim noted that all children everywhere will manufacture mental demons out of their parents, regardless of the method of toilet training used. However, the degree of severity or tolerance with which toilet training is approached, the age at which it is initiated and completed—all these will undoubtedly influence the neurotic nature of these fantasies.

But this is not all. The mother or whoever cares for the small child has the potential enormously to enhance the witch fantasies of the child through her treatment of it. This is why the question of day-care centers is not just a purely mechanical one of providing a room and a sitter. It is crucial that there should not be frequent changes of the person caring for the child, or its feelings of insecurity will increase greatly. Combine impotence with insecurity and the child will have future problems as well as present nightmares and witch fantasies. It might well be that the day-care center supervisor is a much better guardian than the actual mother but we must make sure that he or she is really competent, and that there are not changes of personnel.

An interesting research project, following the work of Theodor Adorno and his colleagues who studied the development of the authoritarian personality discussed in Chapter 12, would be to examine the attachment of those brought up in a rule-oriented home to fantasy beliefs. We can see how the helpless child creates fantasy witches, ogres, and giants because of its active imagination combined with its inability to influence what is happening to it. Comparably, people in small-scale farming societies, unable both to deal with the tensions and frustrations of living with people from whom there is no escape and to influence the natural conditions that control their survival—rainfall, drought, locusts—manufacture a fantasy world of incestuous, perverted, murderous and cannibalistic witches. A child brought up in a rigid, rule-dominated home environment which he or she is unable to control will similarly manufacture fantasy witches and demons. Not only are these people prone to fantasy stereotypes about other racial and religious groups; they will be very prone to look for something like a witch on whom they can blame every misfortune.

Similarly, the rigid structure of rules rather than principles, since it promotes a belief in the omnipotence of those in authority and a tendency toward blind obedience, also encourages belief in religious systems that reflect these attitudes: the kind of intolerant systems that create sharp dichotomies between good and evil, angels and demons, heaven and hell—the sort of systems that establish rigid categories that must be accepted without question, that result in the beliefs in pollution and sin, and find ideas, persons, things, foods, clothes, hair styles, and so on threatening if they do not fall into the established categories.

Not only can child rearing, then, create the environment in which prejudice, intolerance, and cruelty will thrive. It can also produce people who will be politically simplistic and who follow parties that divide the world into heroes and villains, like fascism and communism do. Evidently there will be different levels of fantasy and belief. The rigorously unbending and strict background will tend to produce the conservative or fascist bigot or racial fanatic. The less rigorous but still rule-oriented will produce attraction to irrational beliefs like astrology; it may too create what some consider charming literature like that of the English scholars C. S. Lewis or J. R. R. Tolkien, which a little careful analysis will show to be faintly fascist in orientation, certainly extremely sexist.

The enduring fascination of works like Tolkien's *The Lord of the Rings* lies in its manipulation of childhood fantasy themes— of past golden ages; of tyranny and oppression; of a search for the remembered glories which are securely guarded by awful spider-mothers; dragon-fathers that prevent access to the treasure inside the mountain-mother's womb; terrible magicians-fathers who live in great tower-phalli. And so on. One wonders whether Tolkien was consciously aware of the symbolism involved in his stories. Perhaps not. An earlier generation may recall the adventure stories of the English writer H. Rider Haggard, which used much of the same symbolism and inevitably had a dramatic emotional impact.

In particular societies we have very direct evidence of the results of certain kinds of child rearing. Margaret Mead and her former husband Gregory Bateson gave us one such case history. In 1942 they produced a huge photographic record of life in Bali entitled *Balinese Character*. To the popular mind the very name "Bali" conjures up a vision of an earthly paradise, where gentle, physically lovely people live a tranquil life of ease and gaiety. Yet it was in Bali not many years ago that the gentle, sweet-natured populace suddenly arose and engaged in an orgy of killing of their own people because, it was rumored, Communists were going to take over the island. Thousands were killed. How did such a kindly, lovely people spawn such a horror? Does it, as doubtless the Austrian naturalist Konrad Lorenz and the American writer Robert Ardrey would believe, just go to show that humans are naturally aggressive? Not at all. What it does show is how easy it is to mold the human character in childhood so that a murderous potential comes into being.

If we study the pictures and written text of *Balinese Character,* the answer is there plain to see. Part of the child raising, which is probably justified as building character, consists of an extraordinary alternation. First, the mother teases the child until it is utterly enraged or reduced to frantic weeping. Then the mother changes completely and cossets and cuddles the child to comfort its distress. When it is calmed, the other pattern of teasing starts again until rage and misery is induced. This is followed by further cosseting. What is the result? The people are externally gentle and kind and abhor violence. Doubtless one remembers the kind, loving mother as an ideal pattern rather than the tormentor. But somewhere in the brain is the legacy of enraged frustration—of impotence to prevent torment from the person one most loved and trusted and in whom one *had* to repose trust because of one's helplessness and inability to survive alone. This murderous rage is there still in the brain. Unconsciously, it reveals itself in feelings about the figure of the mother. In the ritualized dances and plays and in traditional carvings of Bali, again and again we find the terrifying and loathsome figure of Rangda the witch. In the plays she is always vanquished, just as the witch in the European folk tales is. But do we have to have a witch at all, one wonders? Does the mother have to appear is this guise, no matter how kindly and loving, just because she is physically so gigantic to the tiny child and because the child has to be frustrated by its very powerlessness?

One of the most influential strands of my childhood was total subjection to a group of about six boys who made my life between five and eleven an endless alternation between physical torture (which was carefully calculated never to leave visible marks) and grudging warmth. Never able to tell anyone for fear of terrifying reprisals, life was made bearable by a loving and extremely happy home, but the scars remain still with me. And I know that I have the potential of perhaps murderous rage toward someone being cruel to a helpless person. Recognition of my potential and its origin at an intellectual level has always allowed me to remain in control. Others are not always so fortunate.

Another major reason for conceptualizing women as witches comes, in my view, from weaning. This is particularly so in those societies that practice a long post-partum taboo on sex, so that the child is with the mother night and day for up to three years and has almost permanent access to the comfort of its mother's breast. At the end of some specified period, as we have seen earlier, the child is evicted from its mother's bed and bosom and replaced by the father. The source of all warmth, comfort, nourishment, and love is found to be untrustworthy, treacherous, and rejecting. We all know the pain that follows rejection by someone we loved and trusted. How much more traumatic it must be to the still helpless child. The child's misery is usually compounded by physical distress from malnutrition, lacking the once source of protein, however small, and transferred often to a totally carbohydrate diet based on the logic that cornstarch in water looks like milk.

If all these possible reasons for seeing a witch in the mother are not enough, there remains one more.

The very rapid evolution of *Homo sapiens,* and particularly the development of the size of the brain, has had three effects: babies are totally helpless and dependent; they have a disproportionately large head compared to the rest of their bodies; they have a head in which the bones are both still soft and not fully joined together. Were all these conditions not fulfilled, it would be physically impossible for children to be born except by Caesarian section. Freud was very aware of these facts and speculated that every form of human anxiety stems from that caused to the infant by being physically born the normal way. His associate Otto Rank, who later broke with him, regarded the process of passing from the warmth, comfort, and security of the uterus to the harsh outer world through the birth canal as being so supremely painful and terrifying to the infant that it gives rise to a whole range of adult complaints from asthma to migraine to claustrophobia.[8]

Rank found that patients in analysis became, as he put it, spiritually reborn as children of the analyst. Toward the end of analysis, patients had frequent dreams of the womb, and "in dreams and reactions they put themselves back into the position of the unborn." How many of us have not adopted a fetal position in bed or under extreme mental duress?

The great point of Rank's theory is that because the physical experience of birth is so agonizing—the expulsion from the womb, the pressure on the body of the mother's tremendous muscular contractions, the compressing of the delicate skull—we successfully repress and continue to deny the possibility that we were born by emerging from the mother's genitals. This, he suggests rather persuasively, is what accounts for all the curious theories about children being brought by storks, or found under bushes or in flowers. Similarly, he shows how, in so many heroic tales, the hero is born in some unnatural manner—being cut from the mother's navel; springing from a father's skull like Athena from Zeus' head, or Sin from Satan's in *Paradise Lost;* leaping from a gap in the mother's side, like the Buddha. He also suggests that it is the actual though suppressed memory of that painful passage down the birth canal which accounts for the frightening sensations some of us experience when we enter a tunnel, look down a long empty passage, look down from a tower or similar high place or down a well, or enter the body of an airplane. Some people have a terrifying feeling that the walls in a narrow street are closing in on them, and this Rank equates with the contractions of parturition, linking it with myths of heroes successfully getting through threatening walls, cliffs, pillars, or tunnels.

The experience of being blissfully secure by floating in the womb contributes to myths of a golden age, a Paradise from which one was driven. Children constantly seek a way back and find security by sometimes curling up in closets and similar places. Rank goes so far as to suggest that the origins of masochism lie in a "conversion of the pains caused by parturition (fantasy of being beaten) into pleasurable sensations." This, he claims, is the origin of the custom of swaddling children and the fascination of some people with bondage. An extreme sadist like Jack the Ripper probably personifies the person whose infantile curiosity about being inside the mother and memory of the pain of expulsion cause him to rip open a woman's belly in the wish to get back.

This may seem farfetched, but consider the hatred of women

which seems to be evidenced by the so-called Boston Strangler in 1962–63 or the murderer of Kitty Genovese in 1964. Susan Brownmiller records one verbatim account given by a sergeant of Marines. After telling how it was routine for his men to rape all the Vietnamese women in a captured village—"It wasn't like they were human . . . They were a gook or a Commie and it was okay"—he told of how a woman had been shot by a American sniper and begged for water. The officer ordered the men to kill her. This they attempted by stabbing her breasts and stuffing an entrenching tool up her vagina. She still begged for water. So they pulled out the entrenching tool, pushed in a branch of a tree, and, finally, mercifully, shot her. What Brownmiller's account makes clear is that this was no isolated incident.[9]

Many people find the idea of the birth trauma hard to accept. How could one possibly remember that? they ask. Consider then this poem by a third-grader reported by a poet working with small children in upstate New York.

> When I dreamed
>   I was a squirrel. . . .
>   I was born in a dark
> hole of a tree. I woke up with
> fear. I heard a shriek. Momma,
> Momma, I cried. The sound was
> silence. Momma had died. Here I
> am in a strange world. I heard
> another noise, this time it was
> Momma. I searched up, down, all
> around, I could not find Momma. I
> soon died. I found Momma in heaven.
> She was crying for me. I was coming
> to an end, Momma wasn't there anymore
> I cried forever. Because of
> Momma.

The regular teacher of the class was amazed and rather disturbed. The child was, she said, usually totally withdrawn and did not like to talk or play with others. Of course, she may have been expressing the misery of a child who has no mother. But it is rather interesting since the child's mother had died giving birth to her.

Rank suggested that the fascination all children have with large animals stems from their curiosity about pregnancy. How many parents have children who are excited by dinosaurs? He suggested that the same curiosity and desire of children to return to the womb is shown by the universal game of hide-and-seek; that swings, seesaws, rocking horses, and rocking chairs derive their attraction for children from their similarity to the sensation of being in the womb; that the fear of and fascination with predatory birds and beasts of prey that children (and adults?) have come from the desire to be eaten and so get back inside a body; that the fear that most women and some men have of small animals like mice, rats, snakes, and frogs comes from these creatures' ability to disappear into small holes and thus a fear that they might enter one's body and grow. Certainly the snake and the frog are both phallic symbols—hence the story of the princess and the frog.

Rank thought that boys believe that everyone has a penis because they wish to deny the existence of the female genitals which caused so much pain. He recounts how many legends exist about the terrors of the toothed vagina or the idea of a hidden trunk which can lash out. Most balanced people, he believed, come to terms with their fears, usually through a successful sex life. It is the ideal of being the first to be able to make a return to the womb that puts so high a value on virginity and defloration. Some male homosexuality, he suggested, is due to "the abhorrence of the female genitals," which only allows an image of woman as "the maternal organ of birth."

Unresolved traumas of birth, weaning and toilet training make the attribution of witchcraft to women and the apparently irrational hatred that so many men hold toward them comprehensible.

Rank's book *The Trauma of Birth,* in which these speculations and theories are explained, appeared in 1929 and some psychologists today find it exaggerated. Undoubtedly some of his explanations of cultural history seem rather farfetched, but his basic idea—that the experience of birth is traumatic—has many modern adherents, chief among whom are Arthur Janov and his associates in the school of "primal therapy."[10] Janov's ideas concern not only the birth trauma, but any other childhood experiences that produce pain. "Each time we open up a neurotic we find Pain," he notes. His observations have a very direct relevance to the questions of child rearing that I have discussed, particularly the universal mythic idea of woman as witch. He writes: "Relatively little fear can make one fearful of authority." If this is true, then how fearful of authority can overwhelming fear, pain, humiliation, and coercion make one? He goes on to say that "relatively little anger at mother can make one dislike women." Consider then the rage engendered by traumatic weaning, eviction from bed and bosom, and the kinds of practices found in Bali. Great repressed anger at one's mother, he considers, can make one want to kill women.

Mother as mother one could not kill, but label the person "gook" or "Commie," as the Marine sergeant mentioned before did, and suddenly the repressed rage of childhood can come leaping out armed and murderous. The Balinese customarily restrained their fury, but label someone a Communist, immediately the unthinkable—killing—becomes more than a possibility—it becomes a duty. And mothers trained all of us to do our duty. Pain, Janov reminds us, can be psychological as well as physical. A combination could be devastating: "In a figurative sense an overload of Pain shuts the gates and redirects the energy elsewhere—from 'mother' to 'women.'" Hatred and inner rage lead some people to take pleasure in pain, as can be seen in the faces of boxing fans. Just look at their expressions. And supposing public executions were to be reinstituted tomorrow, do you imagine that a mass audience would be lacking?

Janov has dedicated his work to two persons: Frederick Leboyer and A. S. Neill. The former is the American obstetrician who delivers babies in a muted light, with no haste, and who allows the infant to lie on its mother's belly until the pulse in the umbilical cord stops beating. His efforts seem to be rewarded by an incalculable reduction of the birth trauma. Photographs of children born by this method show them all smiling serenely in a manner which evokes an involuntary answering smile from the viewer. What a stark contrast to the look of utter misery usually seen on the faces of newborn babies.

Neill, who died in 1973, was the radical British educator who founded a progressive school called Summerhill in 1924 in Suffolk. At this school no rules are made by adults; children from five to eighteen meet weekly to decide on how the school should be conducted. The philosophy of the school is that real education should make children "self-directive" so that they would become happy adults.[11] Children are never required to do anything they do not wish to do and can do anything they wish as long as they do not infringe on the rights of others. That was the key. The aim to produce highly moral people who were moral because they understood the crucial necessity for morality in a world where we have to live in social groups, have to depend on one another, have to assume trust (no matter how often we are betrayed). Not behaving because of the fear of God, of hell, of the rulings of some person claiming divine authority, but only because one understood and accepted rationally the need to restrain appetites in the interests of all, which ultimately means one's own.

The main critics of Summerhill have always said that children raised like this would never be able to cope with the "real" world. Is this true? Not at all, says Emmanuel Bernstein, who interviewed fifty people who had attended Summerhill. Most found no difficulty in adjusting to authority and structure and in fact seemed better at dealing with them than most children reared in "traditional" schools. If transferred to other schools, these children had no difficulty in accepting studies presented in a different way. The only problem most had was in understanding why other children stopped working if the teacher left the room and why they were afraid of the teacher and principal. According to Bernstein, "Yet, teachers never found these former Summerhill students rude: these children made their needs known in polite ways."

Summerhill graduates' ability to handle authority and responsibility continues into adulthood. They seemed to have happy and successful marriages and were bringing their own children up in a self-directed way. "Relationship between child and parent was warm: the children happy and spontaneous," writes Bernstein.

One somehow does not see children born under the Leboyer method, weaned lovingly, interacting with both parents, and being educated under Neill's principles inventing witches like the Rangda of Bali, the terrifying mother goddess Kali of India. Nor can one see them being remembered for horrors like pogroms, Auschwitz, or My Lai. Would they equate sex, incest, and death? Perhaps. But it could probably be in a muted and nondestructive way.

15

Summary and Conclusion

What has all this been about? One tries to bring together the really important points in a coherent brief synopsis, to find that there are several themes when one had thought there was only one. Let me go back to my starting point of the three episodes and from them attempt to build a unified theory. There was the first day in the British Army and the ritual haircut; the coming-out of the Luguru maiden after her long incarceration in the dark; there was Soho's "Filthiest Show in Town."

I have shown that whatever else may be labeled as human universals in behavior, there is no doubt of the universality of language and, arising out of that, a knowledge of our own mortality. Also seemingly universal are fears and anxiety about sex and incest, the concept of incest, of marriage, and of kinship being rooted also in the capacity for categorization inherent in human language. Because we know about death, we fear it. Present in our cultural memory (if not our genetic memory) is the knowledge that corpses rapidly putrefy and produce odors that we, alone among animals, regard as disgusting. Because of our posture, gait, and partially our diet, humans have to clean themselves after defecation, an action that has to be learned. The nature of feces is disgusting to humans, though not to other animals, presumably because of the association made between the smell of feces and putrefying bodies. Thus many mothers inculcate in their children the notion not only that feces, and indeed other bodily emissions, are dirty, but that everything connected with sex is dirty. At one level, then, sex reminds us of death. At another level, all aspects of sexuality prove to be anxiety-provoking because of the perpetual ability of males and females to engage in sex, unlike other animals that have oestrus cycles and mating seasons. The anxiety arises from a fear that incest might take place and thus disrupt and shatter the social structures we have erected based on a prohibition of sex between close kin, a concept of marriage, and the idea of parents, siblings, grandparents, cousins, uncles and aunts, nephews and nieces. The very idea of incest, marriage, and kinship is, as I have noted, totally dependent on language. If sex reminds us of incest, it also reminds us of death because we connect sex with feces and feces with death.

Here then is our "Filthiest Show," our "dirty" joke, our "dirty old man," our "feelthy" postcards. Conversely, we have seen that in many religions, celibacy, virginity, and chastity are extolled as being the essence of spiritual life. If death equals sex, then logically life equals the eschewing of sex. An interesting reflection might be that in Western society and other complex, heterogeneous societies, one finds sexual jokes and pornography, neither of which occur in simple societies where sexual initiation rites take place.* It is established that humans, like apes, do not know naturally how to perform the act of sex. Apes usually learn by physical observation since there is no question of shyness. In societies that have initiation rites, boys, particularly, are given explicit instruction, often with simulated female genitals or chickens used for demonstration. In complex societies where the rites do not take place, it may be that sexual jokes and/or pornography have the function, however inadequate, of acquainting the young with how to perform sexually, which otherwise would be a matter of ignorance to them.

Why did I focus on initiation rites? Because the anxieties surrounding sex exhibit their maximum expression through this medium. We saw that liminality always causes unease because of the inability to categorize. With initiation rites at or around adoles-

* Bawdy jests and remarks abound in simple societies, but one does not commonly find the long fictional tale, e.g., of the "traveling salesman" variety.

cence, not only is the liminal transition period of the rites dangerous, but the participants are dealing with social dynamite: the
transferral of humans from an asexual to a sexual world.

There are other human emotions and characteristics which
come into play too. We explored Bruno Bettelheim's suggestions
about male envy of female procreativity as a counterpoise to the
more commonly discussed penis envy. Part of the explanation for
the confinement of the Luguru girl at puberty seems to lie in the
anxiety of males to prove that they too can bear children or,
rather, adults, which in their own eyes makes them superior to
women, who merely bear babies. It is worth considering whether
the male conceptual invention of penis envy is not just as much a
flaunting of male superiority in society as a real female envy. That
the penis forms a useful symbol for emphasizing the relative statuses of males and females in most societies is hardly ques-
tionable. Wherever we turn, we find phallic symbols representing
authority: maces of office, swords of honor, lances, towers, steeples, minarets, military helmets, and, supreme symbol for many,
the gun. Perhaps it is worth reflecting that those who are gun fanatics, collect knives or swords, or go in for Corvettes and Jaguars are really telling the world how anxious they are about their
own sexual inadequacies, much as the young men who mount
stereo speakers at their windows and regale the public with blasts
of unwanted music are behaving like roosters who seek to boost
their egos with noise.

Certainly Bettelheim's idea about envy by each of the other's
attributes receives considerable support from cases like the "menstruating men" of Wogeo, the Gisu equation of male circumcision
with childbirth, and the Luguru symbolic gestation and rebirth of
girls from men. We should recall that in each of these cases the
effect was also to appear to prove men the superiors of women.
To repeat my previous point, there seem to be more instances of
overt male envy of women than the reverse. Thus the much
debated penis envy seems to be a device designed by males to reassure them of their own position by a belief that women envy
them. One is faintly reminded of the beliefs about anus-plugging
in East Africa. We might also recall that instances of males dressing and acting as females are infinitely more common than the
reverse, particularly in the West. In the case of the English panto-

mime, although a woman does take the part of the "principal boy," her costume is designed to accentuate her feminine characteristics.

A great deal of the book has been concerned with authority and its perverted servant, authoritarianism. Robert Seidenberg's exploration of the effect of the rigid application of the taboo on incest gives part of the key. Those societies, and those persons in society, who are harsh, rigid, and inflexible about incest almost inevitably produce children who in turn will be afraid of sex with their own people and be attracted to but despise and be disgusted by sex with other groups. Not that I am suggesting for one moment that we should abolish the prohibition on incest per se. Rather, it is the constellation of attitudes that go with a harsh inculcation of the taboo and which prove to be cybernetic in nature. One finds not merely a horror and fear of incest but some or most of the following traits: a fear of nakedness; a fear that siblings and parents should see one another naked; a total avoidance of discussion of anything to do with sex within the family (though frequently a great attachment to prurient jokes and discussion outside the family in an all-male or all-female milieu); a great shyness and use of euphemism surrounding urination and defecation and even more around menstruation; an imputation of sexual irregularity and looseness to other economic classes, ethnic or religious groups, and nations; a use of euphemism to describe everything to do with death. Where a culture continues to hold such beliefs, then ideas about witchcraft will often be common. Finally, there will always be strict rules about the head and hair. One could predict with some degree of certainty that those men who insist on a crew cut for themselves or their sons have serious problems with their own sexuality.

Seidenberg's observations and my deductions from them lead straight to the outright discussion of authoritarianism by Theodor Adorno et al. They showed the crucial distinction in child rearing between rules and principles, the latter leading to rational self-control and tolerance and the former to prejudice, bigotry, and cruelty. We saw that those societies that provide harsh and cruel initiation rites have indeed child-rearing practices that would tend to produce authoritarian personalities, who, it should be noted, delight in being punished as well as giving out punishment. We saw, too, that this situation is enormously heightened in many simple societies by a long post-partum taboo on sex and exclusive mother-child sleeping arrangements. This virtually guarantees paternal hostility to the child, since the child takes his place in the mother's bed for from one to three years. It also guarantees great animosity of the child for the father, who forcibly replaces the child at the end of this time. Feelings toward mothers are similarly warped by what must appear as betrayal and rejection. In both cases a fertile ground is created for a lack of trust and a suspicion of those supposedly near and dear, a ground in which the seeds of witchcraft beliefs can germinate and flourish.

The latent possibility of rebellion against the parents' generation under these circumstances, when the children reach sexual and physical maturity, is effectively quelled in many cases by a punitive male initiation rite, which often involves some form of symbolic castration: circumcision, subincision, cutting the head, and almost invariably cutting off the head hair. Even in our own society this latter punishment is still inflicted on army and other service recruits. A recent article in *Ms.* magazine gave an account of a young woman going to West Point. Exactly as in my own case, although she had had her hair cut short in preparation, she still had to have a further haircut. To the authoritarian person, the possibility of rebellion is always a frightening prospect which must constantly be watched for, not seeing that it is his own attitude and behavior that creates the possibility. It is true that in the West we no longer have a long post-partum taboo since we have bottles and weaning foods, but there is no doubt that some of us go on producing authoritarian personalities, whose potential for danger to other people is enormously enhanced in complex societies with sophisticated weapons and surveillance technology. We need only to glance over our shoulders to see Hitler and his servant Eichmann, Stalin and his successors, and the other leaders of fascist and communist countries. Authoritarianism has always sought its solutions of problems by force; reason has no place in its schema. Under the skin, the professional military and the IRA or PLO terrorists are brothers.

But what about women? All this has concerned itself with boys and men. As I tried to explain, it is very unlikely that women could prove a threat in most societies for a variety of reasons, though, of course, there are plenty of authoritarian women around —no one male or female, black or white, has any monopoly on the ability to oppress or exploit. In most nonindustrial societies women have usually been married off at puberty—ostensibly to preserve their virginity. This is partially because women have been regarded as a form of property, partially because of fears in a small society that incest might occur and so the social fabric to unravel. Thus a pattern of male dominance has been extremely easy to establish, based largely on overwhelming physical force. Where any possibility of female autonomy might occur, we find rites like those of the Luguru, well designed to prevent any possibility of rebellion, as with boys.

To ensure the relative positions of the sexes, we find the additional and extremely powerful weapon of pollution rules, rules based in many cases on human fears about sexuality and, I suggest, death. We also have the problem that because human evolution occurred so rapidly, traumatic birth leads to men's fears and anxieties about sex and women. Add to this the fact that humans have to be toilet-trained, and we have a stage set for beliefs about female witches.

Is there any hope for humans? Are we booby-trapped by all this, so that the possibility of more tolerant relations between the sexes or between ethnic, religious, or national groups is doomed to failure? I would rate our chances of success as being directly related to our understanding of all these matters. Most directly, I would say that the primal enemy for a reasonable future for humanity lies in our ability to understand and eliminate authoritarianism. Then a true age of reason could dawn. But looking at the attitudes of most major religions and at the power of political parties of the extreme left or right, the prognosis is not very bright.

Notes

Chapter 2

1. James L. Brain, "Sex, Incest and Death: Initiation Rites Reconsidered," *Current Anthropology*, Vol. 18, No. 2, June 1977.

2. Mary Douglas, *Purity and Danger* (London: Routledge and Kegan Paul, 1966).

3. Marvin Harris, *Cows, Pigs, Wars and Witches* (New York, Random House, 1974).

4. Ernst Cassirer, *Language and Myth* (New York: Dover Publications, 1946).

5. Ibid., p. 45.

6. Unni Wikan, "Man Becomes Woman: Transsexuals in Oman as a Key to Gender Roles," *Man*, Vol. 12, No. 2, 1977, pp. 304–19.

Chapter 3

1. Herman Feifel, ed., *The Meaning of Death* (New York: McGraw-Hill, 1959), p. 122.

2. Paul Theroux, *The Picture Palace* (Boston: Houghton Mifflin, 1978).

3. Herman Feifel, ed., op. cit.

4. Myra Bluebond-Langner, critique of my article in *Current Anthropology*, cited above in note 1, Chapter 2.

5. Helmut Thielicke, *Death and Life* (Philadelphia: Fortress Press, 1970).

6. Gregory Rochlin, *Man's Aggressions* (Boston: Gambit, 1973).

240   NOTES TO PAGES 28-51

7. Herman Feifel, ed., op. cit.

8. Georges Bataille, *Eroticism,* trans. Mary Dalwood (London: Calder, 1962).

9. Rev. Robert G. Grant, Newsletter for "American Christian Cause," Pasadena, California.

10. Martin S. Weinberg, ed., *Sex Research: Studies from the Kinsey Institute* (New York: Oxford University Press, 1976).

11. John C. Messenger, "Sex and Repression in an Irish Folk Community," in Martin S. Weinberg, ed., op. cit.

12. John C. Messenger, "The Lack of the Irish," and Donald S. Marshall, "Too Much in Mangaia," *Psychology Today,* February 1971.

13. E. E. Evans-Pritchard, *Nuer Religion* (Oxford: Clarendon Press, 1956).

14. E. E. Evans-Pritchard, *Kinship and Marriage Among the Nuer* (Oxford: Clarendon Press, 1951).

15. Hans Cory, "The Buswezi," *American Anthropologist,* Vol. 57, 1955, pp. 923-52. (More correctly termed "Bacwezi.")

Chapter 4

1. Maxine Hong Kingston, *The Warrior Woman* (New York: Random House, 1975, Vintage Books, 1977).

2. If gods are indeed immortal, one wonders what happened to all the deities who became obsolete.

3. C. W. M. Hart and A. R. Pilling, *The Tiwi of North Australia* (New York: Holt, Rinehart and Winston, 1960).

4. It does seem that females and males are equally aroused by visual narrative material. See Ashton Barfield, "Biological Influences on Sex Differences in Behavior," in Michael S. Teitelbaum, ed., *Sex Differences* (New York: Doubleday/Anchor, 1976), p. 93.

5. NOW "Legal Defence and Education Fund Letter" of June 1978.

6. Jane Beckman Lancaster, "Sex Roles in Primate Society," in Teitelbaum, ed., op. cit., pp. 22-61.

7. See Richard Dawkins, *The Selfish Gene* (New York: Oxford University Press, 1976); for a genetic discussion relevant to this, see pp. 175-76.

8. Ibid., pp. 135-36.

9. Ibid., pp. 109-10.

10. Jane Beckman Lancaster, op. cit., pp. 22-61.

11. Peter J. Wilson, "The Promising Primate," *Man,* Vol. 10, 1975, pp. 5-20.

12. Dorothy Hammond and Alta Jablow, *Women in Cultures of the World* (Menlo Park, Calif.: Cummings Publishing, 1976).

Chapter 5

1. E. O. Wilson, *Sociobiology: The New Synthesis* (Cambridge, Mass.: Belknap Press of Harvard University Press, 1975).
2. Martin S. Weinberg, ed., *Sex Research*, p. 87.

Chapter 6

1. Otto Rank, *The Trauma of Birth* (New York: Harcourt, Brace, 1929), p. 60.
2. Book of Common Prayer: "Burial of the Dead."
3. John Gardner, *The Sunlight Dialogues* (New York: Knopf, 1972), pp. 413–14.
4. A. M. Hocart, *Caste: A Comparative Study* (New York: British Book Centre, 1951).
5. Richard Davey, *A History of Mourning* (London: Jays, 1890).
6. Jessica Mitford, *The American Way of Death* (Greenwich, Conn.: Fawcett Crest, 1963).
7. John Fowles, *Daniel Martin* (Boston: Little, Brown, 1977).
8. Saul Bellow, *Humboldt's Gift* (New York: Viking, 1973).
9. E. E. Evans-Pritchard, *Nuer Religion*.
10. M. J. Field, *The Search for Security* (Evanston, Ill.: Northwestern University Press, 1960).
11. Monica Wilson, *Rituals of Kinship Among the Nyakyusa* (London: Oxford University Press, 1957), p. 51.
12. John Gardner, *October Light* (New York: Knopf, 1976).
13. Geza Roheim, *Psychoanalysis and Anthropology* (New York: International Universities Press, 1950).
14. Clyde Kluckhohn, *Navaho Witchcraft* (Cambridge, Mass.: Peabody Museums, 1944).
15. V. S. Naipaul, *An Area of Darkness* (London: Deutsch, 1965).
16. Paul Theroux, *The Great Railway Bazaar* (Boston: Houghton Mifflin, 1975).
17. Martin S. Weinberg, ed., *Sex Research*, p. 219.
18. V. S. Naipaul, *India: A Wounded Civilization* (New York: Knopf, 1977).
19. Encyclopedia Americana, Vol. 20 (New York: Grolier, 1976), pp. 867–68.
20. Mary Gordon, *Final Payments* (New York: Random House, 1978).
21. Algernon Charles Swinburne, *Chorus from Atalanta*.

Chapter 7

1. Webster's Third New International Dictionary (Springfield, Mass.: G. & C. Merriam, 1966).

2. Edmund Leach, "Anthropological Aspects of Language: Animal Categories and Verbal Abuse," in Pierre Maranda, ed., *Mythology* (Baltimore: Penguin Books, 1972), pp. 39–68.

3. John Halverson, "Animal Categories and Terms of Abuse," *Man*, Vol. 11, No. 4, 1976, pp. 505–16.

4. E. E. Evans-Pritchard "Some Collective Expressions of Obscenity in Africa," *Journal of the Royal Anthropological Institute*, Vol. LIX, 1929, pp. 311–31.

Chapter 8

1. Robin Fox, *Encounter with Anthropology* (New York: Dell, 1975).

2. Simone de Beauvoir, *The Second Sex* (New York: Knopf, 1952), pp. 650–51.

3. Sigmund Freud, *Three Essays on the Theory of Sexuality*.

4. Sigmund Freud, Foreword, in Theodor Reik, *Ritual* (London: Hogarth Press, 1931).

5. Ralph Linton, *The Study of Man* (New York: Appleton-Century-Crofts, 1964), p. 334.

6. Ellen Weber, "Sexual Abuse Begins at Home," *MS.*, Vol. V, No. 10, April 1977.

7. Pierre L. Van den Berghe and David B. Barash, "Inclusive Fitness and Human Family Structure," *American Anthropologist*, Vol. 72 No. 4, 1977, pp. 809–23.

8. Robin Fox, *Kinship and Marriage* (Baltimore: Penguin Books, 1967).

9. Melford E. and A. G. Spiro, *Children of the Kibbutz* (Cambridge: Harvard University Press, 1958).

10. Arthur P. Wolf, "Childhood Association and Sexual Attraction: A Further Test of the Westermarck Hypothesis," *American Anthropologist*, Vol. 72, No. 3, 1972, pp. 503–15.

11. Nicholas de Jongh, review of *Les Parents Terribles*, in *The Guardian*, June 4, 1978, p. 20.

12. Martin S. Weinberg, ed., *Sex Research*, p. 128.

13. Robert Seidenberg, "Sexual Basis of Social Prejudice," from Edward Podolsky, ed., *Encyclopedia of Aberrations* (New York: Philosophical Library, 1953).

14. H. C. G. Matthews, ed., *The Gladstone Diaries*, Vol. V:

1855–1860; Vol. VI: *1861–1868* (Oxford: Clarendon Press, 1978).

15. Elliott Leyton, "Opposition and Integration in Ulster," *Man,* Vol. 9, No. 2, 1974, pp. 185–98.

Chapter 9

1. Victor Turner, *Chihamba: The White Spirit,* Rhodes-Livingstone Museum Paper 33, Livingstone, Northern Rhodesia [Zambia], 1962.

2. See Alice Schlegel and Herbert Barry, "Cultural Correlates of Adolescent Initiation Ceremonies," paper presented at the annual meeting of the Society for Cross-Cultural Research, Chicago, February 21, 1977, and Schlegel's critique of my article in *Current Anthropology,* cited above in note 1, Chapter 2.

3. Michelle Rosaldo, Introduction, in Rosaldo and Louise Lamphere, eds., *Woman, Culture, and Society* (Stanford: Stanford University Press, 1974).

4. Theodor Reik, *Ritual* (London: Hogarth Press, 1931).

5. Jean Briggs, "Kapluna Daughter," in Peggy Golde, ed., *Women in the Field* (Chicago: Aldine, 1970), pp. 19–44.

6. J. W. M. Whiting, R. Kluckhohn, and A. Anthony, "The Function of Male Initiation Ceremonies," in E. Maccoby, W. Newcomb, and R. Hartley, eds., *Readings in Social Psychology* (New York: Holt, Rinehart and Winston, 1957).

7. See critique by C. Fred Blake of my article in *Current Anthropology,* cited above in note 1, Chapter 2.

8. Sigmund Freud, *Three Essays on the Theory of Sexuality.*

9. Henri A. Junod, *The Life of a South African Tribe* (London: Macmillan, 1927).

10. Camara Laye, *The Dark Child,* trans. James Kirkup, Ernest Jones, and Elaine Gottlieb (New York: Farrar, Straus and Giroux, 1954).

11. Ashton Barfield, "Biological Influences on Sex Difference in Behavior."

12. Ariana Stassinopoulos, *The Female Woman* (Glasgow: Collins, 1974).

Chapter 10

1. Bruno Bettelheim, *Symbolic Wounds: Puberty Rites and the Envious Male* (New York: Macmillan, 1954; rev. ed., 1962).

2. Harvey Graham, *The Story of Surgery* (New York: Doubleday Doran, 1939).

3. Theodor Reik, *Dogma and Compulsion* (Westport: Greenwood Press, 1951), pp. 104–5.

4. Martin S. Weinberg, ed., *Sex Research*, p. 161.

5. Ian Hogbin, *The Island of Menstruating Men* (San Francisco: Chandler, 1970).

6. Vieda Skultans, "The Symbolic Significance of Menstruation and the Menopause," *Man*, Vol. 5, No. 4, 1970, pp. 639–51.

7. Warren R. Dawson, ed., *A Leechbook: A Collection of Medical Recipes of the Fifteenth Century* (London: Macmillan, 1934).

8. Harvey Graham, *The Story of Surgery*.

9. Simon Harward, *Harward's Phlebotomy, or, A Treatise of Letting the Blood* (London: F. Kingston, 1601).

10. The logic of this "diversion" of blood like an electric current through a thicker wire is comprehensible, but one wonders what happened to the poor women.

11. Jean La Fontaine, "The Power of Rights," *Man*, Vol. 12, Nos. 3/4, 1977, pp. 421–37.

12. Jean La Fontaine, "Ritualization of Women's Life Crises in Bugisu," in Jean La Fontaine, ed., *The Interpretation of Ritual: Essays in Honour of I. A. Richards* (London: Tavistock Press, 1972).

13. James L. Brain, "Ritual Rebirth: The Mwali Rite Among the Luguru," *Africa*, Vol. 48, No. 2, pp. 49–61.

14. Ibid., p. 61

15. Gregory Bateson, *Naven* (London: Cambridge University Press, 1936).

16. Alan Dundes, "A Psychoanalytic Study of the Bullroarer," *Man*, Vol. 11, No. 2, 1976, pp. 220–38.

Chapter 11

1. See Marvin Harris, *Cows, Pigs, Wars and Witches*, pp. 84–85.

2. Michelle Rosaldo and Louise Lamphere, *Woman, Culture and Society*.

3. Terry Davidson, *Conjugal Crime: Understanding and Changing the Wifebeating Pattern* (New York: Hawthorn Books, 1978).

4. Susan Brownmiller, *Against Our Will: Men, Women and Rape* (New York: Simon and Schuster, 1975).

5. Quoted in Francine du Plessix Gray, "Erotica and Transcendence in Women's Novels," *Barnard Alumnae* (Summer 1977).

6. Ibid.

7. James Branch Cabell, *Jurgen* (New York: Grosset & Dunlap, 1927).

8. John G. Kennedy, "Circumcision and Excisions in Egyptian Nubia," *Man*, Vol. 5, No. 2, 1970, pp. 175–91.

Chapter 12

1. Theodor Reik, *Masochism in Modern Man* (New York: Farrar, Straus, 1941), p. 203.

2. Ibid., pp. 21–42.

3. Melanie Klein, *Contributions to Psychoanalysis, 1921–45* (New York: McGraw-Hill, 1964).

4. Paul Theroux, *The Great Railway Bazaar.*

5. Theodor W. Adorno et al., *The Authoritarian Personality* (New York: Harper, 1950).

6. Basil Bernstein, "Elaborated and Restricted Codes: Their Origin and Some Consequences," *American Anthropologist,* Vol. 66, No. 6, pp. 55–69. 1964.

7. Mary Douglas, *Natural Symbols* (New York: Vintage Books, 1973.

8. Mircea Eliade, *Myths, Rites and Symbols,* ed. W. C. Beane and W. G. Doty (New York: Harper & Row, 1976).

9. Jean La Fontaine, "The Power of Rights," *Man,* Vol. 12, Nos. 3/4, 1977, pp. 421–37.

10. J. W. M. Whiting, R. Kluckhohn, and A. Anthony, "The Function of Male Initiation Ceremonies."

11. Dana Raphael, critique of my article in *Current Anthropology,* cited above in note 1, Chapter 2.

12. James Woodburn, script of film *The Hadza* (London: Hogarth Films, 1966).

13. G. B. Kolata, "!Kung Hunter-Gatherers: Feminism, Diet and Birth Control," *Science,* Vol. 185, Sept. 13, 1974, pp. 932–34.

14. Ibid.

15. R. E. Frisch and J. W. McArthur, "Menstrual Cycles: Fatness as a Determinant for Minimum Weight for Height Necessary for their Maintenance and Onset," *Science,* Vol. 185, Sept. 13, 1974, pp. 949–51.

16. G. B. Silverbauer, *Bushman Survey* (Mafeking: Bechuanaland Press, 1965).

17. Isaac Schapera, *The Khoisan Peoples of South Africa: Bushmen and Hottentots* (London: Routledge, 1930).

Chapter 13

1. Mary Douglas, *Purity and Danger,* p. 121.

2. Ibid., p. 124.

3. Johann Jakob Meyer, *Sexual Life in Ancient India* (New York: Barnes and Noble, 1953).

4. Fatima Mernissi, *Beyond the Veil* (New York: Wiley, 1975).

5. *The Holy Koran,* trans. Marmaduke Pickthall, 1930 (London: Allen & Unwin, 1954).

6. Al-Amin bin Aly, *Uwongozi* (Mombasa: East Africa Muslim Welfare Society), p. 1. (Passage translated by author.)

7. Nadia M. Abu-Zahra, "On the Modesty of Women in Arab Muslim Villages: A Reply [to Richard Antoun]," *American Anthropologist,* Vol. 72, No. 5, 1970, pp. 1079–88.

8. Ibid.

9. Mary Douglas, op. cit., p. 60.

10. Johann Jakob Meyer, op. cit.

11. Vieda Skultans, "The Symbolic Significance of Menstruation and the Menopause," *Man,* Vol. 5, No. 4, 1970, pp. 639–51; she is quoting from Helene Deutsch, *Neuroses and Character Types* (London: Hogarth Press, 1965).

12. Nora Ephron, *Crazy Salad* (New York: Knopf, 1975).

13. Shirley Ardener, ed., *Perceiving Women* (New York: Wiley, 1977).

14. James L. Brain, "Less than Second-Class: Women on Tanzanian Settlement Schemes," in N. Hafkin and E. Bay, eds., *Women in Africa* (Stanford: Stanford University Press, 1974).

15. Sherry Ortner, "Is Woman to Nature as Man Is to Culture?" in Michelle Rosaldo and Louise Lamphere, eds., *Woman, Culture and Society.*

16. Arnold van Gennep, *Rites of Passage,* 1908, trans. N. B. Vizedom and G. L. Caffee (London: Routledge and Kegan Paul, 1960).

17. James L. Brain, "Handedness in Tanzania," *Anthropos* 72, 1977. See also Carl Sagan, *Dragons of Eden* (New York: Random House, 1977).

Chapter 14

1. I first suggested this at a conference entitled "Anthropology on the Fringe" at SUNY Oswego, in 1969, and later incorporated the idea in a chapter of a *Festschrift* for Lucy Mair; see "Witchcraft: A Hardy Perennial," in M. Owusu, ed., *Colonialism and Change* (The Hague: Mouton, 1974).

2. E. E. Evans-Pritchard, *Witchcraft, Oracles and Magic Among the Azande* (Oxford: Clarendon Press, 1934).

3. Lucy P. Mair, *Witchcraft* (New York: World University Library, 1969).

4. See James L. Brain, "Ancestors as Elders: Further Thoughts," *Africa,* Vol. XLIII, No. 2, 1973, pp. 122–33.

5. Harvey Graham, *The Story of Surgery,* p. 191.

6. Ibid., pp. 110–11.

7. For an easy-to-understand account of the progress of brain size, see Richard Leakey and Roger Lewin, *Origins* (New York: Dutton, 1977).

8. Otto Rank, *The Trauma of Birth.*

9. Susan Brownmiller, *Against Our Will,* pp. 108–11.

10. Arthur Janov and Michael Holden, *Primal Man: The New Consciousness* (New York: Crowell, 1975).

11. Taken from Emmanuel Bernstein, "Summerhill: After 50 Years, the First Follow-up," undated mimeographed pamphlet.

Index

in New Testament, harshness and
submission to, 188–89
in Old Testament, stress upon,
186–88
restricted language codes and,
181–84
source of, 155
weaning as source of
authoritarianism, 190–93

Bacwezi (Tanzania), public rites of,
34, 42
Bad smells, 59
decaying flesh, 65–66, 67, 70,
73–74, 75, 222
decay linked with death, 79, 222
feces, 74–75, 222
Balinese Character, 225, 226
Barash, David, 105–6, 107
Barfield, Ashton, 129
Baryshnikov, Mikhail, 101
Bataille, Georges, 28
Bateson, Gregory, 149–50, 225
Beauvoir, Simone de, 99
Belloc, Hillaire, 154
Bellow, Saul, 70–71, 83
Bernstein, Basil, 180–81, 182, 184
Bernstein, Emmanuel, 232
Bettelheim, Bruno, 117, 134, 136,
137, 141, 147, 150, 151, 180,
235
Black Death, 218, 219
Black Mass, 34, 220
Blood letting. *See* Phlebotomy
Bluebond-Langner, Myra, 26
Body
disposal of, after death, 64–65,
66–71
putrefaction of, 65–66, 67, 70,
73–74
resurrection of, 71–73
Body hair, loss of, 55
Book of Common Prayer
(Anglican), 64
Bride wealth (price), 161–62
Brontë, Emily, 107

Brownmiller, Susan, 156–58,
162–63, 229
Bull-roarers, 128, 150–51
Burton, Sir Richard, 189
Bushmen (Kalahari Desert), 191.
See also !Kung
Byron, Lord, 105

Cabell, James Branch, 200
Cartland, Barbara, 165, 170
Cassirer, Ernst, 14
Caste, in India, 19–20, 66–67, 79,
196
Castration, 192
Celibacy, 197–98, 200
Chaplin, Charlie, 194
Child rearing
and character molding for later
life, 225–26
reason why women identified as
witches, 220–26
Chisungu, 116–17
Chomsky, Noam, 11
Circumcision, 117, 127, 128, 136,
168, 192, 208–9
according to Bible, 186
of girls, 136
public, 145–46
Cleland, John, 86
Clitoridectomy, 135–36, 163, 168
"Cloth Captives?", 61
Cocteau, Jean, 108
Conjugal Crime, 154–55
Coote, Anna, 61
Cory, Hans, 34, 42
Couvade, 119–20
Cows, Pigs, Wars and Witches, 188
Crazy Salad, 206–7
Cultures, 12
differences among, 114–15
language in, 13–14, 115
nature and, 15–16
rituals in, 116–18
symbols in, 12–13, 115, 116, 117,
118
Cupping, 144, 153